BATMAN

AND

PHILOSOPHY

The Blackwell Philosophy and Pop Culture Series
Series Editor: William Irwin

South Park and Philosophy
Edited by Robert Arp

Metallica and Philosophy
Edited by William Irwin

Family Guy and Philosophy
Edited by J. Jeremy Wisnewski

The Daily Show and Philosophy
Edited by Jason Holt

Lost and Philosophy
Edited by Sharon Kaye

24 and Philosophy
*Edited by Richard Davis, Jennifer Hart Week,
and Ronald Weed*

Battlestar Galactica and Philosophy
Edited by Jason T. Eberl

The Office and Philosophy
Edited by J. Jeremy Wisnewski

House and Philosophy
Edited by Henry Jacoby

Heroes and Philosophy
Edited by David Kyle Johnson

BATMAN
AND
PHILOSOPHY
THE DARK KNIGHT
OF THE SOUL

Edited by Mark D. White
and Robert Arp

WILEY

John Wiley & Sons, Inc.

To the memory of
Heath Ledger (1979–2008)

CONTENTS

ACKNOWLEDGMENTS: The Oscar Speech
George Clooney Never Got to Make ix

Introduction: Riddle Me This . . . 1

PART ONE

**DOES THE DARK KNIGHT ALWAYS
DO RIGHT?**

1 Why Doesn't Batman Kill the Joker? 5
Mark D. White

2 Is It Right to Make a Robin? 17
James DiGiovanna

3 Batman's Virtuous Hatred 28
Stephen Kershnar

PART TWO

**LAW, JUSTICE, AND THE SOCIAL ORDER:
WHERE DOES BATMAN FIT IN?**

4 *No Man's Land:* Social Order in Gotham City
and New Orleans 41
Brett Chandler Patterson

5 Governing Gotham 55
Tony Spanakos

6 The Joker's Wild: Can We Hold the Clown
Prince Morally Responsible? 70
Christopher Robichaud

PART THREE

**ORIGINS AND ETHICS: BECOMING
THE CAPED CRUSADER**

7 Batman's Promise 85
Randall M. Jensen

8 Should Bruce Wayne Have Become Batman? 101
Mahesh Ananth and Ben Dixon

9 What Would Batman Do? Bruce Wayne as
Moral Exemplar 114
Ryan Indy Rhodes and David Kyle Johnson

PART FOUR

**WHO IS THE BATMAN? (IS THAT
A TRICK QUESTION?)**

10 Under the Mask: How Any Person
Can Become Batman 129
Sarah K. Donovan and Nicholas P. Richardson

11 Could Batman Have Been the Joker? 142
Sam Cowling and Chris Ragg

12 Batman's Identity Crisis and Wittgenstein's
Family Resemblance 156
Jason Southworth

13 What Is It Like to Be a Batman? 167
Ron Novy

PART FIVE

BEING THE BAT: INSIGHTS FROM EXISTENTIALISM AND TAOISM

14 Alfred, the Dark Knight of Faith: Batman
   and Kierkegaard   183
   Christopher M. Drohan

15 Dark Nights and the Call of Conscience   198
   Jason J. Howard

16 Batman's Confrontation with Death, Angst,
   and Freedom   212
   David M. Hart

PART SIX

FRIEND, FATHER, . . . RIVAL? THE MANY ROLES OF THE BAT

17 Why Batman Is Better Than Superman   227
   Galen Foresman

18 World's Finest . . . Friends? Batman,
   Superman, and the Nature of Friendship   239
   Daniel P. Malloy

19 Leaving the Shadow of the Bat: Aristotle,
   Kant, and Dick Grayson on Moral Education   254
   Carsten Fogh Nielsen

20 The Tao of the Bat   267
   Bat-Tzu

CONTRIBUTORS: The Clown Princes (and Princess) of
   Casuistry and Categorical Imperatives   279

INDEX: From the Secret Files of Oracle, Master
   Indexer to the DCU   285

ACKNOWLEDGMENTS

The Oscar Speech George Clooney
Never Got to Make

We wish to thank the Justice League (Eric Nelson, Connie Santisteban, and the rest of the staff at Wiley) for their stewardship and valuable input; Commissioner Gordon and the Gotham City Police Department (Jeff Dean and Blackwell), under whom this project was started; and Thomas Wayne (Bill Irwin) for his interminable assistance and inspiration. (Never fear, Bill's still alive—who would oversee *Batwoman and Philosophy* if he weren't?)

Mark wishes to thank the legions of writers, artists, and editors who have made Batman come alive for him for decades; and Rob wishes to thank his wife, Susan (even though she's never written a Batman story—not even one!).

RIDDLE ME THIS . . .

We know what you're thinking (because we're smart—we're philosophers): "*Batman and Philosophy*? Seriously? Why?"

Well, since you asked. . . . Because we believe that Batman is the most complex character ever to appear in comic books and graphic novels. Because the stories featuring him over the last seventy years, not only in the comics but also on animated and live-action TV shows and in movies, have provided us with a wealth of philosophical material to discuss. And because we had the chance, along with about twenty other fans, to combine our passion for the character with our love for philosophical mumbling, all to create the book you now hold in your hands. (No need to thank us—we're happy to do it.)

One reason Batman appeals to so many people around the world is that he is "just" a human being, even though he is *nothing* like the rest of us. He has devoted his entire life to avenging the death of his parents and all other victims of crime by risking life and limb to protect his city of Gotham and beyond. He has spent years and sacrificed everything to train his body and his mind to the point of perfection. He is wealthy beyond measure, but denies himself all luxuries (except a butler) in pursuit of a goal that will never be attained. And he does all this dressed like a giant bat. (Well, that we can do, but that's about it!)

What makes a person go to such extremes? Is what Batman does good, or right, or virtuous? And what does his obsession, his devotion to "the mission," say about who he is? How does he treat his partners, his friends, and his enemies? What is it like to actually be Batman? These are all genuine philosophical questions, and when we read Batman stories, we can't help but think about this stuff (and then write down our thoughts). The twenty chapters in this book explore issues of ethics, identity, friendship, politics, and more, using examples drawn from famous Batman stories such as *The Dark Knight Returns, Batman: Year One, No Man's Land, A Death in the Family*, and *The Killing Joke*, as well as the various movies, animated series, and yes, old chum, even the 1960s TV series with Adam West and Burt Ward.

So whether you know every detail of Jason Todd's recent resurrection, or whether you can recite all of Jack Nicholson's lines from Tim Burton's first *Batman* movie, or if you just have fond recollections of Halloweens past wearing the blue cowl and cape, there's something in this book for you. The Bat-signal's shining—let's go!

PART ONE

DOES THE DARK KNIGHT ALWAYS DO RIGHT?

WHY DOESN'T BATMAN KILL THE JOKER?

Mark D. White

Meet the Joker

In the last several decades, the Joker has transformed himself from the Clown Prince of Crime to a heinous murderer without rival. Most notoriously, he killed the second Robin, Jason Todd, beating him to a bloody pulp before blowing him up. He shot and killed Lieutenant Sarah Essen, Commissioner Jim Gordon's second wife—in front of dozens of infants, no less, whom he threatened to kill in order to lure Essen to him. Years earlier, the Joker shot Barbara Gordon—Jim Gordon's adopted daughter and the former Batgirl—in the spine, paralyzing her from the waist down, and then tormented Jim with pictures of her lying prone, naked and bleeding. And let us not forget countless ordinary citizens of Gotham City—the Joker even wiped out all of his own henchmen recently![1]

Every time the Joker breaks out of Arkham Asylum, he commits depraved crimes—the type that philosopher Joel

Feinberg (1926–2004) calls "sick! sick! sick!," or "triple-sick."[2] Of course Batman inevitably catches the Joker and puts him back through the "revolving door" at Arkham.[3] Batman knows that the Joker will escape, and that he will likely kill again unless the Caped Crusader can prevent it—which, obviously, he can't always do.

So why doesn't Batman just kill the Joker? Think of all the lives it would save! Better yet, think of all the lives it would have saved had he done the deed years ago, just among Batman's closest friends and partners. Commissioner Gordon has contemplated killing the Joker himself on several occasions, and Batman is usually the one to stop him.[4] In a terrifically revealing scene during the *Hush* storyline, Batman is *this* close to offing the Joker, and it is Jim who stops him. Batman asks Jim, "How many more lives are we going to let him ruin?" to which Jim replies, "I don't care. I won't let him ruin yours."[5]

So though he may have considered it on many occasions, Batman has never killed the Joker, decidedly his most homicidal enemy. Of course, with the exception of his very earliest cases, Batman has refused to kill at all, usually saying that if he kills, it would make him as bad as the criminals he is sworn to fight. But that seems almost selfish—someone could very well say, "Hey— it's not about you, Bats!" Or . . . is it? Should it be? Usually we think a person is obligated to do something that would benefit many people, but what if that "something" is committing murder? Which is more important, doing good—or not doing wrong? (Ugh—Alfred, we need some aspirin here.)

In this chapter, we'll consider the ethics of killing to prevent future killings, exactly the problem Batman faces when he balances his personal moral code against the countless lives that he could save. In fact, this issue has been raised many times, very recently by both the villain Hush and Jason Todd himself (returned from the dead), and earlier by Jean-Paul Valley (the "Knightfall" Batman), none of whom have the strict moral code that Batman adheres to.[6] I'll do this by introducing some famous philosophical thought experiments that let us trace through the ethics of a situation by whittling it down to its most basic elements, just like Batman solving a cleverly plotted crime. (Well, not quite, but you have to let a guy dream!)

Is Batman a Utilitarian or Deontologist? (Or None of the Above?)

The argument in favor of killing the Joker is fairly straightforward—if Batman kills the Joker, he would prevent all the murders the Joker would otherwise commit in the future. This rationale is typical of *utilitarianism*, a system of ethics that requires us to maximize the total happiness or well-being resulting from our actions.[7] Saving many lives at the cost of just one would represent a net increase in well-being or utility, and while it would certainly be a tragic choice, utilitarians would generally endorse it. (We could add more considerations, such as satisfying the quest for vengeance on the part of the families of his past victims, or the unhappiness it brings to some people when *anyone* is killed, but let's keep things simple—for now.)

Superheroes, however, generally are not utilitarians. Sure, they like happiness and well-being as much as the ordinary person, but there are certain things they will not do to achieve them. Of course, criminals know this and use it to their advantage: after all, why do you think criminals take innocent people as hostages? Superheroes—just like police in the real world—normally won't risk innocent lives to apprehend a villain, even if it means preventing the villain from killing more people later. More generally, most superheroes will not kill, even to save many other lives.[8]

But why do they refuse to kill in these instances? The utilitarian would not understand such talk. "You're allowing many more people to die because *you* don't want to kill one?" In fact, that's almost exactly what Jason Todd and Hush recently said to Batman. Hush asked, "How many lives do you think you've cost, how many families have you ruined, by allowing the Joker to live? . . . And why? Because of your duty? Your sense of justice?" Jason Todd put a more personal spin on it (of course): "Bruce, I forgive you for not saving me. But why . . . why on God's Earth—is he still alive? . . . Ignoring what he's done in the past. Blindly, stupidly, disregarding the entire graveyards he's filled, the thousands who have suffered, . . . the friends he's crippled, . . . I thought . . . I thought killing me—that I'd be the last person you'd ever let him hurt."[9] Batman's standard response has always been that if he ever kills, it will make him as bad as the criminals he fights, or that he will be crossing a line from which he would never return—though he is very open about his strong desire to kill the Joker.[10]

While utilitarians would generally endorse killing one person to prevent killing more, members of the school of ethics known as *deontology* would not.[11] Deontologists judge the morality of an act based on features intrinsic to the act itself, regardless of the consequences stemming from the act. To deontologists, the ends never justify the means, but rather the means must be justifiable on their own merits. So the fact that the killing would prevent future killings is irrelevant—the only relevant factor is that killing is wrong, period. But even for the strictest deontologist, there are exceptions—for instance, killing in self-defense would generally be allowed by deontologists. So killing is fine, but only for the right reasons? Might killing a homicidal maniac be just one of those reasons? We'll see, but first we have to take a ride on a trolley. . . .

To the Bat-Trolley, Professor Thomson!

One of many classic moral dilemmas debated by philosophers is the "trolley problem," introduced by Philippa Foot and elaborated upon by Judith Jarvis Thomson.[12] Imagine that a trolley car is going down a track. Further down the track are five people who do not hear the trolley and who will not be able to get out of the way. Unfortunately, there isn't enough time to stop the trolley before it hits and kills them. The only way to avoid killing these five people is to switch the trolley to another track. But, unfortunately, there is one person standing on that track, also too close for the trolley to stop before killing him. Now imagine that there is a bystander standing by the track switch who must make a choice: do nothing, which leads to the death of the five people on the current track, or act to divert the trolley to the other track, which leads to the death of the single person.

Let's call the person in control Bruce. Is Bruce morally allowed to divert the trolley to the second track or not? If he is, can we also say that in fact he is *required* to do it? Thomson takes the middle road here, concluding that Bruce is permitted—but not required—to divert the trolley. A typical utilitarian would require Bruce to throw the switch and save more lives, while a deontologist would have problems with Bruce's acting to take a life (rather than allowing five to die through inaction). Thomson's answer seems to combine the concerns of both utilitarianism and deontology. Bruce is allowed (maybe even encouraged) to divert the train and kill one person rather than five, but it's valid also for Bruce to have problems with doing this himself.

One way to state the difference between the utilitarian and the deontological approaches is to look at the types of rules they both prescribe. Utilitarianism results in *agent-neutral* rules, such as "Maximize well-being," and utilitarians couldn't care less who it is that will be following the rule. Everybody has to act so as to maximize well-being, and there is no reason or excuse for any one person to say "I don't want to." By contrast, deontology deals with *agent-specific* rules—when deontologists say "Do not kill," they mean "*You* do not kill," even if there are other reasons that make it look like a good idea. This is simply a different way of contrasting the utilitarian's emphasis on good outcomes with the deontologist's focus on right action.

While throwing the switch to kill the one rather than five may be good, it may not be right (because of what that specific person has to do).[13]

Hush Will *Love* This Next Story . . .

Thomson likes to compare the trolley situation with a story involving a surgeon with five patients, each of whom is dying from failure of a different organ and could be saved by a transplant. Since there are no organs available through normal channels, the surgeon considers drugging one of his (healthy) colleagues and removing his organs to use for the transplants.[14] By doing so, he would kill his colleague, but he would save his five patients.

With the possible exception of our bandaged and demented Dr. Hush, few people would endorse such a drastic plan (least of all Dr. Thomas Wayne, bless his soul). You can see where I'm going with this (Batman fans are so smart)—"What is the difference between the bystander in the trolley case and the surgeon in the transplant case?" In both cases a person can do nothing, and let five people die, or take an action that kills one but saves the five. Thomson, and many philosophers after her, have struggled with these questions, and there is no definitive answer. Most people will agree that throwing the trolley switch is justified, and also that the surgeon's actions are not, but we have a very difficult time saying precisely *why* we feel that way—and that includes philosophers!

Top Ten Reasons the Batmobile Is Not a Trolley . . .

How does Batman's situation compare to the trolley story (or the transplant story)? What factors relevant to Batman and the Joker are missing from the two classic philosophical dilemmas? And what does Batman's refusal to "do the deed" say about him?

One obvious difference between the two cases described by Thomson and the case of Batman and the Joker is that in Thomson's cases, the five people who will be killed if the trolley is not diverted, and the one person who will be killed if it is, are assumed to be morally equivalent. In other words, there is no moral difference between any of these people in terms of how they should be treated, what rights they have, and so on. All the people on the tracks in the trolley case are moral "innocents," as are the patients and the colleague in the transplant case.

Does this matter? Thomson introduces several modifications to suggest that it does. What if the five people on the main track collapsed there drunk early that morning, and the one person on the other track is a repairman performing track maintenance for the railroad? The repairman has a right to be there, while the five drunkards do not. Would this make us more comfortable about pulling the switch? What if the five transplant patients were in their desperate condition because of their own negligence regarding their health, and the colleague was very careful to take care of himself? We might say that in both of these cases the five persons are in their predicament due to their own (bad) choices, and they must take full responsibility for the consequences. And furthermore, their lives should not be saved at the expense of the one person in both situations who has taken responsibility for himself.

But the Joker case is precisely the opposite: he is the single man on the alternate track or the operating table, and his victims (presumably innocent) are the other five people. So following the logic above, there would be a presumption in *favor* of killing the Joker. After all, why should his victims sacrifice their lives so that *he* should live—especially if he lives to kill innocent people?

This case is different from the original philosophical cases in another way that involves moral differences between the parties. Unlike the classic trolley and transplant cases, the Joker actually *puts* the others in danger. In terms of the trolley case, it would be as if the Joker tied the five people to the main track, then stood on the other track to see what Batman would do! (Talk about a game of chicken!) If we were inclined to kill one to save five, that inclination would only be strengthened by knowing that the five were in danger *because* of the one!

We might say that the one person on the alternate track has the *right* not to be killed, even to save the other five. While it would be noble for him to make this sacrifice, most philosophers (aside from utilitarians) would deny that he has such an obligation. This is even clearer in the transplant case. The surgeon could certainly ask his colleague if he would be willing to give up his organs (and his life) to save the five patients, but we could hardly tell him that he *had* to. Once again, the difference with the Joker is that he put the others in danger, and it would be absurd—in other words, appropriate for one such as the Joker—to say, "Sure I'm going to kill these people, but *I* should not be killed to save *them*!"

The recognition of the Joker's role in creating the situation also casts light on the responsibility Batman faces. If we said to the Caped Crusader, as many have, "If you don't kill the Joker, the deaths of all his future victims will be on your hands," he could very well answer, "No, the deaths that the Joker causes are his responsibility and his responsibility alone. I am responsible only for the deaths I cause."[15] This is another way to look at the agent-centered rule we discussed earlier: the bystander in the trolley example could very well say, "I did not cause the trolley to endanger the five lives, but I would be causing the death of one if I diverted the trolley."[16]

"I Want My Lawyer! Oh, That's Right, I Killed Him Too"

What the surgeon does in the transplant case is clearly illegal. However, if the bystander switches the trolley from its track, knowingly causing one person's death to save five others, the legality of his action is not clear. Of course, the legalities of the Batman/Joker case are a bit simpler. Let's assume (for the time being) that Batman has the same legal rights and obligations as a police officer. Under what circumstances would a police officer be allowed to kill the Joker (aside from self-defense)? If the Joker was just about to murder someone, then the police officer would be justified—legally—in killing him (if mere incapacitation is impossible and deadly force is the only effective choice). So if Batman came upon the Joker about to kill an innocent person, and the only way to save the person was to kill the Joker, Batman would be justified in doing that. (Knowing Batman, though, I imagine he would still find another way.)

Let's make the case a bit tougher—say Batman finds the Joker just *after* he's killed someone. Batman (or a police officer) couldn't do anything to save that person, but if he kills the Joker, he'll save untold others whom the Joker will probably kill. *Probably?* Well, let's be fair now—we don't *know* that the Joker will kill any more people. "This is my last one, Batty, I promise!" The Joker has certainly claimed to have reformed in the past; maybe this time it's for real. Or maybe the Joker will die by natural causes tomorrow, never to kill again. The fact is, we can't be sure that he will kill again, so we can't be sure we will be saving *any* lives by taking his.

Given this fact, it's as if we changed the trolley example like so: a dense fog is obscuring the view on the main track, but we can see the sole person on the other track. We don't know if anyone is in danger on the main track, but we know that *sometimes* there are people there. What do we do? Or, to modify the transplant case, the surgeon doesn't have any patients who need organs right now, but he guesses that there will be some tomorrow, by which time his healthy colleague will be on vacation. Should he still sacrifice his colleague today?

I imagine that none of us would be comfortable, in either case, choosing to kill the one to avoid the *chance* of killing others. It's one thing to hold the Joker accountable for the people he has killed, and this may include the death penalty (if he weren't the poster boy for the insanity defense), but another thing entirely when we consider the people he might kill in the future. Admittedly, he has a well-established pattern, and he may even say he's going to kill more in the future. What if we have every reason—as Batman clearly does—to believe him? Can we deal with him *before* he kills again?

Punishing people before they commit crimes has been called *prepunishment* by philosophers, and the concept was made famous by Philip K. Dick's 1956 short story "The Minority Report," more recently a movie directed by Steven Spielberg and starring Tom Cruise.[17] While Batman killing the Joker would not literally be punishment—since he has no legal authority to impose such a sentence—we can still consider whether or not prepunishment is morally acceptable, especially in this case. Some would say that if the Joker intends to kill again, and makes clear statements to that effect, then there is no moral difficulty with prepunishing him. (There may, however, be an informational or *epistemic* problem—why would he confess to his future crime if he knew he would be killed before he had a chance to commit it?) But others say that even if he says he will kill again, he still has the choice to change his mind, and it is out of respect for this capacity to make ethical choices that we should not prepunish people.[18] Prepunishment may trigger the panic button in all of us, but in an age in which very many can be killed very easily by very few, we may be facing this issue before long.[19]

So, Case Closed—Right?

So then, we're all convinced that Batman was right not to have killed the Joker.

What? We're not?

Well, *of course* not. Look at it this way—I consider myself a strict deontologist, and even I have to admit that maybe Batman should have killed the Joker. (I hope none of my colleagues in the North American Kant Society reads this—I'll be on punch-and-pretzels duty for a year!) As much as we deontologists say the right always comes before the good, an incredible amount of good would have been done if the Joker's life had been ended years ago. Compare this issue with the recent torture debates—even those who are wholeheartedly opposed to the use of torture under any circumstances must have some reservations when thousands or millions of innocent lives are at stake.

Luckily, literature—and by "literature" I mean comic books—provides us a way to discuss issues like these without having to experience them. We don't have to trick people into standing in front of a runaway trolley, and we don't have to have a real-life Batman and Joker. That's what thought experiments are for—they let us play through an imaginary scenario and imagine what we should or shouldn't do. Unfortunately for Batman, but luckily for Batman fans, the Joker is not imaginary to him, and I'm sure he will struggle with this issue for many years to come.

NOTES

1. Jason Todd was killed in *A Death in the Family* (1988); Lieutenant Essen was killed in *No Man's Land Vol. 5* (2001); Barbara Gordon was shot in *The Killing Joke* (1988); and most of the Joker's henchmen were killed in *Batman* #663 (April 2007).

2. Joel Feinberg, "Evil," in *Problems at the Roots of Law* (Oxford: Oxford Univ. Press, 2003), 125–192.

3. The Joker is the poster child for the insanity defense, so he never receives the death penalty.

4. For instance, after Lieutenant Essen was killed at the end of *No Man's Land*.

5. *Batman* #614 (June 2003), included in *Hush Volume Two* (2003). Unfortunately, I don't have room in this chapter to quote from Batman's internal dialogue from this issue as much as I would like, but it's brilliant writing, courtesy of Jeph Loeb.

6. See Hush in *Gotham Knights* #74 (April 2006), Jason Todd in *Batman* #650 (April 2006), and Jean-Paul Valley in *Robin* #7 (June 1994).

7. Utilitarianism is usually traced back to Jeremy Bentham's *The Principles of Morals and Legislation* (1781; Buffalo, NY: Prometheus Books edition, 1988).

8. Wonder Woman's recent execution of Max Lord in the *Sacrifice* storyline, in order to end his psychic hold on Superman, is a significant exception and was treated as such in

the stories that followed. (See *Wonder Woman* #219, September 2005, also collected in *Superman: Sacrifice*, 2006.)

9. See note 6 for sources.

10. In the scene with Jason Todd he explains that "all I have ever wanted to do is kill him. . . . I want him dead—maybe more than I've ever wanted anything." In *The Man Who Laughed* (2005), as he holds the Joker over the poisoned Gotham City reservoir, Batman thinks to himself, "This water is filled with enough poison to kill thousands. It would be so easy to just let him fall into it. So many are already dead because of this man . . . [but] I can't."

11. The most famous deontologist is Immanuel Kant, whose seminal ethical work is his *Grounding for the Metaphysics of Morals* (1785; Indianapolis, IN: Hackett Publishing Company, 1993).

12. For Foot's original treatment, see her essay "The Problem of Abortion and the Doctrine of the Double Effect," in her book *Virtues and Vices* (Oxford: Clarendon Press, 2002), 19–32. For Thomson's version, see "The Trolley Problem," reprinted in her book *Rights, Restitution, & Risk*, edited by William Parent (Cambridge: Harvard Univ. Press, 1986), 94–116; and also chapter 7 in *The Realm of Rights* (Cambridge: Harvard Univ. Press, 1990).

13. For an excellent treatment of agent-relative rules, see Samuel Scheffler's *The Rejection of Consequentialism*, rev. ed. (Oxford: Oxford Univ. Press: 1990).

14. Never mind the astronomical odds against one of his colleagues being a donor match for all five patients!

15. In *Batman* #614, he thinks, "I cannot . . . I will not . . . accept any responsibility . . . for the Joker." But then he adds, "except that I should have killed him long ago." And finally, after contemplating that the Joker may kill someone close to him again, "he dies tonight by my hand," engaging in a graphic fantasy of several ways he could kill him. Makes you wonder what would have happened if Jim had not been there to stop him. . . .

16. This also brings in the controversial ethical distinction between causing a death through action and causing a death through inaction. Merely allowing a death is usually considered less problematic than directly causing a death—consider Nightwing's choice not to stop Tarantula from killing his archnemesis, Blockbuster, who also happened to pledge to kill many more people in the future (*Nightwing* #93, July 2004). Interestingly, Dick actually did kill the Joker once, although Batman revived him (*Joker: Last Laugh* #6, January 2002).

17. You can find the short story in Philip K. Dick's collection *The Minority Report* (New York: Citadel, 2002). Tom Cruise, in case you don't know, is mainly known for being married to actress Katie Holmes from *Batman Begins*. (To my knowledge, he's done nothing else worth mentioning.)

18. Christopher New argues for prepunishment in "Time and Punishment,"*Analysis* 52, no. 1 (1992): 35–40, and Saul Smilansky argues against it (and New) in "The Time to Punish,"*Analysis* 54, no. 1 (1994): 50–53. New responds to Smilansky in "Punishing Times: A Reply to Smilansky,"*Analysis* 55 no. 1 (1995): 60–62.

19. Of course, Wonder Woman already faced this question with regard to Max Lord, who promised to force Superman to kill, and she came to the opposite conclusion. (Apparently she had read New's papers.) But ironically, it was she who stopped Batman from killing Alex Luthor (who nearly killed Nightwing) in *Infinite Crisis* #7 (June 2006). Even more ironically, who eventually killed Alex at the end of the same issue? The Joker.

IS IT RIGHT TO MAKE
A ROBIN?

James DiGiovanna

What Should a Batman Do?

Batman and Robin, the Dynamic Duo, the Dark Knight and the Boy Wonder—what could sound more natural? But no matter how familiar and right it sounds, you may ask yourself: is it really okay for Batman to train a young boy to be Robin in order to send him out to fight dangerous criminals? To answer this question, we turn to *ethics*, the branch of philosophy that considers questions like "What should I do? How should I live my life? What sort of person should I be?"

Let's say, for example, that you have a superior intellect, an unsurpassed martial prowess, and a haunting memory of watching your parents being killed by a criminal. You might answer these ethical questions by saying, "I should probably put on a cape and cowl and slip into the dark of night to violently stop criminals from engaging in their nefarious deeds." Or perhaps you might answer these questions with "I should get some therapy. I should become a less obsessed and more humane person. I should be a caring nurturer." (But then few people would write comic book stories about you.)

What about this: suppose you find an orphaned boy living on the streets, and you want to help him. What should you do? It seems that the morally acceptable answers include turning him over to social services, finding a home for him, and adopting and caring for him yourself. But what about putting him in a costume, training him to fight crime, and exposing him to constant danger in the name of refining and improving his skills and character? This is what Batman did with Robin . . . twice (Dick Grayson and Jason Todd)! It's harder to imagine that this would be as morally acceptable as turning him over to the state, and so on. And yet, throughout history, many people have taken a similar path in raising children. Ancient Spartans, medieval European royalty, and New Guinean warriors have all exposed young boys to potentially lethal danger in the name of making them into proper adults. While only the medieval Europeans dressed their children in capes and symbols, there's still something rather Batman-like about the behavior of all these people.[1]

Can we justify this sort of child rearing? Can we excuse Batman's penchant for taking young boys and throwing them at vicious criminals who dress up like clowns? These issues form the core of ethical questions concerning the appropriate rearing and education of Robin, and they also form the basis for this chapter.

The Duty of the Superhero

Ethics could be defined as the attempt to live by a set of rules or duties, where it's necessary to follow some of these rules or act on some of these duties regardless of the consequences, simply because the duty itself is most important. We call this *deontological ethics,* from the Greek word *deon,* meaning "duty." The most important deontological ethicist is Immanuel Kant (1724–1804), who famously held that the most important duties must be universal and categorical. "Categorical" means "without exception"—in other words, I can't choose a duty and then think of cases where it doesn't apply, or choose not to apply it in some particular instance. So, for example, Kant says that there's an ethical duty not to tell lies. Suppose that Batman was captured by the Joker, and the Joker wanted to know where Robin was. Batman could certainly say nothing, or dodge the question, but he couldn't lie to the Joker and say that Robin was in some location where Batman had set a trap for the Joker unless Robin was actually there, because that would violate the duty to tell no lies.[2]

"Universal" means that the rule applies to everyone; in other words, we should ask of any given act, "What if everyone did this?" or as Kant puts it, "Act only according to that maxim [the rule I propose to follow] whereby you can at the same time will that it should become a universal law."[3] Kant argues that if your maxim doesn't "universalize" in this way, then it can't be ethical, because everyone has to be able to live by the same moral rules that you do, and no one person can make exceptions for himself.

So let's consider Jason Todd, the second Robin, whom Batman decided to train after he found Jason trying to steal the tires off the Batmobile.[4] If we want to be Kantian deontologists, we'll have to ask, "Is this in accord with a rule that is categorical (has no exceptions) and universal (applies to everyone)?" Batman's maxim could be something like this: "If you see an orphan stealing your hubcaps, you should put him in a bright red-and-yellow costume and send him out to fight the Penguin." This hardly seems universal, so maybe Kant would argue that it's immoral to do this.

But maxims are rarely this specific; after all, if everyone followed the maxim "Become a philosopher," the world would surely screech to a halt, but becoming a philosopher hardly seems immoral. "Become whatever makes you happy" or "Make use of your talents" would be more general and more easily universalized. Likely, we could reformulate the Jason Todd maxim to read "Do what you can to help orphans"—that's certainly universalizable, and it fits with Kant's general duty of helping others. Of course, helping orphans doesn't necessarily include "Send the orphans out to fight psychotic criminals in Halloween costumes." In fact, we would probably think that it should be a universal rule to safeguard children from harm *while* you help them. In this sense, a duty to safeguard children places limits on what you can do to help them. If we accept this, then Batman is not a very good Kantian, at least on this score, because he does expose Robin to harm.

Using Robin for the General Good

Ethics could also be defined as the process of figuring out which of our actions would produce the best outcome, and then following that course of action. This is called *consequentialist ethics*, because it's concerned with the consequences of our actions more so than with their inherent moral rightness. *Utilitarians* such as Jeremy Bentham (1748–1832) and John Stuart Mill (1806–1873) argue that an action is morally good insofar as its consequences promote the most benefit, payoff, or pleasure for the greatest number of people.[5] In opposition to the deontological position that says "Safeguard children," or at least "Don't expose children to grievous harm," the utilitarian perspective could be used by Batman to justify placing Robin in danger if doing so promotes the general good of Gotham City. If training Robins does more good for the citizens of Gotham than it costs in time, punching bags, and injuries, then the utilitarian would find it justified.

But what about the Robins themselves? After all, Jason Todd was famously bludgeoned to death by the Joker. Isn't their sacrifice too high a price to pay, even if their service to Gotham helps many people in return? Utilitarians are notorious for justifying the treatment of persons as means to the greater good of the majority, even if it means harming those persons who are used in the process. For example, if the greater consequence of saving the group from some evildoer requires killing one, two, or even a hundred people in the process, then, on utilitarian grounds, this seems morally correct. So we can presume that Batman may agree that putting his young sidekicks in danger is justified due to the good consequences for the community.[6] But we know Batman will never sacrifice the life of an innocent bystander to catch a criminal. So he applies this logic only to those he trains, who have also volunteered for the job. (But then again, what young boy wouldn't?) So while the training of Robins can be explained by utilitarian thinking on the part of Batman, this thinking only goes so far.

Crime Fighting and Character

Is there another way to understand Batman's ethical decision-making process? His decision to train Robins for crime fighting could stem from *virtue ethics*, which emphasizes general character traits, called virtues or excellences, rather than judging specific acts (as deontology and utilitarianism do). Virtue ethics also takes into account differences, such as differences of character, the different roles people play, and the different cultures in which they live. While he strives to uphold abstract moral principles that he thinks are always right, Batman seems to understand that different sorts of characters demand different sorts of actions. Not everyone should be a Batman or a Robin. The specific character type needed to be a superhero is not suited to everyone, and society demands different roles from each of us.

It might be possible to justify Batman's course of action because he instills in Robin a specific character that, while not appropriate for everyone, is still proper and necessary in its relation to the larger culture.[7] In other words, Robin may have a role to play that makes the world a better place, and Batman may be making Jason Todd a better person by turning him into Robin, even if it's not universally true that men who dress up like bats should turn tire-stealing orphans into living weapons of justice.

Plato (428–348 BCE) was the first Western philosopher to write in the tradition of virtue ethics.[8] He believed that different ethical norms applied to different persons, depending on their role in society. Nonetheless, universal ethical rules applied to everyone, so in certain aspects everyone was ethically the same, whereas in the specific ethical demands of different societal roles, different ethical imperatives would be at play.

Virtue ethics faded into near obscurity in the early modern era. But in the twentieth century, philosophers including Michael Slote, Martha Nussbaum, and Alasdair MacIntyre argued that there were problems with the deontological and utilitarian ethics that were alleviated by virtue ethics.[9] The deontologists and utilitarians could discuss right action, but they seemed incapable of saying how it was that someone came to be able to make right decisions. Deontological and utilitarian theories are sometimes called "act" or "rule" ethics, since they deal with individual actions and the universal rules that apply to them. What they don't deal with, generally, is the training needed to create the sort of character who would be inclined to act morally. Deontology and utilitarianism seem to imply that simply *understanding* the ethical theory should be enough; anyone who knew best would, or should, do best. But it's clear that we can know something is wrong and still do it, through weakness of the will, for example.

Further, it seems clear that certain things that we think are good aren't necessarily good for everyone in every set of circumstances. For example, police officers can arrest people, commandeer vehicles, and use deadly force in certain situations. But we don't want ordinary citizens acting like this. So something about the specific role of the police officer requires some specific ethical rules, even if ultimately all the societal roles must abide by certain overarching rules. Importantly, police officers undergo training to learn about their role, and only after they have been properly trained and, one hopes, instilled with the proper character, are they allowed to act as police officers. This is why the founders of virtue ethics, Plato and Aristotle (384–322 BCE), emphasized building character, noting the importance of *training* someone to be ethical, rather than simply *explaining* how to be ethical.

In his book *After Virtue*, Alasdair MacIntyre argues that character is created over the course of a lifetime by the manner in which we act. MacIntyre agrees with Plato, who thought that first we behave morally, and then we learn morality. In brief, we don't explain ethics to a child, we simply say no. Only when people are older and have already internalized virtuous behavior are they capable of understanding the abstract reasons for behaving virtuously or morally. At that point, one can fully engage in philosophical thinking about ethical behavior and perform the kinds of ethical thought experiments that deontologists and consequentialists think of as the heart of ethics, that is, deducing general rules and effectively thinking about outcomes.

At first, we learn ethics by being reprimanded when we misbehave, and rewarded when we behave properly. If we wish to instill certain specific virtues, like courage, we must test the person who is to be given this character. Courage comes from facing danger. So if a child is to become courageous, he must encounter some dangers. If we see that the child has a natural propensity for courage, he becomes a good candidate for the role of soldier or police officer. We then increase the training in courage, adding other virtues, including gentleness and moderation, to slowly mold the character desired.

Without experience in ethical behavior, and general experience of the world, this sort of thought is likely to be misguided, and without the moral character to carry through on our ethical thinking, it's likely to be ineffective. Without background training in good behavior, no amount of abstract knowledge of good behavior will suffice. No matter how much theorizing we do, without the background in action, our propensity to act selfishly and without virtue will overcome our knowledge of better ways to be.

Can Batman Train Robin in Virtue?

So when Batman takes Robin under his wing, he doesn't just *explain* the superhero ethic to him; he *trains* Robin, teaching him by example and experience the ways of the superhero. But still, we have questions about the moral rightness of this: one could, for example, train a boy to be a thief, giving him the "virtues" of the criminal. Virtue ethics also demands that we decide the kind of training we should use, what sort of ethical character we should try to create. For this we will have to, like the deontologists and consequentialists, appeal to general rules, and like the consequentialists in particular, ask, "What kind of person do we want to train a young person to be?"

Although virtue ethics concerns training, not everyone can receive the training for every role; if someone shows a natural propensity for certain virtues, those virtues can be honed. But if someone strongly lacks certain virtues, it may simply be impossible to train such a person to take on a role that requires those virtues. Take Jason Todd, for instance; Jason had the virtue of courage, but he also had the vices of harshness and rashness. He took delight in roughing up villains and made many impetuous decisions that put Batman and himself in danger. In terms of Jason's ethical training, Batman seems to have failed in two ways: he failed in providing moderating virtues, and also in changing the underlying character of his young ward.

Batman faced a couple of difficulties in training Jason Todd. First, Todd's character was already shaped by his life of crime. Second, Batman's focus has always been on training in fighting, courage, and action. He was simply unprepared to train Robin in gentleness and moderation of courage. Probably as a result of these failures, Jason rushed into battle with the Joker and was killed, a tragedy that has haunted Batman ever since (even after Jason's recent resurrection).

Sometimes Heroes Fail

But how could Robin have been saved? In the end, sometimes moral character will escape us no matter how good our intentions, or those of our teachers. Yet virtue is always worth pursuing; had Batman not made the virtuous choice in his own intense training, he would never have become Batman.[10] While the deontologists' rules and the consequentialists' emphasis on outcomes can help us make moral choices, they make it seem as though morality was simply a matter of making the right choices. Sometimes, virtue ethics admits, even the best intentions are incapable of producing a morally good outcome because of the multitude of constraints upon the development of character. As Jason Todd discovered, sometimes failure is simply a fact of the moral life. Perhaps Jason was simply unfit for the role of superhero, lacking the natural propensity or inclination. (Indeed, after his resurrection, he became more of an antihero, choosing to kill criminals.) In that case, Batman should have placed him in some other role—as it happened, he did ultimately suspend Jason from superhero training late in his career (but by then it was *too* late). Or perhaps Jason Todd simply needed a kind of training that Batman could not give him.

We can now return to a question from the beginning of this chapter: Is Batman's decision to train Robin morally permissible? No matter how you may answer based upon a particular ethical perspective, what seems clear is, in the context of this issue, Batman is a lousy deontologist, a decent consequential-ist, and, most assuredly, some kind of a virtue ethicist. And without being the world's greatest detectives (or philosophers), we'll have to leave it at that!

NOTES

1. See Barbara Greenleaf's *Children through the Ages: A History of Childhood* (New York: McGraw-Hill, 1978).

2. See Kant's *Grounding for the Metaphysics of Morals* [1785], translated by James W. Ellington (Indianapolis: Hackett Publishing Co., 1993). Kant gives almost this exact example in his essay *On a Supposed Right to Lie from Philanthropic Concerns* (1799), where he said that you could not lie to a murderer who asked you the location of his intended victim (who is hiding in your house). (This essay is included in this edition of *Grounding for the Metaphysics of Morals*).

3. Kant, *Grounding for the Metaphysics of Morals*, 421.

4. We'll focus on Jason because of his beginnings as a street punk (at least in post-*Crisis on Infinite Earths* continuity), and because of his tragic end (in 1988's *A Death in the Family*).

5. Jeremy Bentham, *The Principles of Morals and Legislation* [1781] (Buffalo, NY: Prometheus Books, 1988); John Stuart Mill, *Utilitarianism* [1863] (Indianapolis: Hackett Publishing Company, 2002).

6. For utilitarian arguments defending use of people for various means, see Peter Singer, *Practical Ethics* (Cambridge: Cambridge Univ. Press, 1993). Kant argued strongly against this position, requiring that persons must never be used simply as means to an end, without also being considered as ends themselves (*Grounding for the Metaphysics of Morals*, 429).

7. One of the leading figures in twentieth-century virtue ethics is Alasdair MacIntyre, who, in his seminal volume *After Virtue* (Notre Dame, IN: Notre Dame Press, 1984), defined "character" as the fusing of role and personality (p. 28). In other words, in character we have what someone does, which could be their job, vocation, or calling, and their underlying inclinations, desires, and attitudes coming together to form a whole. MacIntyre notes that the Greek word that forms the basis for "ethics" and the Latin word that forms the basis for "morality" both roughly translate as "pertaining to character" (p. 38).

8. See Plato's *Republic*, trans. G. Grube (Indianapolis: Hackett, 1992). The writings of the Chinese philosopher Confucius (551–479 BCE), which predate those of Plato, are often considered in the realm of virtue ethics. Homer (seventh century BCE) also wrote works that contribute to the virtue ethical tradition, but as a poet, and not in the form of philosophical writings that argue for the place of virtue ethics.

9. MacIntyre's *After Virtue* is a sustained attempt to criticize the ethics of the modern world. Martha Nussbaum's *The Fragility of Goodness* (Cambridge: Cambridge Univ. Press,

1986) is less polemical and tries to lay out what a virtue ethic that respected human fragility would look like. Michael Slote's *From Morality to Virtue* (Oxford: Oxford Univ. Press, 1992) tries to recapitulate and justify the movement back toward thinking about the virtues in twentieth-century ethical thought.

10. See the chapter by Ananth and Dixon in this book for more on the ethics of the decision to become Batman.

BATMAN'S VIRTUOUS HATRED

Stephen Kershnar

Batman Hates

Let's face it—Batman hates criminals. In *The Dark Knight Returns* (1986), for example, he's in a position to kill a powerful mutant behemoth, a member of a murderous youth gang that threatens Gotham. But rather than just kill him, Batman decides to fight the behemoth in order to remove any self-doubt about whether he could beat him. Despite breaking the behemoth's nose, Batman loses the battle. After recovering from his injuries, Batman insists on fighting him again. This time, ignoring his conscience, Batman destroys him. In this case (and others), Batman seems to get immediate satisfaction from dominating and destroying the bad guys, although he never seems to get outright pleasure from it.

What can explain this attitude? Well, Batman is plagued by nightmares and tortured memories of helplessly watching while his parents were murdered (for instance, in 1992's

Blind Justice). Also, apart from his butler, Alfred, he lives a solitary life. Of course, he works well with Commissioner Gordon, the various Robins, Catwoman, and others, but he seems to shy away from any interaction that does not focus on fighting crime. In particular, despite flirtations and temporary dalliances with Catwoman (both in and out of disguise), he never makes a life with her. Batman's hatred of evildoers in part explains why more generally he jeopardizes his chance at loving relationships with the various beautiful women in his life. For example, his relationships with Julie Madison, Vicki Vale, and Vesper Fairchild never lead to marriage, children, or even stability. As a result, it seems that his life, however valuable to others, is lonely and unfulfilling.

Vice and Hatred

In judging whether persons are good or bad, we can use the ideas of virtue and vice, which form a central part of the moral philosophy known as *virtue ethics*. Virtue ethics concerns what sort of a person one should be, differing from other schools of ethics that focus on how someone should act (deontology, for example) and on how to evaluate the consequences of an act (utilitarianism, for example).

The philosopher Aristotle (384–322 BCE) put forth the most famous version of virtue ethics.[1] In his view, moral virtues are the most appropriate character traits of a person that make him good and, thus, allow him to make the right decisions. Think of a virtue as a mean between extremes in our actions and reactions. For example, in a situation where one is called upon to fight in a war, a person having the virtue of courage will not go berserk (the extreme of *too much*) or run away like a coward (the extreme of *too little*), but will stand firm and fight (the *mean* between the extremes). There are many other virtues, including prudence, justice, self-control, affability, mercy, generosity, and patience, to name a few. Virtuous people tend to do things in a rationally appropriate and correct way that makes them flourish while at the same time doing what is morally required.

Virtue ethics has been criticized for a couple of reasons. First, one could argue that it's circular in that "virtue" is defined in terms of the tendency to do good things, while at the same time "good things" is defined in terms of what virtuous people tend to do! Second, virtue ethics has been criticized for being impractical because it provides no guidance when two or more virtues conflict. For example, justice and mercy have a tendency to conflict with one another on a regular basis when people try to make moral decisions about an appropriate punishment for a crime. A judge who considers giving a long prison sentence to a repentant Riddler cannot be both just *and* merciful, and virtue ethics tells her little about what to do. (It's a riddle!)

It's not clear that either of these criticisms succeed, however. Virtue need not be defined in terms of the tendency to do good things; instead, virtue might be defined in terms of loving what is good and hating what is bad. And even if virtue is unhelpful in guiding our actions, it might still be helpful with other issues. For example, it's useful in helping a person decide if she is the sort of person that she wants to be. Despite these disagreements, virtue ethics sits alongside deontology and utilitarianism as one of the major ethical systems that philosophers use to evaluate and justify moral decision-making, and it's the one that we'll use to analyze Batman's hatred.[2]

Is Batman Virtuous, or Does He Do Virtuous Things?

There are two popular theories of what makes someone virtuous (or vicious). According to Aristotle, persons themselves are primarily virtuous. A person is virtuous when he tends to do the right thing, and that action is virtuous only if it's the kind of thing that a virtuous person would do. Let's call this theory the "Virtuous-Persons Theory."

For example, if Commissioner Gordon tends to do the right thing—treat his wife and child well, prevent the police from using excessive force, and so on—then he's virtuous. In the Virtuous-Persons Theory, virtue centers on the question of how someone tends to behave. Even when he has an affair with an attractive female officer in *Batman: Year One* (1987), Gordon feels guilty and tells his wife, probably in part to repair his marriage and in part to enable him to fight police brutality and corruption. On this theory, Gordon's actions are virtuous if they are the sort that a virtuous person in Gordon's position would do.

The Virtuous-Persons Theory raises a couple of concerns, though. One is that we normally believe that what makes someone virtuous is what he thinks, not what he does or tends to do. For instance, we think that a person who was paralyzed could be virtuous or vicious even if she were unable to affect others through her actions. So this theory is incorrect to the extent that it focuses on what people do or tend to do, rather than what goes on in their heads.

Another concern is that particular actions can be virtuous or vicious regardless of who takes the actions. For example, consider Carmine "The Roman" Falcone, a mafia don and a source of violence, corruption, and death, whom Batman and Catwoman investigate in *The Long Halloween* (1988). At one point, Carmine puts a one-million-dollar bounty on Batman's and Catwoman's heads, which eventually leads to Falcone's death and the destruction of his empire. But in addition to these bad acts, Falcone truly loves his son (a Harvard MBA and Rhodes Scholar), and this love is virtuous even if Falcone himself is not. Bad guys can have good thoughts and do nice things, and we need our theory of virtue and vice to reflect this.

A second theory of virtue holds that a person's *thoughts and actions* are primarily virtuous (or vicious), rather than the person himself—he's virtuous only to the extent that he has virtuous thoughts or actions. We'll call this theory the "Virtuous-Thoughts-and-Actions Theory." With this theory, a thought is virtuous when it involves a person loving what is good (for example, Gotham residents having happy, healthy, and fun lives) and hating what is evil (for example, Gotham residents suffering because of the Joker or the Ventriloquist). A person loves something when he is pleased that it happens, wants it to happen, or does what he can to make it happen, and he hates something when he has the same attitude toward the thing not happening. Similarly, a person's thoughts are vicious when he hates what is good and loves what is bad. According to this theory, a person is vicious if he has many vicious thoughts, or perhaps many more vicious thoughts than virtuous ones.

The Virtuous-Thoughts-and-Actions Theory is attractive. It lets us judge a thought or action without having to know anything about the person who has it. For example, in *Batman: Year One*, a pimp manhandles a young prostitute in response to her poor judgment in soliciting tricks. Other than his motivation, we don't need to know anything else about the pimp to know that his actions—pimping her out and manhandling her—are vicious. Of course, Batman (disguised as a veteran cruising the red-light district) responds by provoking the pimp and then smashing him with an elbow and a devastating kick to the head. The provocation suggests that Batman is looking for an excuse to injure the pimp, rather than merely trying to protect the young girl. His violence results from his hatred of evil.

The Virtuous-Thoughts-and-Actions Theory, unlike the Virtuous-Persons Theory, explains that virtuous people tend to think and act in certain ways because they love good things and hate bad things. According to this theory, persons are virtuous depending on the number of virtuous thoughts they have, or perhaps their ratio of virtuous to vicious thoughts. This is consistent with how we often think of people, isn't it? We often think that whether someone is virtuous or not depends on what goes on in his head—in particular, it depends on whether he loves good things and hates evil ones.

Batman's Hatred Is Virtuous

Batman hates criminals and loves to see them suffer, and this might suggest that he's vicious. For example, when smashing the pimp with his elbow, he worries about enjoying it too much. But is Batman in fact vicious? Or might this hatred actually be virtuous?

The issue of whether Batman is virtuous is a tricky one, because not all persons are good and not all pain is bad. For instance, we often think that it's good that evildoers suffer. We think that it's good that people get what they deserve, and vicious people deserve pain (or suffering). Because virtuous persons love good things, they may love to see a vicious person in pain—a virtuous person can actually *want* a vicious one to suffer, and be pleased when he does suffer. And if wanting someone to suffer or being pleased that someone is suffering *is the same thing as* hating him, virtuous people can hate. Batman is just such a case.

"Just desserts" explains why we think that Batman's suffering is bad, whereas the suffering of a dirty and brutal cop isn't. Detective Flass in *Batman: Year One* is a former Green Beret who uses his training and size to brutalize men who are doing nothing more than hanging out on a street corner. Flass and fellow officers actually beat James Gordon for not taking bribes or tolerating a dirty police force. Gordon later gives Flass a bat to make the fight more even and severely beats him, stopping just short of sending him to the hospital. He then leaves Flass bound and naked, which sends Flass and the other dirty cops a clear message.

Like Batman, Gordon is obviously a superb fighter, but unlike Batman, it's not clear that Gordon enjoys handing out rough justice or beating people to send a message. We imagine that Batman would probably enjoy beating and humiliating Flass. His hatred is virtuous, but this dark personality stands in sharp contrast to a person like Saint Francis of Assisi and superheroes like Spider-Man and Superman, who are also virtuous but not awash in hatred.

Responding critically, you might claim that a truly virtuous person doesn't hate other human beings. Rather, hatred is a bad thing, an inherently negative attitude, and therefore best avoided. If this is true, then two conclusions might be drawn. It might be thought that because he hates some people, Batman isn't virtuous, or at least he is less virtuous than he could be. Alternatively, we might conclude that Batman, being virtuous, doesn't really hate people. Perhaps he views criminals in the way a soldier might view warriors on the other side, as adversaries who have to be disabled or killed—but not as persons worthy of contempt or disrespect.

I would argue, however, that such criticism is mistaken (though I don't hate my critics for proposing it!). Hatred (that is, having a negative attitude toward something) is an appropriate attitude toward persons who maliciously cause others to suffer. Other points of view, which may be either positive or indifferent, are not appropriate: good persons should not feel benevolent toward evildoers who intentionally hit, poison, or kill others. Nor should a person merely indicate through indifference toward evildoers that she does not care if they act in such ways. Negative attitudes and emotions such as hatred, disgust, or contempt are the morally correct ways to respond to wrongdoing, and therefore they are virtuous.

The analogy to soldiers is also mistaken in that it doesn't capture Batman's actual attitudes toward evildoers. He shows little appreciation for criminals and never expresses regret or remorse when foiling their plans, even when doing so involves serious violence. Criminals, unlike soldiers fighting for their countries, are not worthy of respect or admiration, but are wrongdoers who have earned contempt and hatred. So, I would argue that Batman does indeed hate criminals. And since this is the only appropriate attitude to have toward such people, he is virtuous *because of,* not despite, his hatred.

Batman's Hatred Is Not in His Self-Interest

Even if we accept that Batman's hatred of evildoers is virtuous, it still might not be in his self-interest. Batman's hatred has led him to be so focused on crime fighting that he can't indulge in other things that make a person's life worthwhile, such as family, friends, and hobbies. For example, the fact that Batman has so many ruthless enemies makes it unwise for him to get involved with a woman. Consider what happened to Jim Gordon in *Year One*: Flass and his buddies severely beat him with baseball bats, kidnapped his wife, dropped his baby off a bridge, and exposed his affair—and this is nothing compared to what Bruce Wayne could expect for his friends and family if his identity became known to the Joker, Two-Face, and the rest. Even though it's in the interests of Gotham's citizens for Batman to be consumed with hatred and crime fighting, it's not good for his mental and emotional well-being.

There is something unseemly about having a life revolving around hatred and violence, even if it's directed at persons who deserve it. Perhaps this is best explained by the notion that a virtuous life need not go well. Batman is certainly an example of this. Virtue alone does not guarantee that your life will be a success, because it doesn't guarantee meaningful relationships, true beliefs, and pleasure—all things that are essential for someone's life to flourish. A person whose life is consumed with hatred, even virtuous hatred, might have a less pleasurable life, or lack a beloved partner and friends, and this explains why his life goes poorly. With his brooding and violent outlook and his isolation, Batman seems to be just such a person.

Batman's hatred makes the world a much better place even if it makes his life worse. His pain and isolation pale in comparison to the ocean of death and destruction that would have resulted had Batman not stopped his enemies' nefarious plans. For example, in *The Long Halloween*, the Joker plans to stop a serial killer by gassing everyone in Gotham Square on New Year's Eve. He reasons that "odds are" the killer will be in the crowd, and he seems utterly unconcerned with the massive collateral damage. (Luckily, Batman stops him.) Another example of how dangerous the Joker is comes from *The Dark Knight Returns:* after claiming to have already killed six hundred people, he gasses and kills hundreds more who come to hear him interviewed on a late-night talk show. Batman doesn't stop the Joker every time, but when he does, he saves many lives, and on the balance definitely makes the world a better place, regardless of the effect on his own well-being.

Could Batman choose *not* to hate? It's not obvious that he could: watching his parents being murdered greatly influenced his attitude toward crime and criminals. In *The Dark Knight Returns*, we see that as a boy, Bruce insisted that any criminals in his bedtime reading were caught and punished. In another episode in that story, which may be merely a dream, young Bruce fell down into a hole where he was claimed by a giant bat that instilled hatred and ferocity in him. Without control over his hatred, Batman can't be responsible for it, so we can distinguish the issue of whether Batman is virtuous from whether he is responsible for what makes him virtuous, his hatred of evil.

Lacking Balance

One issue we have not considered is whether a successful life requires a balance between love of the good and hatred of the bad. It might be that a person's life is happier if he has a proper balance between love and hate.[3] In this view, a person who spends too much time loving the good seems oblivious to the suffering and pain that are a part of everyone's life. Similarly, a person who spends too much time hating evil seems insensitive to the many good and beautiful things in life. Given Batman's laserlike focus on fighting crime, he might fit into the latter category. Thus, aside from his isolation and tortured dreams, Batman's life might also be limited by the prevalence of hate in his life. But without his hate, could the Batman exist? Would he be the same Dark Knight? I think not.

NOTES

1. See Aristotle, *The Nicomachean Ethics*, trans. J. Welldon (Amherst, NY: Prometheus Books, 1987), especially Book 2.

2. For a simple introduction to virtue ethics, deontology, utilitarianism, and other ethical theories, see Simon Blackburn, *Ethics: A Very Short Introduction* (Oxford: Oxford Univ. Press, 2003).

3. See the interview with Bat-Tzu in chapter 20 of this book for more on the importance of balance in one's life.

PART TWO

LAW, JUSTICE, AND THE SOCIAL ORDER: WHERE DOES BATMAN FIT IN?

NO MAN'S LAND: SOCIAL ORDER IN GOTHAM CITY AND NEW ORLEANS

Brett Chandler Patterson

No Man's Lands: Gotham City and New Orleans

The average American takes social order for granted. We wake up each day assuming that our institutions—educational, medical, political, and so on—will run smoothly, even if not always in our interests. Terrorism has fostered some doubt, but on the whole, most Americans still assume and enjoy a relatively peaceful existence. Even the United States, however, is not exempt from the large-scale destruction of natural disasters. Hurricane Katrina made this point painfully clear. Earthquakes, floods, tsunamis, hurricanes, tornadoes, mudslides, and meteor strikes—there are still many forces in this universe that are beyond our control, forces that we fear. When that fear strikes during and after these disasters, what happens to social order? Do human beings resort to a more primal, violent nature in our struggle to survive?

This is the topic of perhaps the most masterful Batman storyline to date, *No Man's Land*, which traces the disintegration of social order in an earthquake-ravaged Gotham City.[1] Though the fictional story predates the flooding of New Orleans by six years, the eerie resemblance between the fictional story and the days following Katrina's landfall on August 29, 2005, adds weight to a story that we might otherwise dismiss as exaggerated and melodramatic. *No Man's Land* presents a wide array of responses to the loss of social order and reminds us that despite the colorful rogues' gallery, Batman's true enemy, and perhaps ours as well, is anarchy. The storyline also calls to mind the political philosophy of Thomas Hobbes (1588–1679), who argued that human beings in their natural state are inclined to war and distrust. When the structures of social order are challenged by large-scale disasters, this "natural state" rears its ugly head again, forcing representatives of that social order to step in and fight to reclaim the social contract.

The Road to No Man's Land

Gotham crumbled overnight in 1998's storyline *Cataclysm*, in which a magnitude 7.6 earthquake devastated the city (which had recently been weakened by a widely dispersed lethal virus in 1996's *Contagion*). The only buildings left standing in Gotham after the quake were the ones reinforced by Wayne Enterprises. Wayne Manor, however, was destroyed because that historical structure could not be reinforced (or Bruce Wayne's secret batcave might have been discovered). In the months that followed, Batman and company struggled first in pulling themselves out of the rubble and then in assessing the full extent of the damage. In *Aftershock* and *Road to No Man's Land*, Gotham's elite abandon the city since the infrastructure that supported their industries and businesses has been destroyed. They do not have the will or the wealth to attempt to rebuild it. Meanwhile, the crowds of people in the city panic in various ways, contributing to a bridge collapse that kills hundreds. Though Police Commissioner Jim Gordon tries to keep the peace, he also, in what he perceives later as a moment of weakness, seeks in vain to find a job in another city.[2]

In "Mr. Wayne Goes to Washington," Bruce attempts to persuade the federal government to assist Gotham, pleading for the lives of the seven million people there, while trying to combat the negative rhetoric of Nicholas Scratch, a mysterious public figure (villain) who has targeted Gotham.[3] Yet in a surreal move, the president issues an executive order—followed by congressional approval—that the city must be cut off from the rest of the country, because the damage is too great and too costly. The federal government gives a forty-eight-hour deadline for the people to evacuate the city and then, in a drastic move, blows the other bridges and surrounds the city with blockades and troops. At this point, Gotham officially becomes a "no man's land."

In our world, Hurricane Katrina's storm surge and the subsequent flooding were the undoing of New Orleans in 2005. Around 80 percent of the city flooded (water primarily from Lake Pontchartrain) after the levee system failed. Much of this occurred late at night, surprising those resting in their homes, thinking that the levees had protected them from the worst of Katrina. Although the federal government did not go as far as the one portrayed in the comics, there was a delay of a couple of days before a full-scale rescue effort was put into place, and there were a few politicians who voiced a desire to abandon the city to the swamps surrounding it.[4] Since New Orleans—unlike Gotham—had advance warning of the impending disaster, there were some emergency measures already in place, leading thousands to seek shelter at the New Orleans Superdome and the Convention Center. The breakdown of social order was not as severe as in the fictional Gotham, but much chaos did ensue.

Survival over Justice: Villains, Gangs, and Hobbes's State of Nature

At the time of the declaration of No Man's Land, a significant number of people were unable to leave, or chose not to leave. They found themselves in an environment without technology—no electricity, no heating or air conditioning, no gasoline, no transportation, and no grocery or retail stores. Gotham City resorted to a primitive state, people scavenging off the remains of what Gotham once was. The "No Law and a New Order" story (in *NML* 1) introduces us to No Man's Land, showing a group of children fighting over food dropped into the city by a sensationalist photographer who wants pictures of people fighting. Within a few pages Scarface has shot a young boy over a package of cookies. We soon learn that an elaborate system of barter has developed, as people trade things that are no longer of value (fancy electronics) for basic necessities (flashlights with batteries, fresh produce).

We also learn that people have started to gather into gangs to protect themselves and to provide some system of distributing goods. Tagging—spray painting a symbol of your gang in a highly visible place—becomes essential for identifying whether you are in a relatively friendly or an overly hostile part of the city. In the early days of Gotham's crisis, the major Bat-villains—including Two-Face, Penguin, Black Mask, and the Joker—have each carved out territory from the chaos, celebrating in the absence of the social order that had imprisoned them in Arkham Asylum. During this period, Batman, going through his own crisis as Bruce Wayne, is absent from the city, adding to the general despair among the populace.

The situation resembles the "state of nature" that Thomas Hobbes described in his political philosophy. In *Leviathan* (1651), Hobbes painted a rather dark portrait of the natural state of humanity, claiming that outside society we became brutes at war with one another.[5] Yet his theory grew out of his own experience of living in exile in France during the English civil war in the 1640s, watching his nation's social order break down. Hobbes argued for the value of a centralized authority that would galvanize the rest of the populace. In his opinion, human life is a competition to obtain power; life is a struggle over a limited number of material goods. We are motivated by a fear of death and fear of others' power, no matter how high-minded we might pretend to be. Fear motivates us to seek peace; we agree to a social contract out of a desire to preserve our own lives in a social order; we agree to a system of justice to preserve that order. A sovereign power—"the Leviathan"— preserves that order and protects those subjects who have willingly submitted to that rule. Fear of falling back into the "state of nature" keeps subjects in line.

Though some philosophers have challenged whether such a "state of nature" ever existed, Hobbes would counter that whenever a country plunges into civil war, it falls back to this condition. Several novels in the twentieth century, from Joseph Conrad's *Heart of Darkness* (1899/1902) to William Golding's *Lord of the Flies* (1954) and the current television show *Lost*, have all suggested that going from "civilization" to extremely isolated natural settings can bring out the "wild" side in human beings.[6] Of course, wide-scale natural disasters have the same potential.

In the days immediately following the 2005 flooding of New Orleans, the media reported looting, possible rapes and murders, and conflict among various gangs of people brandishing weapons. Tensions in the city over racism, poverty, and drugs broke out as the populace was in a state of panic, with corpses lying in the city streets. When National Guard troops started evacuating people and restoring order, they discovered that a number of the rumors were unfounded; the media had sensationalized and exaggerated the extent of the criminal activity, particularly at the refuge centers. So New Orleans was not exactly Gotham City, but there were long moments of distrust, and there could easily have been more criminal activity away from these crowds. Some police officers actually abandoned the city and were later disciplined. Twenty-five thousand people waited over five days to be rescued from the Superdome; National Guard troops turned people away from refuges in those later days; hotels turned people out onto the streets; and the sheriff of Jefferson Parish closed the greater New Orleans Bridge to refugees, emphasizing that the suburbs would not fall into the chaos. Many have argued that latent racism affected the handling of the thousands who could not or did not leave the city.[7] It is also noteworthy that one of the first institutions to be restored in the first week was a makeshift jail. Hobbes's "state of nature" seemed to be alive and well.

William Petit versus Jim Gordon: Violence in the Quest for Justice

One of the more thought-provoking threads in the *No Man's Land* storyline is the conflict between Jim Gordon and fellow police officer William Petit, revealing two distinct perspectives on how to oppose the reigning anarchy. Gordon and Petit start out on the same side; they are both seeking to reclaim Gotham and rebuild social trust in the police force. But as the plot progresses, we are gradually shown the radical difference between Petit and Gordon. We come to see that they represent different tactics in reestablishing a sovereign power over the chaos. In *Leviathan* Thomas Hobbes described two different ways that sovereignty can come to power—the people can agree to the rule (a "paternal" power) or the ruler can seize power (a "despotical" power).[8] In certain ways, Gordon is the paternal power, seeking to maintain the standards of justice as he moves back into control of the social order, while Petit is the despotic power who seeks to seize power through intimidation and force.

In "No Law and a New Order," Jim Gordon believes that he is sliding into moral ambiguity by setting off a war between two rival gangs in an effort to weaken them, but Petit pushes even further, calling for murder to solidify the war—and he finds his opportunity in rescuing Gordon from an ambush. Another significant conflict arises within the week: when Gordon's plan works and the GCPD claims the gangs' territories, the police wonder where they are going to put the prisoners. Gordon decides to release them, but Petit demands that they need to be intimidated so that they will not return later in greater numbers. So he executes a gang member before Gordon can stop him. Gordon immediately seeks to discipline Petit, but in feeling that he too has compromised, he offers no answer to Petit's verbal challenge: "Tell me I'm wrong." From this point on, Petit becomes increasingly obsessed with violence, claiming that the only way to deal with Gotham's criminals is to exterminate them.

Gordon's main goal, along with keeping his family safe, is to reestablish social law over the city. In "Bread and Circuses" (in *NML* 2), Gordon expresses the Machiavellian lesson that he must be seen enforcing the law to create social trust again.[9] Jim Gordon's biggest compromise, though, is working with Two-Face in a power play that wins more territory for the GCPD, but which eventually comes back to hurt them.

Gordon and Petit stay together through this, but in "Fruit of the Earth" (in *NML* 3), the conflict reaches a turning point. While facing a hostage scenario in which a gang threatens an officer, Gordon tries to negotiate, but Petit simply shoots the offender. After Gordon's reprimand, Petit goes his separate way, claiming that Gordon is not strong enough to face the challenges of No Man's Land. The Huntress (one of Gotham's heroines) later faces off against Petit, who argues that their tactics must change because they are soldiers in a war. Petit hovers on the periphery of the plotline, though frequently calling for lethal force against Killer Croc, Two-Face (who happens to be imprisoned), and the Joker. The climactic encounter with Joker in "End Game" (*NML* 5) shows Petit finally broken and insane; in seeking to murder the Joker, he ends up killing several of his own men (whom the Joker dressed as clowns).

In "Jurisprudence" (*NML* 4), Gordon literally faces his own trial when Two-Face (former district attorney Harvey Dent) kidnaps him and "prosecutes" him for violating the laws he was sworn to protect. Yet because of his compassion for Harvey Dent, and with help from Officer Renee Montoya, Gordon is able to survive. Then in the last, crucially heartbreaking moment, after Joker has murdered his wife, Gordon faces the maniacal clown, with Batman nearby pleading for Jim not to sacrifice his values (*NML* 5). Gordon does not kill Joker, but he does shoot him in the knee before Joker is taken into custody—showing that the residual impact of No Man's Land is still in play. In the days that follow, mourning the loss of his wife, Jim Gordon wonders if their efforts and triumphs were worth the sacrifices.

The Witness of Nonviolent Humanitarians

Thankfully, there are also a few peace-loving humanitarians in the midst of the story. Two prominent examples are Father Christian, a Catholic priest in charge of a mission, and Dr. Leslie Thompkins, a medical doctor trying to hold together a makeshift hospital for the scores of wounded in the city (and one of Bruce Wayne's oldest friends and confidantes). Their parallel stories are told in "Fear of Faith" (*NML* 1) and "Spiritual Currency" (*NML* 4). In the first of these stories, Father Christian has turned the remains of his church into a refugee center, seeking to provide food, water, shelter, and some degree of safety to those staying there. He has refused to ally himself with anyone else, including the GCPD, which is using force in its efforts to reclaim the city. He also extends his charity to one of Gotham's villains, Scarecrow, despite warnings from the Huntress. Scarecrow sabotages the mission's food supply, forcing Christian to negotiate with another villain, Penguin, who, as a master tradesman, has thrived in the chaos. Penguin gives Christian the supplies he needs in exchange for allowing him to store guns in the basement of the mission. Feeling backed into a corner, Christian accepts the offer, a decision that precipitates a later power struggle in front of the church, where Father Christian's group apparently is saved by the intervention of the GCPD, Huntress, and Batman. At the end of the struggle, Father Christian and company dump the guns into Gotham Harbor, stubbornly refusing to let anyone get their hands on the weapons.

In the second story, Dr. Leslie Thompkins sees her clinic as a place of refuge, even for a notorious killer, the gang lord Mr. Zsasz. Huntress, Petit, and Batman all challenge Dr. Thompkins's decision, but she argues that her commitments are to healing and to pacifism. Huntress tells her that it's easy to make such a stand as long as Batman is protecting her, and in fact, later in the story, Zsasz awakens and Batman is not there. Dr. Thompkins faces the possibility of her death as she tries to appeal to some compassion in him and announces that she will not resist with violence. Killer Croc, who is seeking Zsasz for killing a friend, grabs Zsasz before he can hurt the doctor, and then Batman finally arrives to scare Croc away and take Zsasz to Blackgate Prison. Since she had earlier reprimanded him for his tactics, Batman now apologizes to her for the violence that he uses. Thompkins makes an agreement with him that if he will work for peace in the city, she will help him work for peace in his heart.

Both of these stories contrast greatly with the excessive violence, competition, and hatred expressed in the activity of the gangs and the power maneuvers of various Arkham escapees. Though others like Batman and Jim Gordon help protect these individuals, Christian and Thompkins are prepared to face the consequences of their humanitarianism and pacifism, even to the point of sacrificing themselves for others. In *Leviathan* (Book 3), Thomas Hobbes argues that religious organizations should be subservient to the sovereign power to prevent divided loyalties, thus preserving peace. Church authorities should acknowledge the preeminence of the sovereign rule; otherwise, they will undermine the stable social order enforced by the sovereign.

Christian theologians today, following H. Richard Niebuhr, John Howard Yoder, and Stanley Hauerwas, however, would strongly disagree with this subordination. These theologians have argued for the distinctive social character of the Church; the beliefs and practices of the Christian community set it apart from other communities. Commitment to God should be the centering activity that orients the value of all other aspects of one's life. Christians can serve an earthly sovereign, but their primary loyalty is to God through church communities. These theologians believe that unlike the deist "distant God" perspective of Thomas Hobbes, God is working in the world through the new order presented in the politics of the Church.[10]

Father Christian has a respectful relationship with Jim Gordon and with Batman, but he refuses to be subservient to the social order they seek to reinstitute in violent ways. Concern for his people leads Father Christian to compromise in negotiating with Penguin, but he reasserts the values of the Church later in the story by dropping the guns in Gotham Bay. Though it's unclear whether Dr. Thompkins would consider herself a Christian, she, as a pacifist, also resists becoming a part of Jim Gordon's and Batman's efforts to reclaim the city through coercive means, reprimanding Batman for his violent tactics. Batman and Gordon (and others) need the examples Father Christian and Dr. Thompkins provide. Without such examples they might cycle into insanity like William Petit.

Likewise, although most of the news coming out of New Orleans seemed to focus on the chaos, there were also stories of heroism and humanitarian aid—ministers trying to provide hope to their congregations and doctors trying to keep patients alive under hostile circumstances. Many of the relief workers were themselves trapped in the city. Ordinary citizens also became heroes as they stepped forward to help, creating makeshift shelters, sharing looted water and food, and offering comfort to the elderly and the sick; their heroism became an inspiration to others.[11] Numerous humanitarian organizations made their way into New Orleans following the devastation. Though they worked respectfully with the civil authorities, many of the relief organizations mobilized on their own. New Orleans needed their distinct contributions.

"This Is My Town": Batman and the Restoration of Order

Finally, in "Shellgame" (*NML* 5), we witness the events that lead to the end of No Man's Land, when Lex Luthor enters the city in a shrewd political move, attempting to claim the land of many who died during the earthquake and of those who lack the resources to challenge his claim. To the public, he simply seems to bring the money and national attention needed to pull Gotham out of its decay. Batman faces Luthor twice—once not long after he arrives and again after foiling Luthor's fraud—both times emphasizing that Gotham is *his* town, not Luthor's.

At the start of *No Man's Land*, many characters questioned this assertion because, mysteriously, Batman was nowhere to be found. When Batman finally appears, over three months into the city's isolation, he finds that he must rebuild the mythology that he uses to intimidate criminals and that he must adjust his tactics to the new environment. Eventually he learns to work within the system of gangs, acknowledging that the people feel lost without loyalty to a leader (a sovereign) who can protect them and help distribute goods justly. Batman essentially becomes a gang lord, albeit a benevolent one. He also permits various Arkham residents, like Penguin and Poison Ivy, to maintain roles in the new order similar to the roles they chose for themselves (upon their escape from Arkham), as long as they contribute to the greater good of the city. Gotham is deeply hurt, and Batman invokes a long-range plan (in contrast to Superman's quick fix, which does not work),[12] which eventually incorporates most of his partners and colleagues: Oracle, Huntress, a new Batgirl (Cassandra Cain), Robin, Nightwing, Azrael, Alfred, and Dr. Thompkins, as well as Jim Gordon and the GCPD. It is a long road to the city's healing, to a restoration of the law and order that existed before the earthquake.

Batman's ultimate goal is this reestablishment of order; thus, it is extremely important that he reconcile with Jim Gordon, who previously distanced himself from Batman, feeling betrayed by the Batman's absence those first months. Batman's ongoing relationship with Jim Gordon emphasizes that he is not an isolated vigilante, a law unto himself. He seeks to uphold social justice, and to that end he works closely with Jim Gordon and is also more in tune with the GCPD than at odds with it. He also has a code against killing, and his reprimanding Huntress for her more violent methods parallels Jim Gordon's disciplining Petit. (Huntress, though, redeems herself in the end and witnesses Petit's descent into insanity.)

As a detective, Batman uncovers crimes that run counter to social order; and as a gang lord, he walks the streets during the day and demands tribute to provide rules and structure to those citizens lost in this hostile environment. Batman helps people pull together to share resources in a more just way, as opposed to the exploitative ways of Penguin, Mr. Freeze, Two-Face, and others. Batman must first dismantle their systems of oppression to establish a new order, which will eventually coincide with the work of Jim Gordon and the GCPD. It is a long process, involving the work of the Bat-family in the streets during the long months of No Man's Land, and the money and willpower of Lex Luthor and Bruce Wayne during the turning point, when the executive order is revoked. The rebuilding of Gotham is a long, tortuous road, with many sacrifices along the way.

Years later, in the real world, New Orleans is still rebuilding. Many people still live in temporary housing, and large sections of the poorer neighborhoods are filled with abandoned homes. Each anniversary brings national attention back to the devastation, but then the story fades away in the midst of other news. The people of New Orleans know that the process of rebuilding continues; there is much still left to do. They did not have a Batman with a masterful plan to pull the city back from the brink, but they have had government aid, National Guard troops, police officers, and volunteers of all types coming to their rescue. A hot debate continues as to whether there has been enough follow-up; the devastation was great, and many still suffer.

The Thin Veil

The stories of a ravaged Gotham and a flooded New Orleans leave us with a mixed message. We wonder how close we, in our different communities, might be to anarchy—what would it take to rip that thin veil of order? But on the other hand, we see stories of heroism as people pull together in the face of extreme challenges. Batman's ultimate enemy is chaos: Arkham's criminally insane celebrated in crippled Gotham, a city ruled by anarchy. Batman's crusade is not only against them, but, more important, against what they represent. Though we often take social order for granted, we may also have a deep-seated fear about whether we could survive if that order were ever to crumble. Batman rises as a defender of social order, even as he operates in a questionable world of vigilantism. This image has resonated with readers, whether or not they could voice it, since 1939, and it is one that can still encourage those who listen today to fight to hold back chaos, as we continue to face disasters the size of Katrina. Hopefully we will have our own heroes in these moments of trial, common people who will rise to the challenges.

NOTES

1. Most of this storyline was collected in five trade paperbacks, *No Man's Land, Vols. 1–5* (1999–2001), and these will be cited in the text as *NML* 1, *NML* 2, etc. Some parts of the story were not reprinted in these volumes, and can be found in the various Batman-related titles from 1999 to 2000.

2. These storylines encompass a number of issues from 1998 and 1999. *Aftershock* includes *Batman* #555–559, *Detective Comics* #722–726, *Shadow of the Bat* #75–79, and *Batman Chronicles* #14. *Road to No Man's Land* includes *Batman* #560–562, *Detective Comics* #727–729, and *Shadow of the Bat* #80–82.

3. *Batman* #560–562 (December 1998–February 1999).

4. Allen Breed, "New Orleans in the Throes of Katrina, and Apocalypse," WWLTV .com, September 2, 2005.

5. Thomas Hobbes, *Leviathan* (Norton Critical Edition) (New York: W. W. Norton, 1996), Book 1, chapters 10–18.

6. See Brett Chandler Patterson, "Of Moths and Men: Paths of Redemption on the Island of Second Chances," in *Lost and Philosophy: The Island Has Its Reasons*, ed. Sharon Kaye (Malden, MA: Blackwell, 2007).

7. See Sarah Kaufman, "The Criminalization of New Orleanians in Katrina's Wake." June 11, 2006, http://www.understandingkatrina.ssrc.org.

8. Hobbes, *Leviathan*, Book 2, chapter 20.

9. Niccolo Machiavelli,. *The Prince* (New York: Oxford Univ. Press, 2005 [1532]). One of the main arguments of this work is that a ruler must be aware of his social reputation. It is not enough to *be* virtuous; your subjects must also *see* you being virtuous.

10. See Stanley Hauerwas, *Peaceable Kingdom* (Notre Dame, IN: Univ. of Notre Dame Press, 1983); H. Richard Niebuhr, *Meaning of Revelation* (New York: Collier Books, 1960 [1941]); and John Howard Yoder, *The Politics of Jesus* (Grand Rapids, MI: William B. Eerdmans, 1992 [1972]). Hobbes's political philosophy so removes God from earthly politics that it is easy to see why a number of proponents of his thought have seen an atheistic bent to it, even though Hobbes himself denied such a connection.

11. Chris Carroll, "Hope in Hell: From the Gulf Coast to Uganda—The Reach of Humanitarian Aid," *National Geographic*, December 2005, http://www7.nationalgeographic .com/ngm/0512/feature1/index.html.

12. See "Visitor," in *NML* 3.

GOVERNING GOTHAM

Tony Spanakos

Can somebody tell me what kind of a world we live in, where a man dressed up as a bat gets all of my press? This town needs an enema!

> —The Joker, from the 1989 movie *Batman*

Gotham Made Me Do It

Defeating freaky bad guys, using cool gadgets, and leaving "Ka-Pows" in your wake is pretty impressive. But what is most compelling about the Batman is how and why he took up tights and evening prowls in the first place. The story of Batman's origin has been retold many times and many ways, but it always focuses on the child who witnesses the murder of his parents and grows up to become a crime-fighting bat.

Most analyses of the Batman's actions and motivations—including the movie *Batman Begins* (2005)—focus on the psychological impact of this event on Bruce Wayne/Batman. In this chapter, we'll take a different approach, arguing that

Gotham, particularly its government, is the source of Batman's angst. Thomas and Martha Wayne were murdered because the state was incapable of maintaining law and order, and Bruce Wayne's response was to become the crime-fighting Batman, trying to correct the lack of order in his city. Though extreme, this reaction is not unique. Nearly all of the major characters in the Batman pantheon are reacting against a state that is perceived as either too weak or too restrictive. Batman and Jim Gordon have a more nuanced vision of public safety in that they support the state but reject its exclusive authority in the area of security. This highlights the precarious nature of political rule, and it also explains why the Batman (and, periodically, Gordon) has such a problematic relationship with the state.

Do We Need Any Stinking Badges?
Legitimacy and Violence

"Faster than a speeding bullet, more powerful than a locomotive, able to leap tall buildings in a single bound . . ." These and other powers have always allowed Superman to serve the greater good, justice, and the American way. He is an orphan from another planet, whose loyalty to the country in which he was raised is unquestioning. Superman equates the greater good with the American way like the good citizen/soldier he was drawn to be some seventy years ago. Because of his love for his adopted country, Superman recognizes the authority of the state, and it, in turn, authorizes him to act on its behalf. When Superman saves Gotham City from a nuclear warhead in *The Dark Knight Returns* (1986; henceforth *DKR*), his use of force is licensed and therefore "legitimate" because he is an agent of the state. The crime-reducing activities of the Batman, however, are not licensed and legitimate.

This produces an interesting tension, which Frank Miller explores in *DKR*. Miller's Superman is a golden boy who has decided to play nice with humans and their government.

He struggles to understand Bruce Wayne's quip *"Sure* we're criminals. . . . We've always *been* criminals. We *have* to be criminals." Bruce is a friend, but he understands order, crime, and the world very differently. Despite their friendship, Superman has no misgivings about who to support when the confrontation between the state and the Batman is made clear. He first warns Bruce candidly, saying, "It's like this, Bruce—sooner or later, somebody's going to order me to bring you in. Somebody with authority." Later, as a government representative, he kills (or so he thinks) the Batman.

German sociologist Max Weber (1864–1920) defined the state as *the* institution that holds a monopoly on the legitimate use of coercion in a given territory. Through the police and military, the state—and only the state—may enforce authority. The use of violence by nonstate actors (terrorists, revolutionaries, criminals, vigilantes) occurs, and may even be understandable on occasion, but it can never be legitimate. Most superheroes, even unintentionally, play a subversive role because very few are officially licensed or commissioned by the state to use coercion to guard public order (except during World War II and the Cold War, when heroes such as Captain America and the Justice Society of America worked with the U.S. government to fight off Nazis, Soviets, intergalactic aliens, and other hobgoblins).[1] Batman, however, is particularly subversive, especially in his "Dark Knight" incarnation (in the earliest stories, and again after 1986), because his concept of order and the good goes beyond the state; his use of violence is in addition to, though not in coordination with, the state. The challenge to the state's monopoly on the legitimate use of violence is seen most clearly in Miller's depiction of Batman in contrast with Superman and Commissioner Yindel.

The return of the Batman in *DKR* corresponds with a rise in violent crime in Gotham City (coincidentally, Miller's story debuted in 1986 as crime was cresting in New York, the model for Gotham). The mayor is depicted as a poll-watching, weak politician who has no position on Batman's activities until one is imposed on him by an aide. When the time comes to choose a successor for the retiring Commissioner Gordon, the mayor selects Ellen Yindel. Yindel had a brilliantly successful career fighting crime in Chicago, but Chicago is not Gotham. Yindel's inability to understand Gotham underlies her relationships with Gordon and Batman. She correctly realizes that she is inheriting a situation where there is virtual anarchy. But her effort to impose order depends on a "black and white" interpretation of the law that sees the Batman as a vigilante and, by definition, a criminal. She justifies this position, saying, "[d]espite Gotham's plague of crime, I believe our only recourse is law enforcement. I will not participate in the activities of a vigilante. Therefore, as your police commissioner I issue the arrest order for the Batman on charges of breaking and entering, assault and battery, creating a public menace."

Comic fans might be shocked by this, but it is a highly rational response, especially from a representative of the state who prides herself on "law and order." Our problem, as readers and fans, is that we know that law and order are not perfectly correlated. Sometimes there is so little order that the law does not work well, and that is precisely why we need the Batman in the first place. But Yindel, at least until the end of *DKR*, is blind to this because she understands the state as the only location of law and order. If *only* the state can legitimately enforce the law, and use violence in the process, logically any other violence is illegitimate and criminal, regardless of whether it produces good results. After all, even if Gotham is safer because of the Batman, it is no more "orderly," since it has explicitly accepted the idea that one individual can use violence legitimately. This opens the possibility for copycats with lesser abilities and questionable motivations (as *DKR* shows through the "sons of Batman").

From Crime Alley to Sin City:
Hobbes and Gotham

Young Bruce Wayne learns about the need for someone to enforce order in Crime Alley, beneath a solitary streetlamp, between the corpses of his parents Thomas and Martha. Like the rest of us, he had assumed that the state would keep order, that it would prevent criminal elements from individual and lawless pursuit of their own interests. But the robbery-turned-double homicide changes everything. The Batman is born in a city where the state fails at its most basic responsibility of maintaining public safety, where the "social contract" between citizen and state is most essential. Life in Gotham is scary, tenuous, and cheap; danger lurks everywhere. Of course, no government can prevent all crime, but Bruce knows the government cannot, on its own, ensure order. In 1987's *Batman: Year One*, Miller retells the origin of the Batman. The story opens with Lieutenant Gordon arriving in Gotham by train and Bruce Wayne returning to Gotham by plane. Both know they are entering a fallen city, where government has lost control over crime, and it becomes their personal challenge to solve that. Over the course of *Year One* each will learn how his personal efforts require cooperation with the other, sometimes ignoring, or even challenging, the state.

Without a state to enforce order, life is "solitary, poor, nasty, brutish, and short": that's what Thomas Hobbes (1588–1679) argued in *Leviathan*, published shortly after nearly a decade of civil war in Britain.[2] Hobbes imagined a world that existed before government. In it, humans have unlimited liberty, but they are guided by passions, and liberty soon becomes license, and the state of nature becomes a war of all against all. Then there is neither order nor the possibility of justice. It is so oppressive that man will cede virtually all of his liberties to a sovereign so that order can be established. That, according to Hobbes, is the origin of government.

Most Batman stories begin with Gotham being ungovernable, a place where society has broken down into Hobbesian disorder. Various characters in the Batman series give us insight into how the fall of the state allows disorder and how they individually seek to overcome or exploit this. For instance, when Gordon arrives in Gotham in *Year One*, he is greeted by Detective Flass, a happy-go-lucky cop on the take, who takes him to meet Commissioner Gillian Loeb, who runs the police as an old-boy protection network for powerful city elites, politicians, and drug dealers. When Gordon refuses to take a bribe from a priest, Flass and a few other officers, in disguise, jump and beat Gordon. Later, Gordon returns the favor to Flass and is grateful to Flass for teaching him what it means to be a cop in Gotham City. When Batman first appears, Gordon sets traps to try to catch him, but the commissioner tells him that there is no need to be concerned with Batman: after all, he *is* reducing street crime, which does not disturb Loeb's racket. Only after Batman raids a private dinner of Gotham's elites (including Loeb) and threatens them does Loeb make catching Batman his number-one priority.

Rather than establishing order, Loeb's state perverts it. The impact is so extensive that even Gordon is affected. Personally, he cheats on his very pregnant wife Barbara with a fellow officer, Sergeant Sarah Essen. Professionally, he is conflicted by an order that he cannot understand, especially once he sees and learns more of Batman. He lies in bed, hunched over, stares at the gun in his hand while Barbara sleeps, and thinks:

> I shouldn't be thinking . . . not about Batman. He's a criminal. I'm a cop. It's that simple. But—but I'm a cop in a city where the mayor and the commissioner of police use cops as hired killers . . . he saved that old woman. He saved that cat. He even paid for that suit. The hunk of metal in my hands is heavier than ever.

Like Superman and Yindel in *DKR*, Loeb and his henchmen in *Year One* impose an order onto Gotham City. But unlike
Superman and Yindel, their intentions are hardly praiseworthy,
and as agents of the state, they not only fail to prevent the use
of violence by people other than the police, but they use violence in a profoundly illegitimate way. More important, though
they have the ability to enforce law, establish order, and protect
citizen life, they allow a state of license to prevail in Gotham
because it allows cover for their activities. Rather than the state
ending the chaos of the state of nature, as Hobbes hoped, the
state itself is a participant in the war of all against all.

"Two" Little Security

The failure of the state to maintain its most basic responsibility
provides an explanation for the origin of the Reaper, the villain in *Batman: Year Two* (1988). His beginnings very obviously
mirror Batman's: Judson Caspian and his wife and daughter
were assaulted years ago on their way back from the opera,
and his wife was killed. The failure of the state to provide
order leads Caspian to become the Reaper and his daughter,
Rachel, to eventually enter a convent. (We will focus on the
Reaper here, but it is interesting that both he and his daughter
seek to bring order to a world of sin and license, and both do
so outside of the government.) The Reaper starts his career by
killing four muggers, telling the intended victim of the mugging, "You have naught to fear. Tell the world that the Reaper
has returned . . . and will save this city—with its consent, or
without." A fallen city is in need of saving, and rather than
engaging in collective action or political mobilization, Caspian
takes up arms to begin a one-man war.

The similarities and differences between the Reaper and
Batman are made explicit when the Batman appears as the
Reaper goes after a prostitute: "The Batman, eh? They say
you continue the fight I began. If so, prove it now—stand

aside." Batman refuses because the Reaper seeks "wholesale slaughter" whereas he seeks justice. The Reaper then targets Big Willie Golonka, a mobster in protective security, whom he kills along with his security detail. The state that failed to protect his wife is now protecting a mobster. This is incomprehensible and unacceptable. The police, as agents of the state, "must learn—those who knowingly protect evil . . . must suffer the same penalty as those who commit it!" The state, as the Reaper sees it, has turned the world upside down and forgotten that it exists to prevent a war of man and against man. His "job" is to reestablish order in a Hobbesian world, but he does so as a self-appointed Leviathan. Hobbes's Leviathan, on the other hand, solves the problems of the state of nature through a collective social contract, not brute individual force.

Another one of the most interesting Batman villains is Harvey Dent, otherwise known as Two-Face. Dent is a passionate and incorruptible district attorney who supports Batman and goes after Gotham's greatest criminals, even the politically connected ones (see *Year One*, for instance). When he has acid thrown at him by a mobster during his trial, Dent's face is disfigured and he takes on the new identity of Two-Face. It's not just that half his face is now distorted, but also who he *is* has changed. This is not simply a case of Dr. Jekyll trying to suppress the id and creating the conditions for its irrepressible emergence as Hyde. Harvey Dent cannot bring the world to order through the law. Being a public prosecutor has, in fact, made him a target and turned him physically into the half-monster he is.

Two-Face is yet another Batman character who responds to the failed state's degeneration into a Hobbesian state of war of all against all. In each case, the Hobbesian Gotham is not met by effective state authority. In Loeb, the state consciously chooses predatory action, ushering in a state of war. The Reaper is the individual's brutal and unmeasured response to the failure of the collective security that the state is contracted to provide. And Harvey Dent was a faithful but ultimately ineffective agent of the state. It is the state's incapacity to act, perceived from within, that turns him into someone who tries to bring order through criminality.

The Anti-Batman: Nietzschean Rebellions

Weber's and Hobbes's understandings of the state assume that it is a legitimate institution that brings security, that it is "good." Friedrich Nietzsche (1844–1900), however, sees the state as a threat to individual self-expression and self-overcoming. The state obsessively tries to change its citizens in its own image. In *Thus Spoke Zarathustra*, Nietzsche has the state say, "On earth there is nothing greater than I: the ordering finger of God am I."[3] The Nietzschean state constitutes a "new idol," one that is no less repressive than its predecessors, as it defines good and evil for, and hangs a "sword and a hundred appetites" over, the faithful.

No Batman villain sees this as clearly as Anarky, a teenager seduced by anarchist thought in 1999's *Batman: Anarky*. Anarky aims to bring "freedom" to the people who are enslaved by an order perverted by politics, religion, and capitalism. Like the Reaper, Anarky emerges by combating unpopular figures—a drug dealer, a polluting corporate type, and a big bank that has demolished and cleared an area once inhabited by the homeless. Alfred points out the similarities between Anarky and Batman to Bruce Wayne, who responds quickly, "I know, I know—my own methods aren't always legal, either. But there *is* a difference, Alfred. . . . I only use violence when it's absolutely necessary, not as a form of punishment . . . not lately, anyway!"

Anarky's need to order the world is seen in his long letter explaining to his parents who he "really" is, his teaching anarchism to other juvenile delinquents, and his dream at the end of the graphic novel. In the dream, Anarky tries to "de-brainwash" Gotham, so that its citizens can see the real Gotham, "[w]here administration bigwigs view the world from stretch limos, while families sleep in cardboard boxes— corrupt businessmen flourish, while honest men beg in the gutter—crime explodes. While decent folk are afraid to walk the streets their taxes pay for. All human life is there—from the best to the worst, the kings in their fortresses to the scum in their sties. And all of them believe that it has to be that way. I'm going to show them that it doesn't." In his dream, Anarky creates a dystopia in which there is no state to order things, where politicians flunk a "parasite test" and are interned in ghettoes for being "enemies of the people," and where the people—in the absence of a state—become nasty and brutish. The moral of the tale is that the anarchic order that Anarky tries to impose is worse than the one he tries to replace. His search for an organizing principle that is less repressive than the state fails.

In contrast, the Joker's goals are not nearly as political, but they are nonetheless linked to order. The ultimate Batman enemy is conceived in *DKR* as being a playful harlequin whose vicious acts of crime belie his motivation for lawbreaking: the need to disrupt a boring and restrictive order. The state imposes this order not so much politically as socially, and the Joker responds by trying to undermine *any* order. In *DKR*, the Joker is content to play small-scale pranks in Arkham Asylum until he learns that the Batman has come out of retirement. The return of the Batman necessitates the Joker's return. Batman is too boring, brings about too much order. The Joker has to go back into Gotham to temper the Batman's effect. The duality of the Batman—who is obsessed with order—and the Joker—who needs to challenge order—is best seen when the Joker, speaking of his victims, tells the Batman, "I never kept count, but you did, and I love you for it."[4]

The Real Dynamic Duo:
Batman and Gordon

Batman: Year Two opens with the newly appointed Commissioner Gordon being interviewed on television:

> Interviewer: You seem to be on good relations with Gotham's official police force, but many have questioned your relationship with this masked vigilante, the Batman.
>
> Gordon: My department's relationship with the Batman is strictly—
>
> Interviewer: Many feel that the Batman is no better than the costumed lawbreaker who stalked Gotham's streets twenty years ago, calling himself the Reaper.
>
> Gordon: That comparison has been made, yes, but unfairly.
>
> Interviewer: Some say it was the Reaper's abrupt departure from Gotham that plunged our city into the maelstrom of crime and police corruption from which it's only just emerged.
>
> Gordon: If I can finish: I can't speak for the department of twenty years ago, but the Batman works with the police force, not against us.
>
> Interviewer: And is this "Batman" an authorized representative of force?
>
> Gordon: No, he operates strictly on his own. But he's offered me his services.

This dialogue is a microcosm for the Batman-Gordon understanding of an order that goes beyond the state. The state is not the only agent that can legitimately use violence (as Weber held), and it does play a constructive role in providing order (against Nietzsche). But society also has a role to play in providing security: Batman symbolizes and inspires that, and Gordon knows it.

At the same time, Batman's actions are not wholly legitimate. When Bruce Wayne distinguishes himself from Anarky, he says, "The fact is, no man can be allowed to set himself up as judge, jury and executioner." And, indeed, even though it often seemed silly in the early comics or the television series, Batman always beat the bad guys and tied them up so that the police could imprison them. He regularly surrendered the Penguin, Poison Ivy, the Joker, and so many others to Arkham Asylum, knowing that they would soon walk right out that revolving door. Batman has the ability to pronounce justice and to punish, but he refuses to do either. This speaks volumes about the place of the state (and society) in establishing order and justice.

In *DKR*, the state is weak, infiltrated by touchy-feely organizations and specialists who claim to speak for society but who are entirely alienated from what most people think. The Council of Mothers asks the mayor to arrest Batman as a "harmful influence on the children of Gotham," and the Victims' Rights Task Force demands protection for the victims of the Batman's violence. A psychologist even calls Batman a "social fascist" because of his effort to reorder society in his own image. After considerable fence-sitting regarding the danger of mutants, the mayor says, "This whole situation is the result of Gordon's incompetence—and of the terrorist actions of the Batman. I wish to sit down with the mutant leader . . . to negotiate a settlement." Three pages later, the mayor is killed by the mutant leader in his prison cell after the mayor insisted on having no police protection. He dies because he does not understand the reality of Gotham.

Still, the mayor correctly fingers Gordon as fundamental to the Batman's freedom to pursue his crime-fighting activities. Unlike the mayor, Gordon understands Gotham and he understands Batman. In *DKR*, he tries to explain this to Yindel, but she begins to see this only after she gets a real sense for the kind of crime that predominates in Gotham, and how Batman is a very necessary response to that. Gordon's sympathy to the Batman is rarely perceived as what it is, a significant deviation from law enforcement and dereliction of duty. Very few comic books address this, and none so directly as *Dark Victory* (2001), in which a young, beautiful, liberal, and misguided district attorney named Janice Porter directly confronts Gordon. Referring to a criminal that Batman roughed up, she tells Gordon, "Batman did quite a number on him. In what way weren't his civil rights violated? And from what I understand, you were not only there at the time of his arrest—you stood by and allowed this to happen."

Batman always violates criminals' civil rights, since he has no authority to act as an agent of the law, and Gordon knows that, but he does not place rights and the law before justice and order. You need rights to have justice, but as Lana Lang says in her defense of the Batman in *DKR*, "We live in the shadow of crime . . . with the unspoken understanding that we are victims—of fear, of violence, of social impotence. A man has risen to show us that the power is, and always has been in our hands. We are under siege—He's showing us that we can resist." Throughout *Dark Victory*, Gordon is under pressure because Porter tries to keep him from inappropriate contact with the Batman. This disturbs a fundamental aspect of the Batman mythos, which requires this linkage between the just man inside the legal system and the just one outside of it.

The personal, informal relationship between Gordon and the Batman is essential. Batman will not mete out punishment, and Gordon cannot rely on his police to maintain order and to rein in supervillains. In the process, they install and maintain a precarious order that the reader believes is legitimate. We know that only Batman can handle men in tights with riddles that only a thirteen-year-old former Communist chess master can solve. At the same time, we know Batman ultimately cannot enforce justice, even on Joe Chill, the murderer of his parents. We may cheer for the Batman's righteous revenge, but we pull back and we want him to pull back. As longtime Batman editor Dennis O'Neil says, killing "is not something . . . [Batman] does."[5]

But while this order comforts readers, and lets us know that we can sleep at night because someone is watching over the prowlers in Crime Alley, it is very threatening to the state. The state believes it must monopolize the legitimate use of violence. And more than the villains he fights, it is Batman, and to a lesser extent Gordon, who is a threat to the state, for it is Batman who challenges the state's monopoly over the legitimate use of violence. This is why he is hunted in *DKR* and *Year One*, and why his actions are challenged in *Year Two* and *Dark Victory*. The irony of the Batman's relationship with the state is that the more he reduces crime and contributes to public order, the more he challenges the state, as it becomes obvious that the state's use of violence is ineffective. That makes Gordon necessary to prevent the Batman from being a complete threat. Batman trusts Gordon and will turn over criminals to him, and in return Gordon recognizes him as *the* exception to the state's monopoly.

Theorizing Government

We may wonder to what extent we, as fans, are capable of imagining a gap between order and law. No state can claim that it can guarantee both flawlessly all of the time. Batman and Gordon hold together a world that eludes our sense of logic and justice, and although all characters attempt to impose some sort of order on Gotham, it is the tandem team of Batman and Gordon who do it most legitimately. This renders the state precarious, shows how society must participate in its own defense, and points out how very important personal relationships and trust are in establishing the line between the just use of violence and the proper enforcement of law. Of course, it is possible to theorize about the state, justice, and violence without discussing the Batman, but as the Joker would say—"Why bother?"[6]

NOTES

1. For a more recent exploration of this issue, see how the "Superhuman Registration Act" has influenced the Marvel superhero community in the recent crossover events "Civil War" and "The Initiative." I am grateful to Mark White for suggesting this reference.

2. Thomas Hobbes, *Leviathan* (New York: Penguin Books, [1651] 1985), xiii.

3. Walter Kaufman, ed., *The Portable Nietzsche* (New York: Penguin Press, 1976), 161.

4. For more on Nietzsche and Frank Miller, see Peregrine Dace, "Nietzsche contra Superman: An Examination of the Work of Frank Miller," *South African Journal of Philosophy* 26, no. 1 (2007): 98–106.

5. Roberta E. Pearson and William Uricchio, "Notes from the Batcave: An Interview with Dennis O'Neil," in a book they edited, *The Many Lives of the Batman: Critical Approaches to a Superhero and His Media* (New York: Routledge, 1991), 19. For more on Batman's refusal to kill, see Mark D. White's chapter in this book.

6. I would like to thank Rob Arp, Mark White, Michel Spanakos, and Photini The for the suggestions they gave that strengthened this chapter.

THE JOKER'S WILD: CAN WE HOLD THE CLOWN PRINCE MORALLY RESPONSIBLE?

Christopher Robichaud

Laugh and the World Laughs with You—or Does It?

The Joker isn't playing with a full deck. This isn't news, of course, least of all to the Joker himself. "Don't get ee-ee-even, get mad!" he cackles in Alan Moore's *The Killing Joke* (1988). From poisoning the fish in Gotham Harbor, twisting their faces into a permanent grin just for the sake of copyrighting them,[1] to trying to launch some of Gotham's luminaries into the stratosphere using candle rockets atop a giant birthday cake,[2] the Joker's lunatic schemes have earned him a permanent cell in Arkham Asylum. And while insanity doesn't distinguish the Joker amongst Batman's adversaries—Two-Face, for one, often gives him a run for his money on the crazy-as-can-be count—the Clown Prince of Crime's deranged escapades have certainly earned him the dubious distinction of being the Dark Knight's chief antagonist and foil.

If it all were just about laughing fish and preposterous birth-day celebrations, we might happily leave the Joker to his exploits without further reflection. But as fans of Batman's adventures are all too painfully aware, the Joker's deeds are often as ghastly as they are absurd. Beyond the countless lives he's taken by way of his leave-them-laughing gas, the Joker has beaten Jason Todd, the second incarnation of Robin, to the point of death with a crowbar—in front of Jason's mother, no less—and then blown him up, taking him way past the point of no return.[3] He also shot Barbara Gordon, Commissioner James Gordon's daughter, and then stripped her naked and took pictures of her. When the Joker subsequently captured Commissioner Gordon, he stripped the commissioner naked as well, and put him on an amusement ride where he was forced to see pictures of his daughter naked, shot, and paralyzed.[4] And that, according to the Joker, was done just to prove the point that all it takes is one really bad day to put otherwise good people over the edge.

So the Joker hasn't just done criminal things, he's done unimaginably awful things, things of the utmost moral repug-nance. But how much blame—moral blame—should we assign to him? Perhaps our first reaction is "Are you kidding me? He's a villain, an abomination, and he warrants the most severe moral censure." Perhaps, but then we ought to remind our-selves of the fact we began with: namely, that the Joker really *isn't* playing with a full deck. And there is a strong senti-ment among us—not universally shared, but not uncommon, either—that genuinely insane people often aren't morally responsible for what they do, and therefore don't deserve moral blame for their misdeeds. Maybe, then, the Joker shouldn't be held morally accountable for his actions.

But if that's right, we need to ask *why*. And that's where philosophy enters the picture. In what follows, we'll examine some of the things philosophy has to say about this issue, looking in particular at the light it can shed on the relationship between a person acting freely, on the one hand, and a person being morally responsible for what she does, on the other. We'll focus on this because it seems correct to say that a person is morally responsible only for those actions that she freely performs. So if we want to conclude that the Joker isn't morally responsible for his actions, we'll need to argue that his mental state doesn't allow him to freely do the villainous things he does. Let's get to it!

Clearing Out Some Bats in the Belfry

Any good philosophical exercise should clarify the relevant background assumptions that are being made, and it should spell out important distinctions that will help in exploring the topic under discussion. We'll begin, then, by attending to the most glaring assumption of our investigation, which is that the Joker is truly insane.

Admittedly, issues surrounding insanity are complex and multifaceted, and they often fall more comfortably within psychology and psychiatry than philosophy. Nevertheless, some philosophers, like Michel Foucault (1926–1984), have made very interesting contributions to the field by exposing how groups of persons have been marginalized by being labeled as insane.[5] Engaging as Foucault's discussion is, unfortunately it has led some people to question whether insanity actually exists. We won't go that far; we'll acknowledge that there are several kinds of mental impairments that rightly justify categorizing persons who suffer from them as insane. And we'll further assume that the Joker suffers from one or more of these mental conditions, permitting us to accurately refer to him as insane.

But before moving on entirely, it's worth defending this position against the objection that it's groundless or extreme.

We can agree that we often call folks crazy when we simply find their behavior odd, without meaning that they really suffer from some serious mental derangement. Such is not the case with the Joker, however. Yes, he often does weird things, no question about that—let's face it, putting a Cheshire-cat-grin on all the fish in the harbor is *really* out there—but he also displays some hallmarks of the genuinely disturbed. One example is his attitude toward people: simply put, he often treats them as objects rather than as persons. The Joker didn't blink at shooting Barbara Gordon through her spine and stripping her bare. He wasn't "out to get her." He simply had made up his mind that he wanted to prove a point, and she was a useful object to help him make that point, no more or less meaningful to him than the amusement ride he later used for the same purpose. That's a classic psychotic attitude.

The Joker also lacks a healthy sense of self-preservation. In the *Batman Superman Movie* (1998), there's a wonderful moment when Lex Luthor and the Joker are on a plane together, desperately trying to escape capture by the Dark Knight and the Man of Steel. A box opens, and explosives roll toward Lex and the Joker, about to detonate. Luthor, sanely, cries out in dismay and tries to escape. The Joker simply starts laughing uncontrollably. If these examples aren't enough, perhaps Alfred Pennyworth puts it best in 2008's *The Dark Knight* when he says about the Joker, "Some men aren't looking for anything logical. They can't be bought, bullied, reasoned, or negotiated with. Some men just want to watch the world burn." Clearly, the Joker is insane.

We next need to discuss an important distinction that will help us avoid confusion later, and that's the difference between *causal* responsibility and *moral* responsibility. When we consider causal responsibility, we're simply asking whether a person's action is a cause of a particular event. Suppose that the Joker douses an unsuspecting victim with Smilex gas, killing her. Was he causally responsible for her death? Sure, his dousing her with the gas—that action—was clearly part of the chain of events that brought about her death. Moral responsibility concerns itself with the moral praise and blame connected with an act. Let's say, very roughly, that a person is morally responsible for an action only if she's the appropriate subject of moral praise or blame for that action.

Now with those ideas in place, we may be tempted to conclude that we've already undercut our position: if we grant that the Joker is causally responsible for such things as poisoning people, then it just follows that he's morally responsible for these actions. But that does not follow, and we can cook up much less controversial cases to see why. Suppose Batman starts the Batmobile to head into the city, and it backfires, disturbing the bats in his cave. The bats fly out into the night and disrupt a driver on a nearby country road, who swerves and drives her car into a ditch. It seems true that Batman is causally responsible for the driver going into the ditch—his starting the Batmobile is part of the chain of events that led to the driver swerving—but it doesn't seem right to claim that Batman is *morally* responsible for the driver's minor accident. He simply couldn't have reasonably anticipated the sequence of events that ensued. So a person's being causally responsible for something does not automatically make that person morally responsible for it. And that opens the door to the possibility that the Joker, while quite clearly causally responsible for his villainous deeds, may not always be morally responsible for them.

Putting One More Card on the Table (Don't Worry, It's Not a Joker)

There is one more important assumption to defend, which is that we ordinary folk do in fact act freely. The problem is that if this isn't true—if *none* of us have a free will—then it seems that no one is morally responsible for what she does. And if that's the case, it's rather uninteresting to focus on these issues as they relate to the Joker, since he's in the same boat as the rest of us.

Fair enough, we might think, but what in the world would lead us to believe that we never act freely? Certainly such a claim runs contrary to our ordinary way of thinking—and feeling! The way things seem from within when we're deciding what to do is that we face legitimate options all the time and freely choose between them. Why would we ever think that our beliefs and feelings are inaccurate on this count?

The answer lies with *determinism*: the view that for any moment in time, the state of the world at that time is wholly fixed, or determined, by the prior states of the world (together with the laws of nature that run the whole show). This view is appealing for numerous reasons, one of which is that it seems to conform with a mature scientific understanding of the world. If determinism is true, we are nothing more than a product of events that originated long before we even came into the picture. And facing any apparent choice, it's already determined which course of action we will follow. That doesn't leave much room for free will.

One way to respond to this worry, of course, is to reject determinism. That's an approach that some philosophers happily take, sometimes justifying their position on scientific grounds, by citing facts about the fundamental randomness of quantum mechanics as a reason to believe that the past doesn't perfectly determine the future. Or sometimes they argue simply that determinism runs riot over our common sense, and that's enough to warrant our rejecting it.

Others, though, challenge the idea that determinism is incompatible with the idea of free will. Let's consider an example based on a famous paper by philosopher Harry Frankfurt (b. 1929).[6] Suppose the Joker has devoted huge quantities of money to the construction of a strange machine that tracks Batman's actions and, more interestingly, his thoughts. Moreover, it's able to "control" what Batman does. The Joker's ultimate aim is to use this machine to force Batman to do terrible things, but at present, he just wants Gotham cleansed of all other supervillains. So right now, let's say the machine is tracking Batman as he faces off against Poison Ivy, and the situation is one where a well-placed Bat-a-rang will trip Ivy up enough to allow Batman to capture her.

Here's where things get interesting. *If* Batman chooses to throw the Bat-a-rang—if he makes that *mental* decision—then the Joker's machine will not stop him by sending out the appropriate mind-rays (or whatever) to interrupt that course of action (because the Joker wants Ivy taken out of commission). But if the Dark Knight—for whatever reason—chooses *not* to throw the Bat-a-rang, the machine will intercede and force him to do so. Let's suppose that Batman does choose to throw the Bat-a-rang and in fact does so. We would normally think that in doing so, Batman exercised his free will— he made a free choice and acted accordingly—even though, unbeknownst to him, he had no alternative but to throw the Bat-a-rang. In other words, what he did in this case was actually determined.

So even if determinism is true and what we do is determined by past states of affairs and the laws of nature, there's still room to exercise free will. And as long as there's room to exercise free will, there's room for moral responsibility. Of course, there's much that can be said in response to this line of reasoning. Here's just one concern: it seems that moral evaluation is going to face a certain *epistemological* problem, a problem concerning whether we can ever *know* whether praise or blame is appropriate to attribute to a person. To see why, let's stick with the example sketched above. In order for us to know that Batman deserves praise for his actions, we can't simply attend to what he did, for that was already determined; he was going to do it regardless of whether he intended to or not. We'd have to get inside his head, as it were, and see what choice he made. And crazy Joker-machines aside, getting inside people's heads isn't the easiest thing to do. So we might worry that free will and the moral responsibility that comes with it have been saved only at the cost of making it virtually impossible for us to ever attribute praise or blame, and that cost is too high.

There are responses to this worry, but we must move on. Let's assume, then, that we do have, and can exercise, free will, whether that's compatible with determinism or not. We now turn to the issue of whether there's something wrong with the Joker in particular that prohibits him from exercising free will, and as such, whether this exempts him from moral responsibility for his actions.

Taking the Plunge: The Fall from Freedom

So far we've talked loosely about exercising our free will in terms of making choices. But clearly there's more involved in the performance of free actions than that. Many philosophers believe that exercising free will—and the moral responsibility that comes from it—crucially involves a person being able to think about what motivates her and then using this ability to change her motivations, at least sometimes. The core idea, espoused in various forms by Harry Frankfurt among others, is that one of the things that distinguishes us from other animals is our ability to form desires about our desires: second-order desires.[7] We can take a stance on our first-order desires—the things that drive other animals directly to action—and in this sense, we aren't merely passive in where our wants take us, as it were. Our free will is constituted by our ability to form desires about our desires, to reflect upon and evaluate them, and to change our motivations accordingly.

For example, Batman may find himself so totally exhausted one evening after having spent numerous nights thumping on the Joker's goons that he has a very strong first-order desire to stay in bed and sleep rather than continue to pursue his foe. But Batman also has the desire to bring justice to Gotham, and this is also a first-order desire (though more abstract). Let's suppose it is strongly held, but not as strongly as the first-order desire to stay in bed. What makes Batman free, so the thought goes, is his ability to recognize these two desires in himself and to form a second-order desire that in some sense weights his desire to pursue justice more highly than his desire to stay in bed.

This is a very rough sketch of how free will works and it is not uncontroversial. But it is already enough to help us explain why we think that some persons "aren't in control" in certain matters; that is, why we think they aren't able to exercise their free will. Classic examples involve addicts. We often speak as though people addicted to heroin, say, aren't entirely exercising their free will when they continue to get fixes long after any benefits of the rush have passed, all the time admittedly well aware that they are destroying their lives. The idea, based on what we've sketched above, is that the drug addiction has inhibited their ability to form second-order desires about their desires. One of the influences of the drug, in other words, is that once taken, a person's wanting the drug *cannot* be trumped by a second-order desire to weight one's desire to be healthy over the desire for the drug.

But if such addicts aren't able to exercise their free will when it comes to future decisions to consume the drug, must we conclude that they aren't morally responsible for these future actions? Simply put, *no*, and that's because, at least in many cases, it is reasonable to presume that a free choice was made to start taking the drug. Before a person chose to start taking heroin, she possessed the capacity to rank her first-order desires. Possessing that capacity means that her decision not to rank her desire to stay healthy over her desire to get high was a decision freely made. She's morally responsible for the action that ensued, and that moral responsibility carries over to future actions that aren't free.

However, it might look like this line of reasoning opens the door for us to conclude that the Joker *is* morally responsible for his actions. Let's suppose that his current insanity is best understood as an inability to form second-order desires to quell his first-order homicidal tendencies. So we can agree that once he went mad, all the Joker's further actions were not performed freely. But according to at least one origin story (from *The Killing Joke*), the Joker was first a husband and father who chose to enter a life of petty crime—as the Red Hood—to help make ends meet. A confrontation with Batman resulted in his plunging into a vat of chemicals, forever burning his face into the monstrously clownish visage it now is. *That's* what sent him over the edge (literally). But he entered a life of crime freely—and if so, it seems that the moral responsibility for that action carries over to his present actions, given that his free choice led him to where it did.

Not so fast, though. We need to spell out in more detail why we think that the heroin addict is morally responsible for her future drug-related actions that aren't done freely. And part of that story, it seems right to say, is that we believe that her initial choice to take the drug was not only done freely, but it was done in complete awareness of the likely consequences of her action. One has to go out of one's way to remain ignorant of the effects of heroin. Forget health classes and after-school specials—the novels and the respective movies *Requiem for a Dream* and *Trainspotting* alone make it pretty darn obvious what can happen. We should test our intuitions: if the heroin addict was truly ignorant of the effects of heroin and freely chose to take it, would we be as willing to saddle her with moral responsibility for that and future actions? I don't think we would.

If that's right, we need to ask whether the Joker acted in ignorance upon taking the job as the Red Hood. And here it seems correct to say that while he surely had to be aware of many of the dangers and the ramifications of his actions, it would not be reasonable to expect him to have foreseen that becoming the Red Hood ran him the risk of turning into a homicidal maniac. Notice that that's true even if he somehow could have foreseen that he would take a plunge into a vat of chemicals. He would have to have known a lot more about his psychological makeup to conclude that from the possibility of that chemical plunge, madness would likely ensue. After all, had we made similar choices and had the same thing happened to us, it seems unlikely we would've become the Joker. Unluckily for Batman and for Gotham's citizens, the circumstances that led to his "birth" were one in a million.

Who Has the Last Laugh?

With that objection aside, we can defend our belief that some-one as mad as the Joker isn't morally responsible for his actions. The core idea is that the Joker is not morally responsible because he doesn't perform his actions freely. His craziness has inhibited his ability to form second-order desires about his first-order desires, desires that include very lunatic impulses.

So there we have it. The Joker is crazy, and his craziness, because it inhibits his free will, relieves him of any moral responsibility for his actions. This is a satisfying analysis, but as is often the case, our philosophical investigation has resolved some issues only to allow room for others to arise. For given the Joker's insanity, there remain important questions sur-rounding what obligations Batman and the city of Gotham have toward the Joker. And there are no easy moral answers to the question of how to deal with a genuinely insane person who performs the most vile of deeds. Pity him? Hate him? Institutionalize him? Let him die, if the opportunity arises? The Joker is Batman's nemesis not only because of what he does, but because of what he is. And if the Clown Prince of Crime is able to entertain that thought, there's no doubt he finds it very, very funny.

NOTES

1. *Detective Comics* #475 (February 1978).

2. *Batman* #321 (March 1980).

3. *A Death in the Family* (1988).

4. *The Killing Joke* (1988).

5. See Michel Foucault, *Madness and Civilization* (New York: Vintage Books, 1988).

6. See Harry Frankfurt, "Alternate Possibilities and Moral Responsibility," *Journal of Philosophy* Vol. 66, No. 23 (1969): 829–39; this essay is also available in Frankfurt's collection *The Importance of What We Care About* (Cambridge: Cambridge Univ. Press, 1988).

7. See Frankfurt's "Freedom of the Will and the Concept of a Person," *Journal of Philosophy* Vol. 68, No. 1 (1971): 5–20; also reprinted in *The Importance of What We Care About*.

PART THREE

ORIGINS AND ETHICS: BECOMING THE CAPED CRUSADER

BATMAN'S PROMISE

Randall M. Jensen

The past is never dead. It's not even past.

—William Faulkner

Batman Begins

Where do superheroes come from? Where do they get their powers? What makes somebody adopt the persona of a masked crime fighter, defender of all that is good? Who decides to leave the house wearing tights and sporting a cape?

Every good superhero saga includes an origin story. Such stories are memorable and powerful, coming close to real mythmaking. Origin stories are typically driven by incredible and fantastic events: genetic mutations, strange laboratory accidents, alien encounters, dealings with the devil, and so on. But Batman's beginnings are different. The crucial catalyst—an alleyway mugging gone bad—is all too tragically ordinary. And the rest of the Batman genesis is built upon a boy's extravagant and seemingly foolish promise to his murdered parents that he'll cleanse Gotham City of crime.

The senseless murder of Thomas and Martha Wayne is likely to remind comic fans of the tragic elements in other superhero origin stories. For example, Peter Parker becomes your friendly neighborhood Spider-Man largely because of the circumstances surrounding the murder of his uncle Ben, and Frank Castle turns into the Punisher due to the execution of his wife and children. What's distinctive about the Batman origin story is that the *why* precedes the *how*. When Uncle Ben is killed, a radioactive spider bite has already given Peter his amazing abilities. Likewise, Castle is a scarily competent military operator long before the mob takes out his family. But Bruce is just a boy at the time of his parents' death. He has no reason to think that he can do what he's promising to do. Bruce Wayne doesn't acquire superpowers and then later discover how he ought to use them. No, he first acquires a mission—a vocation or calling, really—and with it, a desperate need for extraordinary abilities. Through his own herculean efforts (and with the help of the enormous financial empire he has inherited, of course!), *he makes himself into Batman* so that he can keep the promise he made.

Unlike so many others, Bruce Wayne doesn't become a superhero by accident, but rather through sheer force of will. Since even the greatest tragedy doesn't transform most children into superheroes, the key element in Batman's origin is not the murder of a mother and father but rather the extraordinary promise of a young boy.

The Nature of the Promise

In the 1939 Bob Kane and Bill Finger version of the Batman origin story, just days after the murder of his parents, Bruce Wayne makes an oath: "And I swear by the spirits of my parents to avenge their deaths by spending the rest of my life warring on all criminals."[1] Much more recently, in Jeph Loeb and Tim Sale's classic *The Long Halloween* (1998), Batman recalls his boyhood promise: "I made a promise to my parents that I would rid the city of the evil that took their lives." In fact, this promise plays a very prominent role throughout Loeb's various contributions to the Batman history, showing up in *Haunted Knight* (1996), *Dark Victory* (2001, the sequel to *The Long Halloween*), *Hush* (2003), and more recently in his run on the popular *Superman/Batman* title (2003–2005). For Loeb, this promise seems to be the defining moment in the life of the Batman. So, what kind of promise is it? What prompts Bruce to make it? And why does it have such an enduring role in the Batman mythos?

One all-too-obvious answer is that this promise is an expression of a desire for vengeance. And indeed in its earlier version, Bruce does speak of "avenging" the deaths of his parents. But it's crucial to recognize it isn't simple revenge he's after; Bruce doesn't promise his parents that he'll kill the man who killed them. Clearly, with either interpretation of the promise, he takes on a much larger task than that—either to war on *all* criminals or to rid Gotham of evil! Furthermore, in the first volume of *Justice* (2006), Batman tells us that "when I was a boy, my father and mother were murdered before my very eyes. I have dedicated my life to stopping that criminal, *regardless of the forms or faces he wears. Really, the form is of no consequence*" (emphasis added).

And in most storylines, Batman never does bring this name-less and faceless killer to justice. Hollywood is the unfortunate exception here. In Christopher Nolan's 2005 film *Batman Begins*, as an angry young man who's just returned home from college, Bruce plots to kill his parents' killer when he's unexpectedly released from prison, only to be thwarted because someone else gets there first. True, he later realizes that there's more to his mission than simple payback, but in the comics he seems to know this even as a boy. To make matters worse, the

1989 Tim Burton film *Batman* makes Jack Napier—the man who'll become the Joker—the very man who killed Bruce's parents. In that film, in one single narrative Bruce watches his parents die as a boy, and then later, as Batman, he watches their killer fall to his death. But that's just the movies—we don't find such a neat and tidy resolution anywhere else in the Batman universe. This isn't a simple revenge story.

However, it'd also be a serious mistake to deny that revenge—or perhaps, better, a desire for *retribution*—plays an important role in Batman's motivation. Retribution isn't the same thing as base revenge, although it proves surprisingly difficult to spell out the differences. Chief among them is that retribution is less personal and more concerned with a wrongdoer's getting exactly what she deserves.[2] In Loeb's *Superman/Batman: Public Enemies* (2005), when Batman uncovers what looks like some evidence that points to the identity of his parents' killer, he confesses, "Nothing haunts me more than finding out who killed my parents." But he immediately complicates matters by adding that "their unsolved murder changed Gotham City." Batman isn't focused only on his personal loss. Yes, he has a keen interest in bringing his parents' killer to justice. But the key point is that he's after a lot *more* than mere payback. Earlier in the story, Superman says, "I've known Bruce for years. I can't decide if it's the hero in him that drives him—which I respect . . . or the dark side that puts him in harm's way—trying desperately to make up for the murder of his parents. That I don't respect."

Yet there doesn't seem to be any good reason to think that these are the only two possible motivations for Batman, or to assume that they're mutually exclusive. Why must we make this choice? And why should we adopt Superman's simplistic conception of what it is to be a hero? Why not acknowledge that Batman is a very complex character whose motives may be numerous and perhaps even difficult to identify at times—especially given how many different people have written his lines! Why not let our heroes be human beings who don't always understand themselves and often aren't easily understood by others?

In addition to a desire for retribution, what other motives play into Bruce's promise and his lifelong struggle to fulfill it? In *Haunted Knight*, Batman remembers his father being called out of bed in the middle of night to respond to some medical emergency, and he asks of himself, while crouching on a rooftop like a gargoyle, "Is that why I'm here?" And this isn't the only time Batman thinks of his role in Gotham as somehow analogous to his father's role as a physician. *Batman Begins* also hints that Bruce wants to continue in his parents' role, this time as the financial caretaker of Gotham City. In a pivotal scene, Rachel Dawes makes the following appeal to Bruce before he's decided to become Batman: "Good people like your parents who'll stand against injustice? They're gone. What chance does Gotham have when the good people do nothing?" But whereas his philanthropic parents fought crime economically by improving Gotham's infrastructure, Batman takes the fight to the streets. This suggests that Bruce wants not only to atone for their deaths, but also to give meaning to their lives by ensuring that their legacy doesn't die with them. If that's right, then Batman isn't just trying to defeat and destroy the evil forces of Gotham; he's trying to build something as well, and this constructive aim further distinguishes him from someone like the Punisher or *Watchmen*'s Rorschach.

On a psychological level, it's likely that Bruce's desperate promise serves to give unity and shape to a life that's just been broken into pieces. As Alfred observes at the outset of *Hush*,

> I cannot imagine the man young Bruce might have become had his childhood not been ripped from him at gunpoint. Suddenly orphaned and alone, a chilling event took place. There would be no grieving for this child. No time would be lost wishing he could

change these events. *There would only be the promise.* That very night, on the street stained with his mother's and father's blood, he would make a vow to rid the city of the evil that had taken their lives. (Emphasis added)

With his parents gone, Bruce needs a new center of gravity in his world, and this life-changing promise provides just that. To fulfill his promise he spends years in study, training, and travel, acquiring the skills and the knowledge he'll need if he's to have any chance at all of living up to the intimidating task he's sworn to perform. Take away that promise and he's still just a boy in shock, kneeling over the bodies of his parents. His promise gives him something to do and, more important, someone to be. Our commitments and projects shape us and define our character. Thus, the young Bruce Wayne grows up to become Batman; as Rachel Dawes sadly observes at the end of *Batman Begins*, the Bruce Wayne billionaire-playboy persona is nothing but a convenient disguise.

Promises and Morality

Much about Batman's mission looks toward the future: he wants to make Gotham a safer and better place to live—a place where children don't lose their parents as he lost his. Batman thus has *forward-looking* moral reasons for his war against criminals. Are those reasons sufficient to justify his actions?

For a *consequentialist*, who believes that consequences are the only relevant factor in deciding what's right and wrong, this all depends on whether Batman's mission brings about the best possible consequences for everyone.[3] If so, then he ought to go to work. And surely Batman does a lot of good, regardless of what critics, like the talking heads in *The Dark Knight Strikes Again* (2002), might say. But if fighting crime as Batman isn't bringing about the best possible consequences, Bruce should hang up the cape and cowl. Wouldn't that mean breaking the promise he made to his parents? And it's wrong to break promises, right?

In fact, consequentialists have a difficult time giving promises the kind of moral weight they seem to deserve. Consequentialist morality is about making the world a better place, and while keeping promises may often do just that—if they're the right sort of promises, anyway—there's really no room to say that we ought to keep our promises even if people are worse off because we do so. Consequentialists aren't very impressed with "Because I promised I would!" as a moral reason, believing that we need to be prepared to set our commitments aside when the greater good calls for us to do so. To put it another way, consequentialists believe that the end justifies the means, and someone with that mentality will probably end up breaking promises along the way.

After all, why should one keep promises? If, for example, when it's time for Alfred to keep a promise, doing what he promised is a good idea, then of course he should keep his word. He would have been glad to do so anyway! But if doing what he promised seems like a bad idea, then why on earth should Alfred go through with it? Because he said that he would? So what? If he's looking to the future, what he may have promised in the past seems relatively unimportant. A potential reason for Alfred to keep his promises might be that he needs people to trust him, and if they find out that he isn't a man of his word, then they won't accept any promises he makes in the future. But that's just a reason for Alfred to make sure that no one finds out that he broke his promise!

All this just underscores the fact that promises aren't fundamentally forward-looking. Batman's promise anchors his mission in the past; his commitment to keeping this promise gives him a *backward-looking* moral reason to carry out his mission, night after night and villain after villain. Furthermore, while it's undeniable that he wants Gotham's citizens to be safe from marauding criminals, Batman clearly also wants wrongdoers to get what's coming to them. And retribution is backward-looking, too. In different ways, then, Batman's war on crime is connected to the past, to his own history, and to the history of the villains against whom he fights. (Notice how he continually returns to the location of his parents' murder, then called Park Row and now dubbed Crime Alley.) This shouldn't surprise us, however, for as witnessed by the architecture of the Gotham cityscape and by the pervasive presence of fear, the unknown, and the uncanny, Batman's story is a truly *gothic* one—and this movement of the past into the present is another hallmark of the gothic.

This also means that Batman isn't a thoroughgoing consequentialist. He's also motivated by *deontological* moral reasons, which are reasons that involve *what someone is doing* rather than *what happens as a result of what someone does*.[4] "Because it would break a promise!" is a deontological moral reason, as is "Because it would be dishonest!" or "Because it would be murder!" Batman's repeated refusal to kill in carrying out his mission, even when it's the Joker, is a perfect illustration of his commitment to a deontological moral reason.[5] Another such illustration is the way Batman is motivated by his resolve to keep his boyhood promise. And as Alfred observes in *Under the Hood* (2005–2006), Batman's enemies fear his incredible resolve more than they fear his appearance or his strength. Batman is a man who *always* keeps his promises—and that makes him more than a man in the eyes of his foes.

Making Promises to the Dead

In spite of the fact that certain aspects of promises may seem puzzling, their importance to our ordinary moral lives is hard to deny. We often make promises to one another, even as young children, and we take ourselves to be obligated by them. There's a further problem in the case of Batman's promise, however. We do make promises *to* someone, right? In fact, that seems to be an essential part of what distinguishes a promise from a more generic commitment. Further, one very natural way of understanding the wrongness of breaking a promise is that in some way it wrongs or harms the person(s) to whom the promise was made. This idea is supported by the fact that if Batman broke a promise to Oracle, for example, he would owe *her* an apology for doing so, and even if he thought he was morally justified in breaking that promise, surely he would at least owe her an explanation. But Bruce's parents are *dead* when he makes his promise to them. Does it even make sense to promise something to a dead person? Can it be wrong to break a promise to the dead in the way it's wrong to break a promise to the living? Can someone who is dead be wronged or harmed? Are the dead inside or outside of our moral universe?

Of course, we can't think for very long about such questions without facing an even larger question: what happens to us when we die? Is death the end of our conscious existence, or is there some kind of conscious life after death? This is a question that confounds any number of religious and philosophical thinkers—and it leaves even the world's greatest detective in the dark! In *Under the Hood*, when Batman begins to suspect that somehow Jason Todd—the second Robin, who was killed by the Joker—has returned from the grave, he seeks out both Superman and Green Arrow to ask them about what it was like to die and then to come back to life. Although he doesn't really understand it, resurrection is a genuine possibility in Batman's world. We mustn't forget about Ra's al Ghul's Lazarus pits, either, for they can also bring the dead back to some kind of life. Whatever may be the case in our reality, death doesn't seem to be the final exit in comics.

Suppose death isn't the end of us. The 1939 version of Batman's promise invokes the *spirits* of Thomas and Martha Wayne. One relatively clear way to make sense of promises to the departed is to say that in some sense the dead still exist among us—as ghosts or spirits of some sort. But while Batman *is* haunted by his murdered parents, he's not usually haunted in *that* way. They don't reappear to fight alongside him in the way that Harry Potter's parents do, for example, and when they do show up, it's typically in the form of a flashback sequence, a memory, a dream, or a hallucination.[6] Batman isn't literally haunted by his parents' ghosts. Rather, he's haunted by his memories of them and of their deaths, by his longing for them, and by the loss of the life he shared with them. And so our question is whether we can understand his making a promise to a mother and father who are dead and *gone*—and who aren't going to show up to express their disappointment if he doesn't do as he's promised to do. As it turns out, that's the most philosophically interesting question here, too, and a number of philosophers have wrestled with the issues it raises.[7]

So, let's suppose, for the sake of argument, that death is the end of us after all. The ancient Greek philosopher Epicurus (341–270 BCE) goes beyond supposition here. His view is that human beings are composed of atoms, body and soul, and that death is literally our dissolution: we simply go to pieces, and that's it. We don't get to reassemble ourselves like Clayface does. Epicurus famously argues that such a death is nothing to be afraid of:

> Get used to believing that death is nothing to us. For all good and bad consists in sense-experience, and death is the privation of sense-experience. Hence, a correct knowledge of the fact that death is nothing to us makes the mortality of life a matter for contentment, not by adding a limitless time [to life] but by removing the longing for immortality. For there is nothing fearful in life for one who has grasped that there is nothing fearful in the absence of life. Thus, he is a fool who says that he fears death not because it will be painful when present but because it is painful when it is still to come. For that which while present causes no distress causes

unnecessary pain when merely anticipated. So death, the most frightening of bad things, is nothing to us; since when we exist, death is not yet present, and when death is present, then we do not exist. Therefore, it is relevant neither to the living nor to the dead, since it does not affect the former, and the latter do not exist.[8]

Epicurus is a *hedonist*, which means he believes that what's good for human beings is pleasure and what's bad is pain. And since pleasure and pain can't exist without being felt, Epicurus says that "all good and bad consists in sense-experience." And since death is the absence of sensory experience, it's nothing to be afraid of. (The process of dying might be really painful, and thus something to fear, but as long as you're still dying "death is not yet present.") Moreover, nothing can be good or bad for the dead, for they experience nothing at all. If Epicurus is right, then it seems like nothing can be good or bad for Bruce's dead parents. And if a large part of the reason not to break a promise is that it's somehow bad for the one to whom the promise was made, that reason simply won't apply in this case, or in any case where the "promisee" is deceased.

But lots of people don't buy this Epicurean argument. For one thing, it seems reasonable to think that even if death itself doesn't involve any bad experiences, it's a bad thing to die precisely because we're deprived of all the good experiences we might have had![9] Furthermore, there are reasons to be suspicious of the idea that all bad things must be experienced. Consider the following words from Aristotle (384–322 BCE): "For if a living person has good or evil of which he is not aware, a dead person also, it seems, has good or evil, if, for instance, he receives honors or dishonors, and his children, and descendants in general, do well or suffer misfortune."[10]

According to Aristotle, then, there are things that are good and bad for the dead. Let's call these things *postmortem benefits and harms*. Aristotle begins by appealing to an analogy: if the living can be harmed but remain unaware of it, then the dead can be harmed as well. Obviously, he flatly rejects Epicurus's claim that "all good and bad consists in sense-experience." Suppose that Selina Kyle (aka Catwoman, for anyone not in the know) is only pretending to be romantically interested in Batman as part of some complicated plot against him. Suppose further that Batman is totally unaware of this and quite enjoys her company—and in fact he never becomes aware of her duplicity. Hasn't he been harmed? Hasn't something bad happened to him although he doesn't know it? If so, then perhaps there are *unexperienced* harms.

This example suggests that deceit and betrayal can harm us quite apart from their effect on our experience. As Thomas Nagel puts it, "The natural view is that the discovery of betrayal makes us unhappy because it is bad to be betrayed—not that betrayal is bad because its discovery makes us unhappy."[11] And Aristotle believes we can be harmed through our reputations and through our friends and families in a way that doesn't depend on our experiencing anything. The idea of an unexperienced harm seems very plausible.

What about a postmortem harm? If a living Batman can be harmed without experiencing the harm, why not a dead one? If Bruce Wayne were to die, and if after his death people wrongly came to believe that he was a horrible villain rather than a terrific hero, wouldn't we think that something harmful—in Aristotle's words, a misfortune—had happened to him? Expressions like "He'd be turning over in his grave" suggest that this is a rather natural thought. Aristotle certainly thinks so, although he concedes that harms to the dead are relatively weak.

Maybe Epicurus is wrong, then, to say that the dead cannot be harmed because they can't experience the harm. But doesn't another of his points still remain? It's one thing to say that a living person can be harmed in a way that doesn't affect her experience. It's another thing to say, as Aristotle does, that a person who no longer exists can be harmed! How on earth can harm befall someone who doesn't exist? Well, in one sense, it surely can't. Nothing you or I do can really harm Bruce Wayne, right? Because he's made-up; he's not a real person. Surely, however, the dead are in a category different from fictional characters! While the latter do not exist and never did exist as flesh and blood human beings, the former are real people who used to exist.

That's the clue we need to make sense of harming the dead. When we wonder whether it makes sense to say that breaking a promise to the dead might harm them, we need to be careful how we characterize the ones we harm. Are we asking whether Bruce can harm the postmortem Thomas and Martha Wayne? If so, we're asking whether he can harm a ghost, or a corpse, or maybe even nothing. And that's just silly. But what if we ask whether he can harm the antemortem Waynes, the living people who cared for him in his early childhood?[12] If that's how we think of it, then there is an appropriate candidate to suffer the harm of a broken promise. The next problem is to figure out *when* the harm occurs and how to talk about a harm that seems to involve *backward causation*, where somehow what Bruce might do in the present might cause harm to his parents in the past. And that's a real philosophical problem, but it seems like the right kind of problem for Batman fans to take up, given the ways in which the Dark Knight's stories always blend the past and the present.

Batman Returns

In *Kingdom Come* (1997), a story depicting one possible future or alternate Earth in the DC Universe, Batman is still fighting crime in Gotham. In fact, it seems that he's winning the war, with the help of a legion of robotic Bat-Knights. He's kept his promise, or close to it. But at the opening of Frank Miller's classic *The Dark Knight Returns* (1986), another futuristic tale, Batman has retired. Why? Not because he's rid the city of evil and fulfilled his promise to his parents. Far from it. Miller's Batman has hung up his cape and cowl not because his mission is over but because of the death of Jason Todd, a former Robin. (Interestingly, Miller wrote this story a couple of years *before* Jason died in the regular Batman continuity, thereby predicting—and probably helping to bring about—the Joker's infamous killing of Robin depicted in *A Death in the Family* in 1988.)

In *The Dark Knight Returns*, Batman's career ends as it began: with a promise. Consider this internal monologue in which Bruce is describing an ongoing struggle with his inner Batman:

> And he [Batman] laughs at me [Bruce Wayne], curses me. Calls me a fool. He fills my sleep, he tricks me. Brings me here when the night is long and my will is weak. He struggles relentlessly, hatefully, to be free—
>
> I will not let him. I gave my word.
>
> For Jason.
>
> Never.
>
> Never again.

Finally, of course, Batman is victorious in this psychic conflict; he comes out of retirement to fight evil once more. Why? Perhaps it's because the older, stronger promise simply cannot be ignored. As Miller puts it, in trying not to be Batman, Bruce has made himself into "a walking dead man." The promise to his parents and the project to which it gave birth define who he is. Without them, he's just a shell of a man. And the past simply cannot be forgotten: "It could have happened yesterday. It could be happening now. They could be lying at your feet, twitching, bleeding." In the end, Batman has made a promise he can never fully keep, yet it's a promise he can't live without.

Batman Forever?

Some philosophers have argued that human beings should be glad they're not immortal, for an endless life would inevitably prove to be boring and thus be a curse rather than a blessing.[13] Surprisingly, then, death might be part of what makes life attractive and appealing. Even a superhero's life might grow tedious; the thrill of fighting evil might wear off after years, decades, or centuries. But Batman's not primarily driven by the thrill of the chase or by the pleasure of victory. He isn't a superhero because he finds the life so exciting and satisfying. In *Superman/Batman: Public Enemies*, he is brutally honest: "It is not a life I would wish on anyone." No, Batman's crusade against crime is motivated by his ongoing commitment to strive to keep the unkeepable promise that defines him. This commitment gives his life a meaning that isn't connected to his own personal satisfaction. In fact, it's connected to his own personal sacrifice. Batman's promise binds him to Gotham for however long she may need him.

NOTES

1. *Detective Comics* #33 (November 1939). This scene is included in Les Daniels, *Batman: The Complete History: The Life and Times of the Dark Knight* (San Francisco: Chronicle Books, 2004), 34–35.

2. See, for example, Robert Nozick, *Philosophical Explanations* (Cambridge, MA: Harvard Univ. Press, 1983), 366–368.

3. Historically, the most important consequentialists are the British utilitarian philosophers Jeremy Bentham (1748–1832) and John Stuart Mill (1806–1873). A useful anthology is Stephen L. Darwall, ed., *Consequentialism* (Oxford: Blackwell Publishing, 2002).

4. The most influential figure in deontological ethics is the great German philosopher Immanuel Kant (1724–1804). A helpful collection is Stephen L. Darwall, ed., *Deontology* (Oxford: Blackwell Publishing, 2003).

5. The chapter by Mark D. White in this book discusses Batman's refusal to kill the Joker in more detail.

6. See, for example, *Haunted Knight*'s third tale, a revision of Charles Dickens's *A Christmas Carol* in which Bruce's father appears as Jacob Marley's ghost; or *The Long Halloween*, where Bruce is gassed by the Scarecrow and lives half in the present and half in the past while he and his mother are trying to escape his parents' killer.

7. See the various essays in John Martin Fischer, ed., *The Metaphysics of Death* (Stanford, CA: Stanford Univ. Press, 1993).

8. From Epicurus's "Letter to Menoeceus," in *Hellenistic Philosophy: Introductory Readings*, ed. Brad Inwood and L. P. Gerson, 2nd ed. (Indianapolis: Hackett Publishing Company, 1997), 29.

9. See Thomas Nagel's "Death" in his *Mortal Questions* (Cambridge: Cambridge Univ. Press, 1979), also reprinted in *The Metaphysics of Death*, 61–69.

10. Aristotle, *Nicomachean Ethics*, 2nd ed., trans. Terence Irwin (Indianapolis: Hackett Publishing Company, 1999), 13.

11. Nagel, *Mortal Questions*, 65.

12. See George Pitcher's "The Misfortunes of the Dead," reprinted in *The Metaphysics of Death*, 159–168.

13. Bernard Williams, "The Makropulos Case: Reflections on the Tedium of Immortality," reprinted in *The Metaphysics of Death*, 73–92.

SHOULD BRUCE WAYNE HAVE BECOME BATMAN?

Mahesh Ananth and Ben Dixon

What to Do with So Much Time and Money?

Bruce Wayne, Batman's alter ego, is rich—*very* rich. *Forbes* magazine's list of the fifteen wealthiest fictional characters slots Wayne at number seven, estimating his net worth to be nearly seven billion dollars.[1] Notably, Wayne was born into wealth, inheriting his parents' fortune after their untimely deaths at the hands of a Gotham City criminal. So when twenty-five-year-old Wayne takes up the very expensive, very risky task of fighting for justice as Batman, he makes a moral judgment that doing so is an appropriate way to spend his time and his inherited wealth. He decides, essentially, that the right thing to do is honor his parents' memory by cleaning up Gotham City's crime. But is this the morally correct decision?

Not Going Gentle into That Dark Knight

> Without warning it comes . . . crashing through the
> window of your study . . . and mine. . . . I have seen it
> before . . . somewhere . . . it frightened me as a boy . . .
> frightened me . . . yes. Father. I shall become a bat.
>
> — Bruce Wayne, age twenty-five, from *Batman:*
> *Year One* (1987)

Batman: Year One's first depiction of Wayne is visually macabre:
a seven-year-old Wayne kneels helplessly before his parents,
his blood-stained father clutching his mother's shoulder, both
parents lying strewn across the ground, motionless. A few pages
later we see a grown-up Wayne kneeling before his parents
once more, this time in front of their graves. Given his sorrow-
ful expression and his hunched posture, Bruce's pain over their
murders appears not to have faded much in the years since.
Indeed, the story quickly unmasks why Wayne, through his
metamorphosis into Batman, decides that no resource should
be spared to fight injustice. Following the examples set by his
father, himself a wealthy heir and Gotham physician, Wayne
must use his own keen intellect and his inherited wealth to
make Gotham a better place.

Batman's crime fighting is largely a way of paying homage to
his deceased parents, as becomes clear in one of the more surreal
scenes in *Year One*. A failed attempt at vigilantism has left Bruce
wounded and nearly bleeding to death; sitting in his Wayne
Manor study, he starts "speaking" to what appears to be a bust
of his dead father, Thomas Wayne. The younger Wayne asks his
father how he can terrify criminals so as to fight crime more successfully, and he makes clear that he has longed for such success
since the night his parents were murdered—the night, he says,
when "all sense left [his] life." His recollection of the details of
his parents' final night is immediately followed by a bat shattering the window of his study, flying into the room, and landing

atop the sculpture of his father. The incident stirs up terrifying memories of a childhood incident involving bats. Inspired by the bat, Wayne then and there decides to evoke similar terror in the hearts of Gotham criminals. Disguised as a bat, he will fight the scum of Gotham. The imagery and dialogue of this scene make obvious the close links between Wayne's decision to become Batman, the loss of his parents, and the desire he has to respect his father's memory by serving Gotham.[2]

"The Singer": Batman's First Real Nemesis

But is becoming Batman the morally best option for Wayne? At first glance, questioning the moral status of Wayne's choice to live as Batman seems odd. Surely his decision to save crime-ridden Gotham City, a place that a newly arrived police lieutenant, James Gordon, dubs "a city without hope" (*Year One*), is not only commendable but reveals a high moral character. Upon close inspection, however, this characterization may be premature.

In his famous article "Famine, Affluence, and Morality," the philosopher Peter Singer (b. 1946) argues that humans have a moral obligation to assist others who are suffering and dying due to a lack of basic needs, such as food, shelter, and medical care.[3] Singer is a utilitarian. *Utilitarianism* is the moral theory that instructs us to perform those actions that will bring about the greatest good or least amount of evil for the greatest number of people, based upon the fact that all people are morally equal.[4] Singer reasons that the following moral principle should clearly be part of our everyday thinking: "If it is in our power to prevent something bad from happening, without thereby sacrificing anything of comparable moral importance, we ought, morally, to do it."

The usefulness and appeal of this principle can be illustrated by an example Singer gives involving a child drowning in a shallow pond. Imagine walking past this pond and observing the drowning child. You further see that it is quite easy for you to wade into the pond and save the child. Although your clothes will get muddy, the damage to your clothes and any other associated inconveniences are insignificant when compared to the life of the child, right? Thus, clearly you should rescue the child.

It appears that Singer's moral principle accurately captures why anyone coming upon the drowning child should offer aid: one can save a life and do so at very little moral cost. What Singer wants us to consider, however, is that acceptance of this principle has profound implications for how we should live day-to-day. Notice that in much the same way as the person in the example can aid the child without sacrificing something of comparable moral worth, so too can affluent Westerners forgo certain luxuries in order to benefit those who are facing disasters, such as famine and treatable diseases. Clearly many of us do not identify ourselves as wealthy, and yet we are often awash in smaller luxuries like CDs, DVDs, name-brand clothing, and fine food. Singer's moral principle forces us to determine whether enjoying these smaller luxuries is more important than saving human lives.

Let's call Singer's argument "the argument from prevention." Basically, he is arguing that if suffering and death from a lack of food, shelter, and medical care are bad and if it is in our power to prevent such bad things from happening, then we as individuals ought, morally, to prevent such bad things. Given that this sort of suffering is bad and we can help, Singer thinks that it is indisputably the case that we, as individuals, ought to prevent such bad things from happening. Singer takes it to be true that suffering at the hands of starvation, disease, poor shelter, and such things, is bad. Indeed, he claims that if you disagree with the truth of this claim, then stop reading his article! For the sake of our discussion, we will assume (along with Singer) that this claim is true.

Now it's important to understand Singer's rendering of "giving." Specifically, how much are we to give of ourselves in an effort to assist those in such great need? A young Wayne clearly decides to live some version of a sacrificial life, insofar as Batman's nocturnal activities will aim at preventing the suffering and death of his fellow Gothamites. Surely this is enough sacrifice, right? But Singer's own words as to "how much is enough" are startling:

> One possibility [the strong version]. . . . is that we ought to give until we reach the level of marginal utility—that is, the level at which, by giving more, I would cause as much suffering to myself or my dependents as I would relieve by my gift. This would mean, of course, that one would reduce oneself to very near the material circumstances of [the starving poor]. [Alternatively,] I proposed the more moderate version—that we should prevent bad occurrences unless, to do so, we had to sacrifice something morally significant—only in order to show that, even on this surely undeniable principle, a great change in our way of life is required.[5]

Singer makes clear above that there are two versions of giving, a strong version and a moderate version (note that he is skeptical of the latter, but he is willing to adopt it for the sake of argument). The strong version claims that we're morally obligated to give until we reach the point where we would cause as much suffering to ourselves as is present in those we are helping, unless in doing so we had to sacrifice something of *comparable moral significance*. The moderate version, in contrast, claims that we're morally obligated to give until we reach the point at which we sacrifice something *morally significant* as a result of our degree of giving.

Batman versus the Singer: The Battle over Aiding Gotham

It's unclear how much weight, if any, a young Wayne places on the option of giving away most or all of his inherited wealth. Perhaps an incident occurring later in his life gives some indication of his general attitude toward such charitable giving. The comic story *A Death in the Family* (1988), which chronicles the Joker's killing of the second Robin (Jason Todd), includes a scene in which Bruce Wayne encounters famine-stricken refugees in Ethiopia. While reflecting on this human tragedy, Wayne thinks to himself: "The Refugees flock into the camps by the thousands each day. It's utterly heartbreaking. When I return to Gotham, I'll send out another check to help the effort and try to forget what I've seen here. I'm no different from anyone else. There's only so much even Bruce Wayne—and Batman—can do."

Notice Wayne's skepticism as to how effective his donations can be, and also his desire to forget the suffering he sees in Ethiopia, a desire upon which he will act, presumably after he cuts yet another check. Were these general beliefs and attitudes present in Wayne's thinking as a younger man? If so, and if they represent that which is both factual and morally permissible, perhaps they can help to meet the challenge Singer presents. That challenge is whether or not Wayne can become Batman in the light of either the strong version of giving or the moderate version of giving.

With respect to the strong version, the challenge is clear: Wayne must give away most of his income—including both his inheritance and his existing income from Wayne Enterprises—to those in dire need, unless he can show that what happens after he becomes Batman is of comparable moral worth. A utilitarian like Singer can acknowledge that if Wayne is successful as Batman—and that's a very big *if*—he can provide a considerable amount of crime-fighting support for Gotham City, which likely will result in a reduction of some suffering. But such help likely pales in comparison to the benefits he can immediately bring to the masses of poor and needy around the world, especially considering the probability of his fortune's being put to good use by a reputable aid organization. Again, this is opposed to the likelihood of success he will achieve dressing up as a bat, fighting bad guys wielding high-tech weaponry, and keeping up the facade of a billionaire playboy. The implication here is that Wayne *cannot* defend the choice to become Batman according to Singer's strong version of giving.

Responding to the strong version, Wayne could acknowledge his moral obligation to give to the needy but insist that if he were to abandon the life of Batman, then he would be abandoning something of equal moral worth. Specifically, he may claim that his desire to honor his parents' memory by benefiting Gotham reasonably counts as "equal moral worth." Such a reply, if true, would perhaps allow him to become Batman and *charitably* assist the less fortunate.

Singer, however, has a reply to this argument based on two implications of his brand of utilitarianism. The first implication is that neither version of giving acknowledges the proximity or the distance of those who need help.[6] The second implication is that neither version of giving entails the idea that giving to the starving is a matter of charity.[7]

In true utilitarian form, Singer makes clear that location, especially in our richly interactive global market, is irrelevant with respect to moral decision making. Every person morally counts as one, and that's it. So, the suffering of Gotham's "first-world" citizens at the hands of crime, while important, is outweighed by the needs of huge numbers of starving poor in impoverished nations facing certain death. Thus, Wayne's familial ties to Gotham allow for no additional "points" in a utilitarian calculation that weighs harms versus benefits. The idea here is that Wayne cannot use the supposed rightness of honoring his parents' memory by focusing on helping Gotham, even when it has the benefit of alleviating some suffering there, as any kind of trump against a utilitarian like Singer.

The knowledgeable fan, armed with a formidable grasp of the Batman mythology timeline, may wish to point out that once Wayne establishes himself as Batman, it's not too long before he starts encountering villains who wish to cause destruction and suffering well beyond Gotham's city limits. Like utilitarians, bad guys are not so concerned with proximity and distance, not when they realize there's money and power to be had away from home! According to the sophisticated Batman fan, then, it is a bit unfair to say that Wayne's efforts as Batman will benefit only Gothamites.

Remember, though, that in this chapter we are analyzing only Wayne's *initial* decision to become Batman. What we want to know is whether *that* particular decision is morally reasonable from a certain moral theoretic perspective. Certainly utilitarianism will require Wayne to take a hard look at what will be the most reasonable way to utilize his vast resources given the knowledge he has *at the time* his young self is making this decision. Thus, it's still the case that, very early on in Wayne's decision making, the utilitarian will cast a skeptical eye on Wayne's option of fighting crime as Batman.

Batman versus the Singer (Round Two): No Supererogatory Superheroes

What would Singer say to Wayne's invoking a notion of charitable actions that are above and beyond the call of duty? Wayne could argue that his desire to honor his parents' memory and the city his father once practically saved from ruin should have more than a modicum of moral legitimacy, so much so that his aid to others in need (outside of Gotham City) should be viewed as charity. In ethical terms, Wayne could insist that his charitable assistance to others is clearly *supererogatory*—that is, his charitable contributions should count as going beyond the call of duty. From this perspective, Wayne can claim himself not only to be moral and heroic, but also *super*-moral and *super*-heroic, to be acting beyond moral duty.

The utilitarian would reject this, however. Typically, according to utilitarianism, charitable or *super*erogatory acts do not exist because such acts, when all is said and done, turn out really to be obligatory anyway. Such acts are just plain "erogatory"! As another moral philosopher, Lawrence Hinman, writes, "One is always obligated to do the thing that yields the greatest amount of utility, and it is precisely this obligation that constitutes duty. . . . For the utilitarian, there is no room for supererogatory actions, for duty is so demanding that nothing above it is greater."[8]

Singer thinks that at the very least, the moral weightiness of the suffering due to lack of food, shelter, and medical care is so great that efforts to alleviate it are not reducible to "charitable giving."[9] Thus, Wayne's donations to alleviate such suffering, which could be greater, of course, if not for the costs of being Batman, constitute neither charity nor supererogation. It should be clear now that the utilitarian's moral life is an exacting one—and this is precisely Singer's point. Singer can ultimately reply to Wayne, then, that his argument from prevention remains untouched by Wayne's counterarguments. So, based upon the strong version of giving, Wayne is morally obligated to abandon becoming Batman in favor of giving his fortune to the needy. If he chooses to ignore the strong version of giving, then his choice to become Batman and his corresponding actions will be viewed as immoral from this utilitarian perspective.

In terms of the moderate version of giving, Wayne would have to show that he's justified in giving only to the point at which he doesn't have to sacrifice his life as Batman and *all* that comes with this life—a life that he would have to argue is morally significant. The problem here is that it's not clear (even in Singer's analysis) what necessarily counts as "morally significant." One could argue that our many luxuries in life are morally significant because they provide a degree of happiness. Clearly, some constraints on what counts as "morally significant" are needed to avoid the implication that any luxury valued is of moral significance. Following Singer's lead, we suggest that something should count as "morally significant" if and only if such a possession brings about happiness for oneself and its cost does not prevent substantial reduction of suffering for those in dire poverty.

So according to this definition people are allowed to keep a portion of their material gain as a result of their way of life, but they must relinquish some of it to assist others. In keeping with the spirit of Singer's account, however, the definition rules out (for the most part) the acquisition of many "frivolous" material items, because they are likely to come at the expense of reducing a substantial amount of suffering for those living in famine-stricken nations.

The Singer's Victory: Letting the Light of Reason Illuminate the Bat-Cave

In response to Singer, Wayne could offer a reasonable defense of his choice to become Batman by way of both the moderate version of giving and the definition of "morally significant." First, the fact that he's able to save many people's lives and provide security to Gotham City makes clear that his way of life is (in general) morally significant. After all, even if he achieves only minor successes, his efforts reduce suffering and death, precisely what Singer clearly identifies as morally significant. Second, it's clear that the income Wayne receives from Wayne Enterprises offers him the kind of financial security and technology to become the Dark Knight, and also allows him to give to the needy through the Wayne Foundation. So, although Wayne goes to great financial lengths to conceal his identity as Batman and come off as a lazy playboy, his expenditures are allowable, indeed necessary, to his morally significant way of living. Thus, Wayne could defend his choice to become Batman as a morally acceptable choice within the domain of the moderate version of giving.

Despite the moderate version's possible validation of Wayne's decision to become Batman, Singer does not really see any reason for privileging it over the strong version. He writes:

> I can see no good reason for holding the moderate version of the principle rather than the strong version. Even if we accepted the principle only in its moderate form, however, it should be clear that we would have to give away enough to ensure that the consumer society, dependent as it is on people spending on trivia rather than giving to famine relief, would slow down and perhaps disappear entirely.[10]

This dissatisfaction isn't surprising, given Singer's status as a true utilitarian. Typically, utilitarianism has a maximizing/minimizing element, such that what is moral is bringing about the *greatest* good, or the *least* bad, for the greatest number. The moderate version of giving is really not utilitarian (traditionally speaking) in nature; therefore, the invocation of the moderate version to support the decision to become Batman isn't the same thing as invoking a Singer-type utilitarianism in support of it.

But there is another reason why Bruce Wayne's decision runs afoul of utilitarianism, and this reason has stalked Bruce's choice from the beginning: the fact that he looks to the *past* to justify becoming Batman. For a utilitarian, however, the relevant aspect of an action is tied to its consequences *in the future*, so they would not approve of Bruce's looking to his parents' deaths and their commitment to Gotham City as sufficient reasons to fight crime. Only beneficial consequences in the future could justify Bruce's decision, and we've already cast a lot of doubt on that! Once again, "the Singer's" utilitarian arguments would force Bruce Wayne to jettison his morally charged memories, sell his rudimentary bat costume and utility belt, and give away virtually all his money to the starving poor.

But This Ruins Everything!

If you are a fan of the Batman character, like us, you probably don't like the possibility of young Bruce Wayne's acting on utilitarian advice and never becoming Batman. "It is much too demanding and thus unreasonable," you may think to yourself. But utilitarianism represents a powerful way of approaching morally difficult problems, especially when those problems present a choice between sacrificing the well-being of a great number of persons, and sacrificing some good that involves fewer persons, even when some of those few are loved ones.

In fact, a mature Bruce Wayne, as Batman, sometimes invokes utilitarian thinking when approaching such problems. Recall, for example, the time when the Joker stole medical supplies and replaced them with his deadly laughing gas, looking to leave his mark by wiping out an entire Ethiopian refugee camp. Having discovered the Joker's plot, Batman must intercept the convoy of trucks carrying the Joker's deadly cargo. However, in deciding to pursue the trucks, he must leave Robin (aka Jason Todd) behind, knowing that his protégé may very likely be hurt or killed by the Joker. In deciding to leave Robin, Batman makes a moral choice between saving hundreds of persons in immediate danger or remaining with his friend and partner, Robin, to face the Joker. Thus, Batman chose to prevent the death and suffering of the greater number of persons; as Batman puts it to himself, "I didn't have any choice, really" (*A Death in the Family*).

It's ironic that this very way of thinking would have prevented Wayne from becoming Batman in the first place! Perhaps what this illustrates, though, is how tempting it is to invoke utilitarianism when difficult moral choices present themselves, choices that involve harm that is so great, so immediate, and so palpable, that we feel tremendous rational pressure to alleviate that harm. But Peter Singer's point is that such harms are constantly occurring all around us. Internalizing this fact within our own minds presents us with a difficult moral choice: should we emulate the younger Bruce Wayne and privilege our commitments to those closest to us while pursuing our own self-interests? Or, like the older Wayne, should we be prepared to sacrifice the well-being of those very same persons, including our own, by trying to do the greatest good for the greatest number of persons?

NOTES

1. Michael Noer and David M. Ewalt, "The Forbes Fictional Fifteen," Forbes.com, Nov. 20, 2006: September 28, 2007. See: http://www.forbes.com/2006/11/20/forbes-fictional-richest-tech-media_cx_mn_de_06fict15_ intro. html.

2. Regarding Batman mythology, our understanding of Bruce Wayne's decision to become Batman is informed by Frank Miller's *Batman: Year One* and the movie it inspired, Christopher Nolan's *Batman Begins* (2005), which similarly displays Bruce Wayne's loyalties to his slain parents.

3. Peter Singer, "Famine, Affluence, and Morality," *Philosophy and Public Affairs* 1, no. 3 (Spring 1972): 229–243.

4. See John Stuart Mill, *Utilitarianism* (Indianapolis: Hackett Publishing, 2005).

5. Singer, "Famine, Affluence," 241.

6. Ibid., 231.

7. Ibid., 235.

8. Lawrence M. Hinman, *Ethics: A Pluralistic Approach to Moral Theory* (Belmont, CA: Wadsworth, 2003), 143.

9. Singer, "Famine, Affluence," 235.

10. Ibid., 241.

WHAT WOULD BATMAN DO? BRUCE WAYNE AS MORAL EXEMPLAR

Ryan Indy Rhodes and David Kyle Johnson

Moral Exemplars

How can I live a good life? One prominent answer to this question involves *moral exemplars*—people who embody moral virtues. By examining moral exemplars we can discover the virtues, and by *emulating* the moral exemplars we can live a good, virtuous life. But who are these moral exemplars? To start we might make a list of noted men and women who have worked for positive change in the world: Jesus, Buddha, Gandhi, Mother Teresa, and the Dalai Lama among others.

What about Batman—could he be on the list too?[1] Batman—although fueled by revenge—is thought by most fans to be morally good. He is one of "the good guys," dedicating his life to protecting people from supervillains like Joker,

Penguin, Riddler, and Bane—not to mention common crooks and street thugs. Like other heroic fictional characters, such as Sir Galahad, Robin Hood, and Momotaro (from Japanese folklore), Batman fights to make the world a better place. So it makes sense to think that if we were more like Batman, we would be better people and would make our world a better place as well. However, some philosophers argue that fictional characters such as Batman cannot serve as moral exemplars. In this chapter we will answer their objections and argue that Batman can indeed fill that role.

Batman's Virtues

Although most readers probably don't need reminding, let's consider some examples of how Batman exemplifies moral virtues. Justice is a constant aim of his activities, not only in the general sense of fighting crime and protecting the innocent, but in more particular endeavors. For example, in *Batman Chronicles* #7 (Winter 1997), Batman investigated a condemned woman's case based on last-minute doubts about her guilt. In the epic *No Man's Land* story arc, he made duplicate copies of title deeds in order to stop Lex Luthor from acquiring most of Gotham City with forgeries.[2] In the movie *Batman Begins* (2005), Batman's beneficence is on display when he sacrifices his own reputation—and by extension, his late father's—in order to save his party guests from impending violence. We see Batman's generosity in the numerous charitable trusts he funds, as well as in cases like *Azrael* #2 (March 1995), where he gives his vanquished ally-turned-adversary several million dollars to aid in rebuilding his shattered life. Examples of courage are so ubiquitous in Batman's character that it is difficult to choose a single example. From infiltrating the underworld, to confronting madmen, to diving through the air on a rope to catch a falling innocent, practically everything he does requires the utmost bravery.

The Unrealistic Objection

Rather than deny that Batman is virtuous, some people suggest that Batman's depiction is so unrealistic that emulation is impossible. No one can really do the things that he does, and thus he is an unsuitable exemplar for human behavior. This is less of a concern for Batman than it would be for certain other superheroes, of course. Batman is much more realistic than his DC counterparts such as Superman, Green Lantern, and Wonder Woman. Batman is not an alien, he has no magic ring that creates objects from his willpower, and he was not blessed with superpowers by the gods. In fact, a large part of Batman's appeal is that he *is* just a human—an extremely intelligent human with exceptional physical skills and lots of money, but a human nonetheless. All of his "powers" derive from his training, intelligence, and the devices and vehicles that his great wealth enables him to buy or build.

Still, some of his feats cannot be realistically emulated. Few (if any) people could withstand the *psychological* burden of constantly fighting killers, thieves, and psychopaths—to say nothing of the physical prowess involved. Batman is "the world's greatest detective," solving mysteries that leave Commissioner Gordon and the rest of the Gotham police baffled. He is one of the best hand-to-hand fighters in the world, able to engage and defeat several armed opponents at once. In his own words, he "evades gunfire on a nightly basis,"[3] can hold his breath for four minutes while swimming,[4] and always develops plans that are not only five steps ahead of his enemies, but plans that all have "five contingency plans, and five backup plans for those contingencies."[5] Though not technically superhuman, Batman's peak mental and physical abilities far surpass those of most mortal men.

However, emulating a moral exemplar doesn't require exact duplication of specific actions. Rather, it is essential to emulate his or her *virtues*. I don't need to miraculously heal the sick to model the virtues of Jesus Christ; by aiding the sick in whatever ways I am capable of, I can exhibit his compassion. In the same way, I need not be able to sneak into a fortified compound and free a political prisoner, single-handedly fight and subdue a group of rapists, or give millions of dollars to a struggling acquaintance in order to practice the virtues of Batman. By actions like writing letters for Amnesty International, supporting self-defense programs for women, and distributing food to the impoverished with the Salvation Army, I can emulate his justice, beneficence, and generosity. I may not do exactly what Batman does, but I can still improve myself and the lives of the people around me by cultivating his virtues.

The Language Objection

Since Batman is a fictional character, it would seem that he cannot be referenced by language. That is, because Batman is not real, sentences about him do not operate in the same way as they do about things that really exist. Consider the following two statements: (1) "Bruce Willis is wealthy" and (2) "Bruce Wayne is wealthy." The first sentence is true because it makes reference to an actual existing "thing": the actor Bruce Willis. Willis either does or does not have the property of "wealthiness." Willis's bank account is what makes this statement true or false—it is the statement's *truthmaker*. As happens to be the case, Bruce Willis's bank account is quite full, so the statement is true. But if there were no person named "Bruce Willis," the sentence wouldn't have a truthmaker—how could it? It wouldn't be referring to anything! So if Bruce Willis didn't exist, a statement regarding his wealth could be neither true nor false.

So it would seem that the second sentence, "Bruce Wayne is wealthy," is likewise neither true nor false. There is no actual person existing named "Bruce Wayne" who puts on a cape and cowl to strike terror into the hearts of superstitious, cowardly criminals. As such, it can't be true or false that Bruce Wayne is wealthy or—more to the point for our discussion—virtuous. If Batman does not exist, the objection goes, it cannot be true of Batman that he is virtuous. Consequently, it would be a mistake to put him on the "moral exemplar" list.

However, this argument fails to take into account an important feature of how we use language. Of course it is true that Batman doesn't exist: there is no actual billionaire named Bruce Wayne who fights crime with a combination of martial arts, detective work, and an amazing collection of gadgets. Nevertheless, in talking about the *character* Batman, it is still correct to say that Batman's real name is Bruce Wayne, his parents were murdered when he was young, he wears a suit with a cape and a cowl when he fights crime, and so on. If someone denied or disputed those claims, we would rightly say that they lacked knowledge of who Batman is *as a character*. So even though Batman doesn't exist, those statements about him are true—just not in a literal sense.

But what could that possibly mean, "not literally true"? Isn't that the same as saying it isn't true at all? Not exactly. Consider the statement "Dragons breathe fire." This seems to be true even though dragons don't exist. Why? Well, when we say "Dragons breathe fire," we don't literally mean: "There is at least one living creature called a dragon and that creature breathes fire." We know better; the literal understanding is false. We really mean something like "Our conception of dragons includes their breathing fire." Perhaps more accurately we mean, "The stories that contain dragons depict them as breathing fire." And that is true!

So contrary to the objection, when we say "Dragons breathe fire," we aren't failing to refer to anything real and thus failing to say something that could be true or false. We are making reference to a real existing entity: the *stories* about dragons. Our statement "Dragons breathe fire" is saying something about the content of those stories. The main difference between the two kinds of sentences—"Dragons breathe fire" and "Bruce Willis is wealthy"—is that what the former refers to, namely "dragons," is not made explicit by the sentence's subject. Given that we do understand such statements, we must already know that the statement is not meant to be taken literally and, instead, means something else.

In the same way, when we say "Batman is virtuous," we don't literally mean, "One of the existing things in the universe is a person named Batman and that person is virtuous." Instead, we are saying something about the Batman stories: Batman is depicted in a virtuous way within them. This, in fact, is true. Thus it seems that—even though Batman doesn't exist—it is still true that he is virtuous. In that regard, the fact that he is fictional has no bearing.

The Exaggeration Objection

Another possible objection to holding fictional characters like Batman up as moral exemplars is that just as Batman's physical and mental skills are shown by the writers and artists to be far greater than those of most people, his virtue could also be elevated beyond anyone's reach. In the case of real-world historical exemplars like Jesus, Buddha, Mother Teresa, Gandhi, and the Dalai Lama, the example must be attainable because the exemplars themselves actually lived up to it. The argument is that fictional characters are unsuitable as exemplars, not because they lack virtue, but because their writers can give them so *much* virtue that no one could really achieve their impossible standard.

This objection fails, however. Many historical exemplars were not as virtuous as we all imagine them to be. In fact, we dare suggest, when it comes to "historical exemplars," most of the time the persons we place on the "exemplar list" aren't historical at all, but exaggerated (mythical) renditions of historical people. Although Buddha was certainly virtuous, undoubtedly much of his discourses, rules, and life story were embellished and exaggerated in the four hundred years of oral tradition that preceded their written recording. For example, the tale of Buddha's four signs is most often taken to be symbolic, not historically literal.[6] Even though a shorter time elapsed between Jesus' life and the writing of the gospels, something similar might be said about the records of his life and teachings. Even when we think about Socrates—a favorite exemplar of philosophers—we hold up Plato's depiction of him despite knowing that it is at best a roughly accurate reflection of what he actually said and did. This is the case with modern exemplars, too. Perhaps even Gandhi and Mother Teresa weren't quite as "history" depicts them.[7]

So, the "version" of a person's life that qualifies him or her for the moral exemplar list is often not purely historical. Those who do make the list are at least partially as fictitious as Batman himself. But this doesn't mean that the historical Buddha, Jesus, Gandhi, and Mother Teresa were bad people. Of course not! They were *good* people—it's just that the idea of them that we hold up as a moral exemplar may not be entirely historical. Additionally, our point is not that the exaggerated version of these historical characters should be taken off the exemplar list. Quite the opposite: they should be left on! The point is that the embellishments in the life of an exemplary figure don't affect the question of whether that person should be emulated. Suppose that Buddha didn't sit under the banyan tree seeking enlightenment some time after seeing, in exact succession, an old man, an ill person, a funeral procession, and a sage. This would not mean that enlightenment is an unworthy ideal, nor would it diminish the value of Buddha's search for it. In the same way, even though no historical figure has ever shown courage, justice, and the like in precisely the ways that Batman does, we can still improve ourselves by imitating the character traits he exhibits. Batman, although unhistorical, is a moral exemplar.

To the Defense: Incomplete Information

So far, we have addressed objections that suggest that nonfictional exemplars are preferable to fictional exemplars. Now let's look at an argument that suggests the opposite, that fictional characters (at least in one sense) make *better* moral exemplars. As we discussed, the truth about historical moral exemplars is often less impressive than the exaggerated ideal, but many of these persons are still worthy of emulation. However, there is clearly a point at which it would no longer be feasible to continue to view someone as admirable.

Imagine a counselor for troubled youth, whose apparent compassion, determination, and insight have made her a highly esteemed member of the community and a personal hero to the children she has helped. If we discover that despite her best efforts, her own children are severely troubled and constantly running afoul of the law, we might amend our assessment of her, but we would probably still consider her worthy of praise and emulation. However, if we discover that she actually has a low rate of success with patients and gained her reputation by falsely claiming credit for the work of others, we would rightly conclude not only that she fails to be a moral exemplar but also that she is a vicious person. The point of this example is that unless we know everything about our exemplars' lives, we run the risk of considering someone virtuous who actually isn't. Even if the person in question did not turn out to be morally bad, as in the example above, we might still find out that those we once believed to be heroes were in fact morally unremarkable.

Because Batman is a fictional character, however, he is not subject to this problem. We can have full access not only to everything he does, but all of his internal states and motivations as well. If a real person helps someone in need, we might wonder whether he did it because he was truly compassionate or only because it served his self-interest. With Batman, we can read the thought balloon and settle the issue. If we hear someone high-mindedly praising nobility and courage, we can wonder whether her actions bear this out, or whether she is a hypocrite. With Batman we can simply read his stories and see all of his actions for ourselves. If someone is virtuous now, we can wonder whether he will continue to be virtuous in the future, or whether one day his resolve will fail him and he will fall from grace. With Batman, the writers can ensure that he always remains true to his mission. For all these reasons, Batman as a fictional character serves as a better moral exemplar than real people. Unlike real people who suffer from human frailties, Batman can forever represent indefatigable virtue. Like Bruce says in *Batman Begins*: "As a man I'm flesh and blood, I can be ignored, I can be destroyed. But as a symbol? As a symbol I can be incorruptible. I can be everlasting."

But Then Again . . .

By the same token, however, Batman has a weakness that historical people do not have—a different kind of incomplete information. With a human being, there is only one person deciding what actions she takes, and what is true of her is strictly limited to what she has actually done. In addition, when her life is over, there is no more room for change—her traits and actions, whether virtuous or vicious, were what they were. But with Batman and other fictional persons, there is not only always the possibility for change, there are multiple people defining the character and potentially engineering that change. We just noted that the writers *can* ensure that Batman always remains true to his mission, but there is no guarantee that they *will* do so. The more Batman stories that are written, by more and more people, the higher the chance that these stories will not represent a consistent, cohesive character, let alone one that always lives up to the same standards of moral excellence.

Not only is this potentially true of future stories, but it is a problem for past ones. While many features of Batman's character are fairly common throughout, there are exceptions. For example, most Batman stories depict him as refusing to use guns, and as never being willing to kill. However, when he was first created, Batman did use guns and had few compunctions about administering fatal justice to the criminals he battled. A potentially very serious objection arises then: Batman cannot serve as a moral exemplar, because there is no way to pick out the *true* Batman from among competing, equally viable alternatives. How can this objection be answered?

We might first try by excluding tales that aren't considered part of the Batman "canon." Some comics are not part of mainstream continuity, but merely serve to envision characters in fun and different ways. In the DC Universe, these were known as "Elseworlds" tales, which took place either in alternate timelines or on alternate Earths. In Batman's case, this includes such works as "Dark Knight of the Round Table" (1999), which places Bruce Wayne in Camelot, and "Castle of the Bat" (1994), where Bruce is a Dr. Frankenstein–type character. However, to exclude noncanonical comics is insufficient to answer the objection for two reasons. First, that exclusion would not solve the problem of future releases within mainstream continuity, which could potentially change the character (as we've seen in the "softer and gentler" Batman after the events of *Infinite Crisis* and *52*). Second, there are some depictions of Batman that, while outside continuity, are widely considered to capture Batman very well. Frank Miller's *The Dark Knight Returns* (1986) is praised not only for its portrayal of Batman, but as one of the most important publications in comics. Similarly, while *Batman: The Animated Series* (1992–1995) is clearly a separate incarnation from the comics, it enjoys near universal acclaim among Batman fans for truly getting Batman right as a character. So we must look for another answer.

There may be a clue in the phrase "getting Batman right as a character." If there is a way to get Batman right as a character, there must also be a way to get him *wrong* as a character—but how do we determine this difference? Could it be simple fan majority? No, because if it is based on the majority, then it could change, and we are looking for a stable, "true Batman." Perhaps, then, the true Batman is whatever is consistent with his original depiction. But as we saw above, this would be different from what most of us today would consider some of Batman's essential properties—the properties that Batman must have in order *to be* Batman. And that seems to be what the whole question comes down to: can a fictional character such as Batman *have* essential properties? And if so, how?

Batman the Icon

It makes sense to talk about Batman's essential properties, insofar as Batman has become an *icon*. True, his portrayal when he was first created was different from how most of us conceive of him now. However, like Superman and many other fictional heroes both inside and outside of comics, the concept for Batman grew and matured into something different and greater. Those new, matured concepts of those characters are what have become *iconicized* as part of our modern mythology. As such, there is a very strong sense in which that version became the *true* Batman. There is a psychological power in that character—one that appeals to our literary consciousness as an archetype—and that is why the character has endured and continues to inspire.

There is room, of course, for continued growth as future Batman stories are written. As with any established character in literature, however, we can view such growth in the context of preserving the character's essence. Just as learning enough new information about a person can make it impossible to continue viewing him as a moral exemplar, if the changes to his character are sufficiently drastic, we could not plausibly continue to call him "Batman." Insofar as Batman exists as an icon, and not just as a character, he has come to possess a mythological status for us. As such, he has evolved into what we can rightly call his true persona. The resulting consistent character, a modern literary hero, can guide us in becoming more virtuous.[8]

Batman *Is* a Moral Exemplar

The fictional nature of Batman should not impede our striving and desire to be like him. After all, fictional stories have morals, don't they? Often they are a call to behave as the characters in the story did. Like our "historical" exemplars, Batman's ideal may lie beyond our reach. But even so, by studying and emulating Batman, we can develop courage, justice, benevolence, and the like. A shadowy dark knight from a fictional city can actually help us live a good, virtuous life in the real world.

NOTES

1. As *The Simpsons'* Comic Book Guy says, "What would Batman do?" (See Matt Groening, "T-Shirts from the Back of the Closet," in *Comic Book Guy's Book of Pop Culture* [New York: Harper Paperbacks, 2005].)

2. *No Man's Land*, vol. 5 (2001).

3. *Gotham Knights* #27 (May 2002)

4. *Detective Comics* #663 (July 1993).

5. *Shadow of the Bat* #92 (December 1999).

6. See John M. Koller and Patricia Joyce Koller, *Asian Philosophies*, 3rd ed. (Upper Saddle River, NJ: Prentice Hall, 1998), 136–137. Similar claims are made by Gananath Obeyesekere. See "The Buddhist Meditative Askesis; Excerpts From the William James Lecture for 2003–2004," at http://www.hds.harvard.edu/news/bulletin/articles/james_04.html.

7. See Christopher Hitchens, *The Missionary Position: Mother Teresa in Theory and Practice* (London and New York: Verso, 1995); Aroup Chatterjee, *Mother Teresa: The Final Verdict* (Lake Gardens, Kolkata, India: Meteor Books, 2002); and G. B. Smith, *Gandhi: Behind the Mask of Divinity* (Amherst, NY: Prometheus Books, 2004).

8. For more on the different "versions" of Batman over the years and across various forms of media, see the essay by Jason Southworth in chapter 12 of this book.

PART FOUR

WHO IS THE BATMAN? (IS THAT A TRICK QUESTION?)

UNDER THE MASK:
HOW ANY PERSON CAN
BECOME BATMAN

Sarah K. Donovan and Nicholas P. Richardson

So, You Wanna Be Batman?

Well, do you? If so, you cannot believe that there is any real depth to who you are as a person. You must accept a world without religion or a higher power of any sort. You must surrender any moral code that you have that is based on religion or God. You must believe in your heart of hearts that you are wholly and completely alone in determining your fate. You must live among criminals. You must dress like a bat, in tights with underwear over them. If you're on board—or if you're at least curious—then read on. (If not, read on anyway—you already paid for the book!)

We'll be looking at three works that demonstrate Batman's construction of himself in his early, mid-, and late career: *Batman: Year One* (1987), *Arkham Asylum* (1989), and *The Dark*

Knight Returns (1986). Drawing on Friedrich Nietzsche's and Michel Foucault's views of identity and power, we'll see that Batman's identity and reality are constructed, and that a hero of the night must be aware of this construction and embrace it.

Will the "Real" Batman Please Step Forward?

But before we can start giving you the information you'll need to become a dark knight, we need to set up a few ground rules based upon the ideas of Friedrich Nietzsche (1844–1900)[1] and Michel Foucault (1926–1984).[2] We will also look at one of the branches of philosophy that they are criticizing: *metaphysics*, which deals with that which is beyond what we can touch, such as God, the soul, objective moral values, or purely rational, absolute truths.

We can sum up Nietzsche's and Foucault's ideas by listing a few short points. They do not believe humans have souls that determine who we are or what we will become.[3] There is no God or afterlife—you die with your body. Neither biology nor genetics properly explains or determines what you will call your *identity* (or self, or personality, or subjectivity—choose your own favorite label because they are all irrelevant now!). Who you are is a product of both your environment and how you understand and create yourself within that environment. There is no deep meaning to your life (some of you may have already realized this). You are nothing more than the multiple (and sometimes conflicting) identities that you live, or become, each day or even moment to moment. According to Nietzsche and Foucault, our day-to-day grind numbs us to these truths, and this lack of insight limits and constrains our freedom. But Batman is able to lift the veil and embrace these truths.

Let's stop for a second and clear up a language issue. When we talk about Bruce Wayne creating Batman, we are not claiming that Batman is Bruce Wayne—we are simply using this language because it's the easiest way to understand what we're talking about. Hypothetically, Batman could have created Bruce Wayne, so that Batman would be no more Wayne than Wayne is Batman. Following Nietzsche and Foucault, we think that both Bruce Wayne and Batman are performances. We are rejecting the idea that there is some "true" self underneath Wayne or Batman that connects them. Obviously the two identities overlap and are aware of each other through memory, but there is much more to it than that.[4]

As Foucault demonstrates in books such as *The History of Sexuality: An Introduction*, identities, bodies, and knowledge do not exist in a pure state outside of history and power relationships. We are not born with identity; identities are products of power (this could be the power of a state or society) or power relationships (such as the relationship between Batman and the Joker). Foucault challenges us to understand all aspects of our lives in terms of a very specific "definition" of power. In particular he focuses on how we are unwittingly controlled by rules, laws, and social norms.

Many of us follow rules without questioning them, or even knowing that we are following them. Even more interesting is that individuals create rules without questioning why they are doing so. Turning to the world of Batman, we can consider the example of Two-Face, who makes decisions based on the flip of a coin. In *Arkham Asylum*, when Batman returns the coin to him, Two-Face uses it to decide Batman's fate, and even the Joker follows the rule. Looking at the same graphic novel, the Joker lays out the rules for Batman when he is in the asylum, giving him one hour to hide, and Batman follows this arbitrary rule. According to Foucault, following rules leads to the construction of a person's identity.

Likewise, Bruce Wayne's constructed identity reflects his affluent life. As a child he was sheltered from the grim realities of life in Gotham, lived with parents who loved him, and clearly had a carefree childhood. But Wayne soon becomes a victim of circumstance—the murder of his parents woke him up to the nature of the vicious and senseless world around him. In *Batman: Year One* he describes that day as the day that "all sense left my life." As we see in *Arkham Asylum*, the young boy who saw his parents murdered and who would eventually become Batman lost faith in rules and civilized society. As an adult, Wayne decided to stop being afraid and to create his own order.

Building a Batman

In *Year One*, we watch as Batman comes into being. Wayne's creation of Batman is telling. Batman is not some sort of heroic force inherent to Wayne that emerges in times of need. Let's consider three examples from *Year One* that show Wayne's conscious decision to create the identity of Batman.[5]

First, when Bruce Wayne is training on his family estate before creating Batman, he says, "I'm not ready. I have the means, the skill. . . . I have hundreds of methods. But something's missing. Something isn't right." Second, after his first failed attempt to defend a young girl from her pimp, he starts to put his finger on what is missing. As he thinks about his missteps during the evening, he says, "God . . . fear of God . . . fear . . . I have to make them afraid." And as he sits seriously injured in his home and wonders how to incite fear in others, a bat crashes through his window, and he says, "Yes, Father, I shall become a bat"—the idea of Batman is born. Third, Wayne begins to don the costume and practice being a Dark Knight. As Police Commissioner Jim Gordon remarks, Batman works "his way from street level crime to its upper echelons, from junkie mugger to pusher to supplier—and along the way, to any cops that might be helping the whole process along." We still sense Wayne's hesitation when he crashes a party at the mayor's mansion in order to incite fear in corrupt politicians: "The costume—and the weapons—have been tested. It's time to get serious. Chauffeur by chauffeur, I make my way toward the Mayor's mansion."

Wayne's actions construct the identity of Batman. Both Nietzsche and Foucault would agree that identity is always under construction and therefore capable of radical reconstruction. When Wayne witnessed the murder of his parents, he had the financial means to leave Gotham forever. However, he chose to remain and to reconstruct himself physically, mentally, and emotionally as Batman.

Arkham Asylum and the Construction of Truth

If you've made it this far into the chapter, then you really are serious about becoming an avenging force. We now must reveal another key piece of information: there is no absolute truth. Nietzsche and Foucault criticize historical philosophers who insist that there are absolute truths about the way the world really is, who we are as individuals, and how we ought to live. For both philosophers, people with power determine what counts as truth. As Nietzsche says in *Philosophy and Truth*, "What then is truth? A movable host of metaphors, metonymies, and anthropomorphisms."[6] In the same way that Nietzsche believes that Christians made God in their image but then said that it happened the other way around, Nietzsche believes that humans create truths but then pretend that truth exists outside of our minds to be discovered.

Agreeing with Nietzsche's basic insight about truth, Foucault applies this analysis to social issues.[7] Foucault argues that we divide our experiences into normal and abnormal. Normalcy is constructed, and it cannot exist without the "abnormal" (which is also constructed). Abnormal must be sustained in order to bolster the "normal."

Let's take Foucault's logic about the constructed and mutually dependent relationship between categories such as normal and abnormal, and apply it to *Arkham Asylum*, replacing the categories of normal and abnormal with "sane" and "insane." Accepting that sane and insane are both constructed and therefore inherently unstable categories, let's focus on how these two categories construct the identity of both the Joker and Batman respectively. While most people consider the Joker insane and Batman sane—we did say *most* people—*Arkham Asylum* questions this, highlighting the larger themes that both identity and reality are constructed.

In *Arkham Asylum*, the inmates have literally taken over the asylum. In a bargain to release the hostages, Batman enters the asylum and faces the criminals, the most famous of whom he bested and busted. Some of the asylum staff voluntarily stays, and psychotherapist Ruth Adams explains to Batman the treatments that villains like Two-Face have undergone. When Batman points out that therapy has had no effect on the Joker, Adams says that it may not be possible to define the Joker as insane. She says,

> It's quite possible we may actually be looking at some kind of super-sanity here. A brilliant new modification of human perception, more suited to urban life at the end of the twentieth century. . . . Unlike you and I, the Joker seems to have no control over the sensory information he's receiving from the outside world. . . . He can only cope with that chaotic barrage of input by going with the flow. . . . He has no real personality. . . . He creates himself each day. He sees himself as the lord of misrule, and the world as a theatre of the absurd.

The Joker is an extreme and undesirable example of the previously discussed theory about identity. However, Dr. Adams's analysis of the Joker shows that the label "insane" is constructed from society's definition of insane. Joker is insane only because

Gotham's rules (which are constructed truths) have labeled him as such. As Adams hints, in a society with vastly different rules from our own, he might be considered sane.

Your Turn, Batman!

In the same way in which Joker's insanity is called into question, so is Batman's sanity. (Imagine that!) *Arkham Asylum* begins with the following epigraph from Lewis Carroll's *Alice's Adventures in Wonderland*, "'But I don't want to go among mad people,' Alice remarked. 'Oh, you can't help that,' said the Cat: 'We're all mad here. I'm mad, you're mad.' 'How do you know I'm mad?' said Alice. 'You must be,' said the Cat, 'or you wouldn't have come here.'" Note that this is another example of a constructed rule, where madness is defined based upon location. What we find in *Arkham Asylum* is that Batman, like Alice in Wonderland, enters only because he is ultimately similar to the criminals. According to the theories of Nietzsche and Foucault, whether we recognize it or not, we all have the potential to be classified as "insane."

We can demonstrate that the sanity of Batman can be called into question if the rules are changed. First, Batman ultimately knows that he shares traits with Alice when he remarks before he goes in to the asylum, "I'm afraid that the Joker may be right about me. Sometimes I question the rationality of my actions. And I'm afraid that when I walk through those asylum gates. . . . It'll be just like coming home." This is not the first allusion to Alice in Wonderland in these three graphic novels—in *The Dark Knight Returns*, Wayne falls into the cave while chasing a rabbit!

Second, *Arkham Asylum* is not just the story of Batman confronting his enemies. It also chronicles the life of Amadeus Arkham, which eerily parallels the life of Bruce Wayne. Both left Gotham and their family estates and returned after twelve years. Both returned to try to bring order to Gotham (Arkham in the form of an asylum for the mentally ill, Wayne as a vigilante who fights crime). Both Arkham and Wayne feel guilty about the deaths of their mothers (Arkham because he killed her, and Wayne because he was the reason that his parents left the movie theater that fateful night). Both of them went through the shock of their family members being murdered. And both saw visions of a bat. However, Arkham was classified as insane, and Wayne created Batman to fight the criminally insane. In the context of *Arkham Asylum*, these direct parallels encourage us to consider who should be classified as sane and insane. They also challenge us to question Arkham's construction of himself as opposed to Wayne's construction of himself.

Finally, at the end of the graphic novel, we read notes written by all of the inmates, including Batman. Of interest are the following lines: "Mommy's dead. Daddy's dead. Brucie's dead. I shall become a bat." Batman has constructed his own identity and considers himself to be different from Bruce Wayne—or at least Brucie Wayne—who he may feel is dead.

So if you do decide to become Batman, please be aware that you may very well be labeled insane for running around in a costume at night, but once you've created a cadre of villains as your foes, society's definition of sanity will be expanded to include you and exclude the villains.

How Batman Sees Through the Lies about Identity and Reality

You've made it this far—congratulations! You've accepted that identities are constructed, and that even truth is constructed. So what's the next piece of the puzzle to complete your transformation? The key to cracking this part of the puzzle resides with Nietzsche. We read *Batman: Year One*, *Arkham Asylum*, and *The Dark Knight Returns* as a chronology of Batman's life, and if you want to become a Batman yourself, you must embrace Nietzsche's philosophy—as Batman has.

Nietzsche states that we are instinctual creatures and our identity is constructed out of our desires for survival and power. Nietzsche coins the phrase *will to power* to describe these desires.[8] A companion concept to this is the *eternal recurrence* (also known as *eternal return of the same*). This is the ability to welcome *both* the highest peaks and the deepest, darkest valleys of our individual lives. Nietzsche praises the person who fully embraces these concepts.

In *Thus Spoke Zarathustra*, Nietzsche poetically captures the essence and the difficulty of the eternal recurrence in "On the Vision and the Riddle" when he describes the following scene as a vision and a riddle to be deciphered:

> Among the wild cliffs I stood suddenly alone, bleak, in the bleakest moonlight. *But there lay a man.* . . . A young shepherd I saw, writhing, gagging in spasms, his face distorted, and a heavy black snake hung out of his mouth. Had I ever seen so much nausea and pale dread on one face? He seemed to have been asleep when the snake crawled in his throat, and there bit itself fast. My hand tore at the snake and tore in vain; it did not tear the snake out of his throat. Then it cried out of me: "Bite! Bite its head off! Bite!" Thus it cried out of me—my dread, my hatred, my nausea, my pity, all that is good and wicked in me cried out of me with a single cry. . . . The shepherd, however, bit as my cry counseled him; he bit with a good bite. Far away he spewed the head of the snake and he jumped up. No longer shepherd, no longer human—one changed, radiant, *laughing*! Never yet on earth has a human being laughed as he laughed.[9]

Nietzsche believes that life is full of real suffering (as represented by the snake in the riddle) and joy (as represented by the triumphant bite of the shepherd and his subsequent laughter). Most people "sleep" through their lives (as the shepherd is doing when the snake bites him), but an individual who lives according to Nietzsche's philosophy of the eternal recurrence can embrace both suffering and joy. This person loves life so much that he or she does not regret or wish away even the most painful moments. In the same way that no one could save the shepherd except the shepherd himself, we are all the captains of our own lives.

Much like the snake in the vision, in the world of Batman the bat is a symbol for everything frightening, tragic, and ruthless in life. Only Batman is able to confront the bat, embracing it and overcoming the despair that it symbolizes. Others have also witnessed the bat; when they fail to embrace the bat, they have two options: one, they may pursue a life of crime or evil deeds (this may include criminal insanity), or two, they may be utterly terrorized and become withdrawn.

To see a failed encounter with the bat, consider in *Arkham Asylum* when Amadeus Arkham chronicles his own descent into madness and also the insanity of his mother. After his family is brutally murdered, he uncovers a repressed memory in which we once again see the vision of a bat. Arkham recalls that he visited his mother before her death. His mother is frightened and tells him that something is there to take her. At first Arkham thinks that she is mad, but then he says, "But God help me, I see it. I see the thing that has haunted and tormented my poor mother these long years. I see it. And it is a bat. A bat!" Arkham murders his mother in order to save her from the bat. Recollecting this, he says, "I understand now what my memory tried to keep from me. Madness is born in the blood. It is my birthright. My inheritance. My destiny." Here the vision of the bat terrorized both Arkham and his mother.

Dr. Cavendish similarly descends into madness upon reading Arkham's journal. He frees the prisoners of Arkham Asylum and forces Batman to read the passage from Arkham's journal in which he speaks of a bat. He accuses Batman of having a partnership with the "hungry house" in which he supplies the asylum with "mad souls." Cavendish says, "I'm not fooled by that cheap disguise. I know what you are." He suggests that Batman is a mystical force when he says of Arkham that he "studied Shamanistic practices, and he knew that only ritual, only magic, could contain the bat. So you know what he did? He scratched a binding spell into the floor of his cell." Arkham died once the binding spell was complete. While Cavendish does not literally see the bat, the vision conveyed to him by Arkham's journal drives him to madness.

Batman and—Well, Uh, You Know—Bats

The vision of the bat has an effect on Bruce Wayne that is different from its effect on the others who have seen it. While Batman's sanity is called into question in *Arkham Asylum*, none of the other graphic novels causes us to seriously doubt that there is a moral distinction between his actions and those of criminals such as the Joker. We read about Bruce Wayne's struggles to come to grips with both the vision of the bat and his identity as Batman. This is a Nietzschean struggle to face the madness and suffering that is a part of life. At the end of *The Dark Knight Returns*, we see Bruce Wayne finally come to terms with the bat.

Bruce Wayne and Batman have four significant encounters with the bat in the three graphic novels. First, in *The Dark Knight Returns*, Wayne dreams about a childhood experience in which he sees a bat. While chasing a rabbit, Wayne falls into the rabbit hole and into what will later become the Batcave. Here he encounters what he describes as an ancient bat. He says, "Something shuffles out of sight . . . something sucks the stale air . . . and hisses . . . gliding with ancient grace . . . unwilling to retreat like his brothers did . . . eyes gleaming, untouched by love or joy or sorrow . . . breath hot with the taste of fallen foes . . . the stench of dead things, damned things . . . surely the fiercest survivor—the purest warrior . . . glaring, hating . . . claiming me as his own." When the adult Wayne awakens, he finds that he has been sleepwalking and is in the Batcave. In this graphic novel, he recounts the dream as if the childhood experience determined the course of his life—even though he would not understand the significance of seeing the bat for many years.

Second, Wayne sees the bat crashing through the window of his study at the Wayne Manor on two occasions that mark a birth and rebirth of Batman. In *Batman: Year One*, the vision prompts him to create the identity Batman. In *The Dark Knight Returns*, the vision incites him to come out of retirement and once again don the mask and become the Dark Knight. As he says soon thereafter, dressed in his Batman costume, "I am born again."

Third, in *Arkham Asylum*, if we follow the visual cues of the artist, Batman is the vision of the bat as seen by Amadeus Arkham and his mother. Batman is consistently drawn as a shadowy figure, almost always without a face. Here, Batman himself is the walking vision of the bat.

Finally, in *The Dark Knight Returns*, Batman sees the bat, drawn in the exact same manner as it is drawn from his childhood memory when he looks at Two-Face (compare pages 19 and 55 of the graphic novel). This reinforces the earlier idea we suggested, in which exposure to the bat can lead to one's becoming a hero if the bat is embraced, or a villain if the bat is rejected. Just like Nietzsche's shepherd has embraced and overcome the snake, Batman has embraced and overcome the bat.

Can You Face the Bat?

So having accepted that your identity is constructed, that truth and reality are constructed, and then going so far as to fully embrace these concepts, you have the philosophical underpinnings to become Batman yourself. But if you follow the steps we have outlined and, instead of becoming a Batman, you become a Joker or a Two-Face, we assume no liability whatsoever. For this is the risk one must take on the road to becoming the Bat.

NOTES

1. With regard to Nietzsche, our citations and references are from Friedrich Nietzsche, *Beyond Good and Evil*, trans. Walter Kaufman (New York: Penguin, 1966); *On the Genealogy of Morals*, trans. Walter Kaufman (New York: Penguin, 1967); *Thus Spoke Zarathustra: A Book for None and All*, trans. Walter Kaufman (New York: Penguin, 1978); *Philosophy and Truth: Selections from Nietzsche's Notebooks of the Early 1870's*, ed. and trans. Daniel Breazeale (New Jersey: Humanities Press International, 1995).

2. With regard to Foucault, our citations and references are from Michel Foucault, *Language, Counter-Memory, Practice*, ed. Donald F. Bouchard, trans. Donald F. Bouchard and Sherry Simon (Ithaca, NY: Cornell Univ. Press, 1977); *The History of Sexuality. Volume 1: An Introduction*, trans. Robert Hurley (New York: Vintage, 1990); *Discipline and Punish: The Birth of the Prison*, trans. Alan Sheridan (New York: Vintage, 1995).

3. As Foucault says, "The soul is the effect and instrument of a political anatomy; the soul is the prison of the body" (*Discipline and Punish: The Birth of the Prison*, 30).

4. We should also consider a point made by Judith Butler, a philosopher influenced by Nietzsche and Foucault. She said that just because identity is a performance does not mean we can change it like a pair of tights. For example, you cannot wake up one morning and decide to be Batman; rather, you must rehearse the performance. See her book *Bodies That Matter* (New York: Taylor and Francis, 1993).

5. Keep in mind that by saying that Wayne creates Batman, we are not implying that Wayne is any less constructed than Batman. We might refer to Batman as the construction of a construction, as Bruce Wayne is himself a construction.

6. Nietzsche, *Philosophy and Truth*, 84.

7. Foucault's essay on Nietzsche entitled "Nietzsche, Genealogy, History" (included in *Language, Counter-Memory, Practice*) demonstrates Foucault's understanding of Nietzsche's genealogical approach to truth.

8. Nietzsche discusses the will to power in books such as *Beyond Good and Evil*, *On the Genealogy of Morals*, and *Thus Spoke Zarathustra*.

9. Nietzsche, *Thus Spoke Zarathustra*, 159–160.

COULD BATMAN HAVE BEEN THE JOKER?

Sam Cowling and Chris Ragg

A Modal Question

Suppose that you and I are citizens of Gotham City, who read the *Gotham Gazette* with all its Batman-related headlines and have suspicions about the identity of Batman. We're convinced he's either billionaire playboy Bruce Wayne or—courtesy of a grandiose conspiracy theory—the criminal mastermind known only as the Joker. One day, the *Gazette* announces, "Batman Unmasked: Billionaire Wayne Is the Dark Knight!" Our suspicions have been confirmed; we now know Bruce Wayne is Batman. Despite this, it certainly seems to be true that the Joker *could* have been Batman. But is this really the case?

There are many ways to make sense of the claim "Batman could have been the Joker." The way that will be relevant to our discussion is as follows: "It is possible that the Joker is identical to Batman." Claims of this sort—claims about possibility, necessity, and impossibility—are *modal claims*. Typically, modal claims assert that the universe could have turned out a certain way. For example, "Batman could have two side-kicks" and "Catwoman couldn't fight crime if her suit were any tighter" are modal claims about what sorts of things are possible for Batman and Catwoman. In ordinary language, these sorts of claims usually include terms like "would" and "might." The truth or falsity of modal claims depends on facts about what sorts of things are possible and, in the particular case we're interested in, on whether Batman could bear a certain relation—the *identity relation*—to the Joker.

In this chapter we'll tackle a single modal question: Could Batman have been the Joker? Answering this question requires a fair bit of modal investigation and some serious metaphysics. Fortunately, *metaphysics*—the study of what exists and how it goes about existing—is the realm of philosophy that has the most in common with comics. It often gets complicated, not to mention absolutely bizarre. But before we consider whether the Clown Prince of Crime might have been identical to the Dark Knight, we'll try to bring together a few key pieces of a very complex modal-metaphysical puzzle. And after introducing some (we hope) plausible metaphysical assumptions, we'll consider an argument aimed at showing that, perhaps surprisingly (and perhaps not), Batman could not have been the Joker. Finally, we'll raise some problems for anyone who accepts this argument and suggest why answering modal questions involving fictional characters like Batman and the Joker is a trickier matter than one might expect.

Some Not-So-Secret Things about Identity

Let's start by introducing the first and most important piece of the metaphysical puzzle: identity. We often say things like "They have identical haircuts" or "Their outfits were identical." These sentences involve a notion of identity between two separate yet extremely similar things. It's important to note that the notion of identity we'll be discussing is different in a very important way—in fact, it's a relation that things bear only to themselves. The notion of identity we're interested is expressed when we say things like "Dr. Jekyll is identical to Mr. Hyde" or "Chicago is identical to the Windy City." So, while a painting and its forgery might be identical, in the sense of being extremely similar, it's not the case that they're identical in the way that we'll be concerned with. After all, you might own one but not the other.

So, when we consider whether Batman could have been identical to the Joker, we're interested in whether they can be one and the same individual in the same way that you're identical to yourself and would be distinct from your twin, if you had one. We're not interested here in whether the Joker might undergo extensive surgery, purchase a new costume, and near-perfectly resemble Batman. Rather, we want to know if Batman and the Joker could have been the very same, identical individual.

Here's one thing we know for certain about identity: everything is identical to itself (or *self-identical*) and not identical to anything else. Given that every thing is self-identical, many philosophers endorse a principle called the *Indiscernibility of Identicals* (let's call this "IOI" for short). According to this principle, in order for things to be identical, they must share each and every property they have. So, for example, you and yourself have all the same properties: you're both human, you're both literate, and you both know who Batman is. Because you and yourself share each and every property, you and yourself are identical. Now suppose that you have a twin sibling and that your twin was born a minute later than you. You and your twin are distinct: you do not share the property of being born at the very same instant.

Similarly, if Bruce Wayne and Batman are identical, we can say that if Bruce Wayne is a billionaire, IOI entails that Batman is a billionaire. While the fact that Batman is

Bruce Wayne's "secret identity" might make this claim seem somewhat counterintuitive, it's important to realize that the sense in which one might think that Batman is not a billionaire is likely a looser, more metaphorical sense than we're interested in. Because IOI entails that identical things never differ in what properties they have, it will be helpful to keep IOI in mind when we attempt to determine whether Batman could have been identical to the Joker.

Picking through Possible Worlds

Modal questions are framed in terms of "possible worlds." Despite the name, these possible worlds—other ways this world could have ended up—are more like alternate universes than alien planets.[1] By using possible worlds as a tool, we can distinguish between different ways for sentences to be true. For example, it is true that dinosaurs *might* not have become extinct, since there is a possible world where we live side-by-side with dinosaurs. Similarly, it is true that the automobile might never have been invented, because there is a possible world where there are no cars. Our world, the actual world, is just one of these many, many worlds.

We can use possible worlds to explain important concepts like *necessity*. If a sentence is *necessarily true*, then it is true in every possible world. "2 + 2 = 4" and "Triangles have three sides" are both necessarily true; so, in every possible world, 2 + 2 = 4, and triangles have three sides. If a sentence is only *contingently true*, then it is true in some, but not all, possible worlds. "Butlers exist" and "Superheroes exist" are both contingently true, since there are some possible worlds where butlers and superheroes exist and other possible worlds where there are no butlers or superheroes. Another category of sentences, including "2 + 2 = 3" and "Triangles have only one side," are necessarily false; it is impossible for these sorts of sentences to mean what they actually mean and still be true.

Possible worlds represent what we could or couldn't have done, so when investigating modal questions, we have to look to possible worlds for answers. Curious about whether there could have been invisible planet-sized penguins? Well, if there is a possible world where there are such things, then it is true that there could have been invisible planet-sized penguins. In addition, when someone asks whether you could have been late for a meeting, we can use possible worlds to determine the answer. Very roughly: if there is a possible world (very similar to the actual world) where you were late for the meeting, then it is true that you could have been late for the meeting.

You might wonder how this person who was late for a meeting is indeed identical to you. After all, you have different properties: one of you was late for the meeting, one of you wasn't. These are thorny issues, but one way to understand this is by thinking of yourself in other possible worlds as you would think about yourself at other times. Five minutes ago, you were standing; now you're sitting down. Despite this change, however, you're still identical to yourself now and to yourself five minutes prior. In what follows, we won't discuss the metaphysical details of how things can be identical over time without violating IOI. Instead, we'll just assume that individuals can be identical across different worlds just as they are identical across different times.

One further thing to note before continuing is that for most of what follows, we'll assume that Batman, the Joker, and the rest of DC Universe are *merely possible entities*. Merely possible entities exist in possible worlds, but not in the actual world. Given this assumption, the world could have turned out in such a way that Batman, Gotham City, and Two-Face would have existed. We'll also be interested in a particular possible world: the possible world where all the usual truths about Batman and the rest of the DC Universe are true. For short, we'll call this New Earth, as the current mainstream universe is called in DC. Having introduced notions like necessity, possibility, and possible worlds, we can now put these notions to good use in trying to answer the question at hand: could Batman have been the Joker?

If the correct answer to this question is yes, then there is a possible world where Batman and the Joker are numerically identical. This will be a possible world where Batman and the Joker exist as one and the same object. Put differently, in some possible world, the object *picked out* by our term "Batman" is identical to the object *picked out* by our term "The Joker." This talk of terms "picking out" objects is actually shorthand for some philosophy-speak, and while the philosophy-speak is complicated, it's important for getting to the bottom of matters modal in nature.

First, terms like "The Joker" and "Batman" are *names*, and names have a unique feature: when they refer to, or "pick out," a particular object, they refer to that very object in each and every possible world. This unique feature isn't shared by *descriptions*. To see why, consider the description "the police commissioner of Gotham." On New Earth, the object that this description refers to is Jim Gordon. In other possible worlds, where things went rather differently, Alfred Pennyworth is the police commissioner of Gotham, so in these sorts of worlds, "the police commissioner of Gotham" refers to Alfred. Descriptions are, for this reason, very different from names in the way that they refer to objects. So, while "Harvey Dent" refers to the Harvey Dent in all possible worlds, "the former district attorney of Gotham" does not.

Second, the question we're investigating isn't merely about whether Batman could have been called "The Joker" and the Joker could have been called "Batman." There is good reason to think that the English language could have developed so differently that the word actually used to refer to Batman could, in fact, have been used to refer to the Joker. What we're interested in are the modal properties of the objects in question: Batman and the Joker. Like you and I, these objects both possess and lack certain modal properties. For example, many philosophers believe that you and I lack the modal property of possibly being a poached egg, but we do possess the modal property of possibly being an inch taller than we actually are. The fact that the terms "Batman" and "The Joker" are names doesn't change the modal properties of these objects. Rather, the fact that these terms are names helps us better understand what reality must be like for sentences like "Possibly, Batman is identical to the Joker" to be true.

Necessary Secret Identities

Modal logic is a formal language—much like mathematics— used to simplify the way we reason about possibility and necessity. In modal logic, certain logical rules (axioms) are near-universally accepted. Here are few examples: If something is necessarily true, then it is possibly true. If something is true, then it is possibly true. A more complicated example would be the following: if something is possibly true, then it is necessarily possibly true. An absurdly complicated example is this: if something is necessarily possibly necessarily possibly necessarily true, then it is necessarily true!

The ins and outs of modal logic aren't of crucial importance here, but one thesis of modal logic is important: the *Necessity of Identity* (hereafter, "NI"). If NI is true, then identity claims—claims that include the identity symbol "="—are necessarily true, if they're true at all. Actually, NI is more specific. It applies only to certain identity claims. Specifically, NI says that identity claims that have names on either side of "=" are necessarily true if they're true, and necessarily false if they're false. For this reason, NI guarantees that "Harvey Dent = Two-Face" and the equivalent sentence "Harvey Dent is identical to Two-Face" are necessarily true. NI does not, however, guarantee that "Harvey Dent = the former district attorney of Gotham" is necessarily true. NI doesn't apply to this sentence, since "the former district attorney of Gotham" is a description rather than a name.

Why should we believe NI? Because of IOI and the obvious claim that, necessarily, everything is identical to itself. Imagine that x and y are like variables in algebra; they stand for objects. Now, if everything is necessarily identical to itself, then, in every possible world, $x = x$. And if $x = y$ in some possible world, then IOI entails that x and y must have all of the same properties. This means that if x = Batman and y = Bruce Wayne and $x = y$, IOI guarantees that Batman and Bruce Wayne share all the same properties. Well, one property x has is the property of being necessarily identical to x itself; therefore, IOI entails that y must also have the property of being necessarily identical to x. In Bat-terms, if Batman and Bruce Wayne are identical in some possible world, then, since Batman has the property of necessarily being identical to Batman, Bruce Wayne must also have the property of necessarily being identical to Batman. The conclusion of this compact but complicated argument is this: when things like Bruce Wayne and Batman are identical, they are necessarily identical.

If NI is true and "Batman" is a name, then we can make an argument showing that Batman couldn't have been the Joker: Batman and the Joker aren't identical on New Earth. Since Batman and the Joker aren't identical on New Earth, "Batman = The Joker" isn't necessarily true. But, given NI, if an identity claim is true, it must be necessarily true. Because "Batman = The Joker" isn't necessarily true, we can conclude that "Batman = The Joker" can't possibly be true. And, since "Batman = The Joker" can't possibly be true, Batman couldn't have been the Joker! (Wasn't that easy?)

"The Batman" and "The Robin"

Okay, we admit it—we've offered up a rather complicated argument for why Batman couldn't possibly be the Joker. It relies upon some unfamiliar, although plausible, assumptions about identity and necessity. So here's an objection against the argument we've formulated, and thankfully, it relies on vastly less complicated premises. Let's call it the *Robin Argument*. We've assumed that "Batman" is a name, and we've concluded that "Batman" couldn't have been anyone other than Bruce Wayne, much less the Joker. It seems, however, that "Batman" and "Robin" are the same sorts of terms, so, if one is a name, then they're both names. If one is a description, then they're both descriptions. As a matter of superheroic fact, there has been more than one Robin. Dick Grayson, Jason Todd, and Tim Drake (among others) have all been Robin at one time or another, so it isn't necessarily true that Robin is identical to Tim Drake, or to Jason Todd, or to Dick Grayson. And if identity claims involving "Robin" aren't necessarily true or necessarily false, then "Robin" can't be a name, given what we know about names. So "Batman" can't be a name either. And if "Batman" isn't a name, then the above argument fails: NI just doesn't apply to sentences involving "Robin" or "Batman," since they're descriptions rather than names.

There is something appealing about this conclusion. It seems that different individuals can take up different secret identities, and one way to explain why this is possible is by holding "Batman" and other "secret identities" to be descriptions. For example, "Robin" might be shorthand for "the guy—or girl, in Stephanie Brown's case—wearing the Robin outfit." In fact, one might think that this is fairly obvious. First of all, Bruce Wayne is often called "*The* Batman" and one might imagine that "Batman" is merely an abbreviation for a certain description. Second, others (such as Jean-Paul Valley and Dick Grayson) have donned the cape and cowl and have "been Batman" in Wayne's stead. Third, the fact that "Robin" and other terms are so similar to "Batman" in use, and that "Robin" and other terms might not be names, provides reason to think that "Batman" is not a name.

But there are also good reasons to think "Batman" is not a description and is, in fact, a name. First, most descriptions pass a certain linguistic test. As with most linguistic tests, there are exceptions, but this test is nevertheless a generally good one. If certain terms show up in the description, certain inferences are usually good inferences. Consider the description "the ugliest criminal in Gotham." If this description picks out an individual, we can reasonably draw certain conclusions about the individual in question. In particular, we can infer that that individual is ugly, a criminal, and located somewhere in Gotham. "Batman" seems to fail this test—we cannot reasonably infer from the fact that "Batman" refers to an individual that the individual is a bat. While this consideration isn't conclusive, it at least gives us good reason to suspect that "Batman" isn't a "disguised description." According to some philosophers, disguised descriptions are commonplace. For example, if "Bruce Wayne" were a disguised description, "Bruce Wayne" would really just be a shorthand version of "the son of Martha Wayne and Dr. Thomas Wayne."

Second, and more important, descriptions refer to objects by virtue of specifying certain properties. "The ugliest criminal in Gotham" picks out Killer Croc because Killer Croc is ugly, a criminal, and located somewhere in—or under— Gotham. But, if some individual wanted to, that person could strive to become uglier than Killer Croc, a criminal, and a citizen of Gotham. If he accomplished this rather strange goal, this description would then refer to him. Notice that "Batman" doesn't work quite this way: no matter how good a costume you assemble, or what cave you build under your house, "Batman" will refer to the fictional character Batman rather than to anyone else. For this reason, "Batman" doesn't seem to behave like a description.

It seems, then, that the Robin Argument gives us some reason to believe that "Batman" is not a name, which means that the argument involving NI fails. But there is also good reason, as shown by the two arguments just considered, to believe that "Batman" isn't a description. For this reason, it seems that "Batman," whatever it is, is a strange term indeed.

There are a few ways one might go about resolving this problem and determining whether "Batman" is a name or a description. One might argue that despite failing these tests, "Batman" is really a description and, since it is a description, it could refer to the Joker in some world other than the New Earth. One might also argue that although it seems like there have been multiple individuals that "Robin" refers to, there have really been multiple individuals with different names that are always "abbreviated" in some disguised way. If Batman and the Joker are merely possible individuals, then in order to figure out whether Batman could have been the Joker, we would need to resolve this issue. That said, we'll close by discussing exactly what sorts of entities Batman and the Joker are rather than whether "Batman" is a name or a description. Ultimately, we'll suggest that certain metaphysical considerations seem to suggest that Batman could indeed have been the Joker.

Fictions and Possible Worlds

Up to this point, we've assumed that although New Earth and its inhabitants are not actual, they still could have existed. According to this assumption, "Batman" and "The Joker" are merely possible entities like your merely possible twin brother or a merely possible galaxy-sized piece of French toast. If these entities did exist, they would be a lot like the physical objects that make up our universe. They would be *concrete objects* like you or me or this book or the Empire State Building. Most of the objects that we're familiar with are concrete; they're subject to the laws of physics and they're located somewhere in time and space.

But fictional characters, like Batman and Robin, aren't concrete. They're more like numbers and stories; it just doesn't make any sense to say that you have the number five in your pocket or that Hamlet is located on Coney Island. For these reasons, fictional characters are *abstract objects* like numbers rather than concrete objects like this book. There's good reason to think that concrete entities are very different from abstract entities, but *fictional* abstract objects, like Batman and the Joker (but not the number two), seem especially different from concrete objects. One way that fictional abstract objects might be particularly unique is in the way that they possess modal properties.

The modal properties of everyday, concrete objects like tables, shoes, and books are determined by objective facts independent of what anybody thinks about them. In our argument, we treated Batman and the Joker like concrete objects, but as we have just indicated, they are quite different; they are abstract fictional entities. Still, if characters like Batman aren't concrete inhabitants of merely possible worlds, it isn't clear how we can make sense of the modal claims we make about them. Despite this, we can say that of the modal claims about fictional entities, some are true and some are false. Batman could have killed the Joker. Mr. Freeze couldn't survive walking on the sun (or even Miami Beach). So how do we make sense of the modal properties of abstract fictional characters? Perhaps fictional characters like Batman have their modal properties in a very special way: they have these properties because they are created by authors and artists like Bob Kane, Grant Morrison, Jim Aparo, and Jim Lee.

More precisely, because abstract fictional characters aren't merely possible entities, we can't use possible worlds to make sense of their modal properties. This means that an alternative account of how fictional characters have modal properties is needed. Here's one account we're fond of: the modal properties—the properties of contingently or necessarily being a certain way—of fictional characters are stipulated by those characters' authoritative creators. The modal properties of

Batman are unlike the modal properties of giraffes and gazebos: the former are stipulated by authors like Bob Kane, while the latter are fixed independently of anyone's intentions. If this is true, the things that Batman can and can't do are determined, not by what possible worlds there are, but by what the *authors* of Batman comics believe to be possible for him.

Fleshing out this proposal more fully will prove a very complicated affair, but the consequence for the question we've been interested in is clear. Whether or not Batman could have been the Joker can't be determined by our usual methods of modal investigation. To answer this question, we need to know what modal properties the creators of the stories involving Batman believe Batman and the Joker to have. It seems, then, that one way to answer this question is by old-fashioned investigation: reading.

Well, we did the reading—after all, that's what we do—and the results are in: Batman and the Joker could have been identical. Why? Because in *Batman: Two-Faces* (1998), Batman and the Joker are one and the same. This Elseworlds tale—a Batman story that seems to takes place outside the typical continuity of the DC Universe, or on an Earth other than New Earth—describes a scenario where Batman and the Joker are, in fact, numerically identical, much like Dr. Jekyll and Mr. Hyde. So this particular case provides us with good reason to think that fictional identities (secret or otherwise) might not be quite *so* necessary as we would have thought.

All Joking Aside, This Is a Modal Muddle

At the beginning, we set out to answer the question "Could Batman have been the Joker?" We assumed from the get-go that "Batman" and "The Joker" are names of merely possible individuals—things that exist in other possible worlds—and, given these assumptions, we argued that there's reason to think Batman couldn't have been the Joker. Despite this, there are some reasons to believe that "Batman" might really be a description and, if it is, then Batman could very well have been the Joker. We then suggested that Batman and the Joker might be strange, abstract, fictional entities rather than merely possible individuals.

Some philosophers might complain about both of these options. These philosophers, sometimes called *nominalists*, prefer a sparse, desertlike view of reality. They deny that there are merely possible individuals or abstract entities. They take seriously the metaphysical maxim that "less is more" and believe only in actual entities and concrete individuals. While there are attractive features of the nominalist metaphysical picture, the nominalist has to bite at least one unappealing bullet: since the nominalist denies the existence of abstract or merely possible entities, the nominalist must deny that Batman, the Joker, and Robin exist at all. This consequence might make nominalism seem unattractive, but interestingly enough, you might think that Batman himself ought to be a nominalist. After all, if nominalism were true, there would be no crime in Gotham. That said, there would be no Gotham at all.[2]

NOTES

1. The "alternate Earths" of the DC Universe (before *Crisis on Infinite Earths* and after *52*) are a lot like what philosophers call possible worlds; they are separate, alternate universes where reality took a different turn somewhere in the course of history.

2. Thanks from the authors to Chloe Armstrong, Barak Krakauer, Eitan Manhoff, and Chris Tillman for discussion and helpful comments.

BATMAN'S IDENTITY CRISIS AND WITTGENSTEIN'S FAMILY RESEMBLANCE

Jason Southworth

What does it mean for somebody to be Batman? Is there something that is required for us to identify someone as Batman? Is there a quality or attribute such that if an individual has it, then that individual must be Batman? In this chapter we'll tackle these questions. Along the way, we'll see that a useful way to capture the meaning and identification of Batman, or anything for that matter, is through the idea of "family resemblance."

Comics, Conditions, and Counterexamples

Philosophers have terms for the types of conditions that let us identify something as being essentially what it is, or defining it as part of a group of things. If an attribute or quality is required for being part of a group, we say that it is a *necessary condition*. Think of an apple: if something is an apple, then it is neces- sary that it be a fruit, or being a fruit is a necessary condition for being an apple. Notice that this does not mean that being a fruit is enough for being an apple. Apples also have to be apple-shaped, have stems, and not be oranges, to name some other necessary conditions of "applehood." All this means is that something can't be an apple without being a fruit; all apples are fruit, but not all fruits are apples.

On the other hand, if meeting a particular requirement *is* enough to be included in the group, then that requirement is a *sufficient condition*. Consider the case of animals. The fact that something is a cat is enough—it is sufficient—for that thing to be an animal. Notice that there can be many different suf- ficient conditions for being an animal. It is also sufficient for something to be an animal that it be a bird, or a salamander, or a human; all cats are animals, but not all animals are cats.

So can we identify necessary and sufficient conditions for Batman? Thanks to widely read stories such as *Batman: Year One* (1987) and *The Dark Knight Returns* (1986), along with the various animated series and live-action movies, many possibilities immediately come to mind. Batman is a man, Bruce Wayne, who dresses up in a costume that represents a bat, and fights crime. Batman acts in this way to avenge the death of his parents, who were killed when he was a child. Since his parents were murdered with a gun, Batman doesn't use a gun, and he also never kills. This is a fairly traditional and uncontroversial picture of Batman's attributes. But riddle me this: are these necessary conditions, sufficient conditions, both, or neither?

The simple answer is . . . no. No part of this conception of Batman qualifies as a necessary or sufficient condition for a person to be Batman. To see this we'll use a method of argu- ment that philosophers call *counterexample*. We'll first consider a candidate for a necessary or a sufficient condition, and then we'll give an example or two that shows why this candidate fails. A counterexample for a necessary condition will be an example of Batman that lacks the feature, which shows that the condition is not essential to Batman. A counterexample for a sufficient condition will be an example of the feature being present in something that is not Batman, which again shows that the feature is not exclusive to Batman.

Let's start with the claims that Batman doesn't kill and that he doesn't use guns. A counterexample to the proposition that these are necessary conditions can be found in Batman's fifth appearance. *Detective Comics* #32 (October 1939)—just look for it, I'm sure you have one—contains the second part of a story where Batman fights a vampire named the Monk. In this story, the Monk and an accomplice have hypnotized Batman's girlfriend (Julie Madison) and are holding her hostage. Batman solves this problem by shooting them both with silver bullets and killing them while they are sleeping, showing that someone that is Batman has used a gun.[1] Neither of these conditions is sufficient for being Batman either, which is even easier to show. There are obviously many things that do not kill or use guns and who are not Batman, ranging from other comic book characters, like Detective Chimp, to people, like Gandhi, to inanimate objects, like my stapler.

It's often suggested by casual Batman fans that being Bruce Wayne is both necessary and sufficient for someone to be Batman. Readers of Batman comics in the early 1990s, however, know better. During the *Knightfall* story arc (1993–1994), Bruce Wayne gives up the mantle of Batman after his back is broken by the villain Bane. To the shock and horror of fans everywhere, Bruce chose Jean-Paul Valley (the hero Azrael) to replace him, and in the subsequent *Prodigal* arc (1994–1995), he chose Dick Grayson (Nightwing, and the first Robin, whom fans were *much* happier with). So, for over two years, someone who was not Bruce Wayne was Batman, on authority of Bruce Wayne himself. Furthermore, during that period, Bruce

Wayne was not Batman, showing that being Bruce Wayne is neither necessary nor sufficient for being Batman.[2]

Perhaps the next most likely candidate for a necessary condition of Batman is that his parents have been murdered. Those who have read the Elseworlds story *Batman: Castle of the Bat* (1994), however, know that this is not the case. This story begins like the traditional Batman origin with the death of the parents of Bruce Wayne. In this story, a twist on the classic Frankenstein tale, Bruce Wayne grows up to become a great scientist and devotes the bulk of his research to the reanimation of dead tissue. Ultimately, Bruce manages to resurrect his father with the help of biomaterials that came from—you guessed it—a bat. Bruce then sends his bat man, whom he calls (no surprise) "Batman," to avenge his dead parents. The murdered father of Bruce Wayne is the Batman in this story, so "Batman's" parents were not murdered in this version. And once again, the case for sufficiency is even harder to make: murdered parents are common in superhero comics. Just to name one example, Helena Bertinelli's parents were murdered, but this caused her to become the Huntress, not Batman.

It's often said of Batman that he is a loner, choosing to work alone and teaming with others only when absolutely necessary. Upon reflection, there are a number of counterexamples to this claim. Very early in Batman's history he started working with others. In *Detective Comics* #38 (April 1940), Robin the Boy Wonder was introduced as Batman's sidekick, and the number of allies have exploded since then. In Batman comics today, you will occasionally read a reference to "team Batman" or "the Batman family," the large group of people on whom Batman has come to rely (including Robin, Nightwing, Oracle, and others). And it should be obvious that being a loner is not sufficient for being Batman (consider Saint Anthony and Ted Kaczynski [the Unabomber], for example).

Since one of the nicknames for Batman is the Dark Knight, some might suggest that it is necessary for Batman to be dark and brooding. But consider the Silver Age Batman stories.[3] During this period, thanks to the Comic Code Authority, superhero comics were cute and campy, and the stories usually turned on a gag or a gimmick. An example of one such story is *Batman* #108, where the Silver Age Batwoman (Kathy Kane) makes her first appearance. This is the beginning of a series of stories featuring the courtship of Batman and Batwoman, with typical romantic comedy tropes: Batman struggles to protect his bachelorhood while Batwoman agitates for marriage. Silly? Yes. Dark? No.

What about the "fact" that Batman necessarily fights crime? As you might have guessed, there are counterexamples for this as well. My favorite example of a Batman who commits crime rather than fighting it is a two-part story from *Justice League of America* #37–38 (August and September 1965). In this story, we are introduced to Earth-A, an earth where new versions of Silver Age DC superheroes form the Lawless League. In this story, the Justice Society (from Earth-2, for those keeping track at home) fights the Lawless League in classic DC world-jumping form. (An amusing visual choice in this story is that the Batman of Earth-A looks exactly like Silver Age Batman except that he has a five o'clock shadow.) So clearly being a crime fighter is not a necessary condition for being Batman. Again, the claim for sufficiency is obviously false, because all superheroes—even Booster Gold—fight crime.

Wittgenstein and Language Games

Without any necessary and sufficient conditions, you might wonder how we can successfully identify instances of Batman. One answer is found in Ludwig Wittgenstein's (1889–1951) *Philosophical Investigations*.[4] Wittgenstein admits that in attempting to identify things as "language," he's in a situation like the one we're in with Batman: "Instead of producing something common to all that we call 'language,' I am saying that these phenomena have no one thing in common which makes us use the same word for all, but they are *related* to one another in many different ways. And it is because of this relationship, or these relationships, that we call them all 'language.'"[5]

The relationship he is writing about is one of similarity. What makes all the different things called "language" language is that they are *similar* to each other. This similarity is called *family resemblance* by Wittgenstein, because you see this type of similarity in families. Consider your own family—if you are biologically related, you will resemble your parents and siblings to some extent. If we had to find ways in which you *all* were similar, however, we would fail. For instance, you and one of your sisters might have red hair like your dad, but the rest of your family does not. You, your sisters, and your mother might have brown eyes, but your dad does not. You might have a nose that doesn't look like either parent or sibling. This same point can be made if you consider body and face shape, complexion, and ear size.

Wittgenstein uses the case of games to make this point. There are many different types of games. What is common to these things? If you start with board games, you might think that all board games have pieces that move around boards. Adding card games into the mix, you will notice that neither of these things is necessary. Video games and solitaire show that there doesn't have to be more than one player. You might think all games are fun, but what about the game adults try to make children play—"Let's see who can be quiet the longest"? Some games involve skill to play well, like tennis, while others, like roulette, do not. What about Russian roulette? This is an example of a game that is very dangerous, unlike most games (although there are still definite winners and losers). Some games, however, don't even have winners and losers, like ring-around-the-roses. So, it seems that there is nothing common to all games—all we have are sets of similarities that are a part of different sets of games.

Wait a minute—some people may say that some of the examples of games I have given are not games at all, especially ones like Russian roulette and ring-around-the-rosy. There seems to be good reason to count Russian roulette as a game, though. After all, casino-style roulette is a game. If betting with money that a random spin of a wheel will stop where you want it to is a game, why would betting with your life instead of money stop it from being a game? Ring-around-the-rosy also seems a plausible candidate for a game. It has many of the elements other, less controversial games have: it is physical, fun to play, and has a set of rules. The reason for wanting to reject ring-around-the-rosy is that there is no winner, but by this criterion, single-player Tetris is not a game. None of this is meant to prevent you from drawing a line and saying something is not a game; it is just meant to show that there is nothing about games that points to a line to draw. The difference is that you might say, "Ring-around-the-rosy is not a game," but that will just be a feature of how you choose to use the term, not a feature of the actual concept.

Games and Gotham

We can make a similar response to the objection that we should not count Elseworlds stories as instances of Batman. When you draw a line and say that Batman can be understood as a set of necessary claims about the Batman from mainstream continuity, or the general public's conception of Batman, you are choosing to fix a description on the concept of Batman. This, however, is different from the concept's actually having that concrete description.

Some readers might object that without a firm boundary for what is and is not a game, the term would not be useful at all. This doesn't seem to be the case, however. We all use the word "game," and as we have seen, no such boundaries can be given. This is also the case with Batman. Earlier we saw that there are no necessary and sufficient conditions for being Batman. Since this is the case, we can't give a concrete definition of Batman in the same way that we can't give such a definition for "game." Still, we use the word "Batman" easily, and we understand others who do so. So, it seems the term is perfectly useful without firm boundaries.

But how should we explain to someone what a game is? Wittgenstein says that we describe different particular games to the individual, and then add "and things similar to this are 'games.'"[6] This seems to be a plausible account of not only how we would explain a game on Wittgenstein's account, but also of how we actually explain what a game is. If a child asks us what a game is, we point to examples the child knows, saying, "Monopoly, Candyland, and baseball are games, and other things are games if they are like these things."

Let's now consider this in terms of Batman. If someone asked us what/who Batman was, we would give a brief origin story for Batman in much the same way I did at the start of this chapter. We might then go on to describe some interesting stories we have read. This person would then be able to see what is common between these instances of Batman. She might then run into some of the strange cases of Batman that I have mentioned, and she will have to consider "is this an instance of Batman?" The person will be able to see what is common between these new instances of Batman and his previous conception, just like a child who stops to consider if catch or Marco Polo are games.

Robin? Who's That?

You might balk at the idea that every term of our language is understood in terms of a family resemblance, but Wittgenstein has two more arguments meant to convince you. First, consider someone saying, "There is no Robin." This might mean any number of things. Maybe it means that Batman has no sidekick, but it might also mean that Dick Grayson is no longer his sidekick. Some philosophers think that the name "Robin" can be fixed by a series of descriptions. Some such examples might be "the boy whose parents were killed when their trapeze act was sabotaged" and "the boy whose sexual advances were rebuffed by Barbara Gordon." Switching between these definitions with the claim "There is no Robin," however, changes the claim.[7]

Wittgenstein goes on to make this point another way. If the definition of "Robin" is fixed by these descriptions, and then it is shown that one part of the description is false, it means that there was never a Robin. So, if Robin's history were "retconned" so that his sexual advances *were* accepted by Barbara Gordon (as is the case in post-*Zero Hour* continuity), and we stuck to our previous claim that they were not, then it would mean that there was never a Robin! This isn't what happens when we find conflicting information, however. What happens is that we no longer hold that the disconfirmed claim is true of Robin. The point of this argument is that language is used all the time without a fixed meaning. Before reading this chapter, some of you probably thought it was a necessary condition of Batman that he didn't kill. After being shown that this is false, you didn't deny that the character was Batman; instead, you modified your picture of Batman.

Wittgenstein relies on one more example to make his point. Imagine someone says, "There is a Batarang," and then as the person gets closer to it, it disappears. We might say that the Batarang was never there and that it was an illusion. But imagine further that the Batarang reappears, and we are now able to touch it. We might now say that the Batarang was real and that the disappearance was an illusion. What if the Batarang disappeared again, only to return intermittently? Is this thing a Batarang or isn't it? If you don't know how to respond to this question, don't feel bad. Most people don't have an answer ready to this question. This, however, is enough to make

Wittgenstein's point. The fact that we don't know how to rule on this case shows that we can use the word "Batarang" without having the rules of use fixed. If that's true, we use language without having the meaning of the words fixed, and the only plausible reason for this is that we understand all things in terms of a family resemblance.[8]

Batman and superheroes generally provide actual cases of the example of the disappearing Batarang. New stories are constantly being written, and many of these purposely change the status quo. Consider the case of *The Dark Knight Returns*. Before this story was written, people most likely thought that Batman and Superman were friends and that they were both good guys. This story, however, puts the characters at odds, with both of them defending opposing positions to which they are morally committed. They can't both be good, given this situation. So what did we do when we read it? We let our conception of the characters change with the new information provided in the story.

Keeping It in the Family?

In closing, let's consider what the family resemblance account means for other areas of philosophy. For starters, if Wittgenstein is right, then it will serve as an objection to moral theories that attempt to use fictional characters as moral exemplars (as in the chapter by David Kyle Johnson and Ryan Rhodes in this volume). If there is no fixed description that can be given of a character, then you can't make reference to specific traits of that character, or to how that character would behave in a given situation. In other words, saying, "You should behave like Batman" doesn't help us decide how to act, because "Batman" may act in different ways in the same situation in different versions or time periods. You can always stipulate what you mean by Batman by referring to specific character traits, or to how he would act in specific situations. But if you do, then there is no reason to refer to Batman as a moral exemplar—you can just refer to the character traits. Great philosophical ideas are rarely limited to one area of philosophy, and often a question in moral philosophy, for example, can lead to a metaphysical or episte-mological mystery. In that sense, all philosophers are detectives, but not all detectives are . . . well, you get the idea.[9]

NOTES

1. However, you might argue that he hasn't really killed, because they are vampires, and therefore already dead. Fine—but in *The Dark Knight Strikes Again* (2001), Batman actu-ally kills Dick Grayson (who has become a killer himself, murdering aged superheroes) by dropping him into a pit of lava.

2. My favorite counterexample actually shows that both the claim of necessity and the claim of sufficiency are false. In *World's Finest* #167 (June 1967), we are shown a world where Clark Kent is Batman and Bruce Wayne is Superman!

3. The Silver Age of comics is the second major period of comics (the Golden Age was the first), which ran from the late 1950s to the early 1970s.

4. Ludwig Wittgenstein, *Philosophical Investigations*, trans. G. E. M. Anscombe (Blackwell: Oxford, 1953). All citations in the chapter will refer to this work.

5. Ibid., Remark 65.

6. Ibid., Remark 69.

7. Ibid., Remark 80.

8. Ibid.

9. For their helpful comments I would like to thank Ruth Tallman and Clarice Ferguson.

WHAT IS IT LIKE TO BE A BATMAN?

Ron Novy

You had a bad day once, am I right? I know I am.
I can tell. You had a bad day and everything changed.
Why else would you dress up like a flying rat?
—The Joker, *The Killing Joke* (1988)

I could never kill you. Where would the act be
without my straight man?
—The Joker, *Batman* #663 (February 2007)

Answering the Batphone

Imagine yourself doing whatever Batman does. Would the experience let you know what it's like to *be* Batman? Like a lot of kids with the impulse to leap off furniture and spring through doorways, it only took a bath towel pinned around my neck for me to become the Caped Crusader. Sliding across the kitchen linoleum in my pre-nonflammable footie pajamas, I would provide my own soundtrack with the "nah-na nah-na, nah-na nah-na" theme from the 1960s TV show. At that time, I had no doubt that this was a thoroughgoing Batman experience. As it turns out, I was wrong.

In fact, if you or anyone besides Batman could know what it's like to be Batman, you would need to meet at least two conditions: first, you'd need to be as extraordinarily and psychologically damaged as Batman; second, you'd need to have the same experiences and relations to the world as Batman. As we'll see, the only person who comes close to meeting these conditions is the Joker, and even he doesn't really know what it's like to be Batman.

What It's *Not* Like to Be Batman

The term *phenomena* refers to the subjective appearance of material objects in your own conscious experience. So, while reading this sentence, your senses register a variety of stimuli: dark marks on a light field, a particular weight and texture in your hands, perhaps also the smell of freshly brewed coffee and the sound of rain at the window. While the weight of the book or the trace of Arabica in the air can be objectively measured, your experience of these phenomena is subjective—something to which only you have access.

Now, acting *like* Batman is quite different from actually knowing *what it's like* to be Batman. At best, one can "do as Batman does"—brood in the Batcave, admire the long curve of Catwoman's calf, or tumble down an alley with some of the Joker's henchmen. Insofar as your actions mirror those of Batman, with a little practice you could do a pretty fair job of behaving as Batman behaves—but this is not the same as knowing what it's like for Batman to be Batman. Your late-night patrols, undertaken with your Keatonesque, Kilmerite, Baleian, or even West-like physique packed firmly into a Kevlar-and-Lycra costume worn by an actual ice-skating stunt double in the movie *Batman and Robin*, may even garner an above-the-fold story from a cub reporter on the *Gotham Gazette* police beat.

Nonetheless, your phenomenal experiences are yours and only yours—even those that occur while you're imagining yourself to be Batman and performing "Batman deeds." To actually know Batman's experience of such events—that is, to know what it's like to be Batman—would require knowledge of Batman's subjective experiences, knowledge to which (it seems) Batman *alone* has access.

We all find ourselves limited in this same way regarding the subjective experiences of other conscious beings. So, to clarify an old chestnut, when it's claimed that we can't understand another's perspective until we have "walked a mile in her shoes," this doesn't mean we can come to know what that experience is actually like for that other person, but rather that we can *imagine* what that experience may be. Nevertheless, this can often deliver the desired understanding, not because we have actually experienced what it's like to be her, but rather because we are imaginative and empathetic creatures. We can understand one another because people are alike in many ways: we share common experiences, physiology, and so on.

In this way, despite our never having met, you have a reasonable chance of having a phenomenal experience similar to mine when, say, you strike your thumb with a hammer. I say "reasonable" not merely because you have experienced or can imagine experiencing such a thing, but because we share the sort of physiological, psychological, and social background that together brings forth a shooting pain, a yelp of surprise, and some slight embarrassment at having whacked oneself in the distal phalanx. You could reasonably expect that I would shake the injured hand and let fly a string of naughty words, again not necessarily because you had ever hurt yourself in precisely this same way, but because you have had other experiences similar enough to mine to imagine your own reaction.

This all seems quite commonsensical *until* you discover that you aren't like me in some relevant way: perhaps your thumb lacks nociceptors—the embedded sensory neurons that translate stimuli into action potentials and transmit this information to the central nervous system—while my thumb does not. Without a shared capacity to feel pain, you would have no grounds on which to claim that you have much of an idea what it's like for me to have that whacked-by-a-hammer experience. This is so even if you've learned to perfectly mimic my pain-related actions such as jumping up and down in a frenzy, weeping, and muttering profanities.

Like us, Batman is "just" a man, with no superpowers: no gifts from mythological benefactors, no alien physiology, no beneficial accident involving experimental radiation. Instead, his body is like ours: his "power" is a product of rigorous physical training, the ability to unnerve criminals, and access to what Jack Nicholson's Joker called "those wonderful toys." And yet, Batman is profoundly not like us.

Bats and Thomas Nagel

To my knowledge, Thomas Nagel (b. 1937) isn't a superhero, and he's never been accused of being the Batman, but he is a renowned philosopher and the author of "What Is It Like to Be a Bat?"[1] In this essay, Nagel argues that even a complete accounting of the physical object "brain" will nonetheless fail to fully describe what we mean by the term "mind." Perhaps most important, such a reduction of "mind" to "brain" would be unable to account for the central feature of *consciousness*— the subjective character of our experience. As Nagel puts it, "An organism has conscious mental states if and only if there is something that it is like to be that organism—something it is like for that organism."[2]

To use Nagel's example, you and I can't know what it's like to be a bat. The average *Chiroptera* experiences the world quite differently from the way we *Homo sapiens* do: it sleeps hanging head-down from a cave roof, it pursues insect delicacies on leathery wings, and it navigates complex flight paths by way of echolocation.[3] While you and I can imagine what it would be like for us—as humans pretending to be bats—to hang upside down or to eat bugs as wind whistles through our hair, our experiences will *never* be interchangeable with those of the bat. Our subjective experience, even of the same physical phenomena encountered by a bat, relies both upon our particular senses and upon our particular histories.

For Nagel, this inability to capture subjective experience necessarily gives us an incomplete account of consciousness. While Nagel was focused on attacking the hypothesis that subjective experience and consciousness could be fully understood as "merely" a physical event of the brain, it should be stressed that one doesn't have to take the presence of echolocation in bats and its absence in humans to be crucial for his point. Nagel's focus on the bat's echolocation capacity, an ordinary "sense" for the bat yet truly alien for us, makes our inability to "know what it's like to be a bat" quite stark. Yet, unless we are willing to grant that any *Homo sapiens* can know what it's like to be any other *Homo sapiens*, there must be something besides difference in body type underlying the issue. Surely a lack of shared experience, not a lack of a shared body type, is what is required.

Suppose that Barbara Gordon, also known as Oracle, the brilliant hacker and brains behind the Birds of Prey (not to mention a former Batgirl), had begun her career not as a coy librarian with a crime-fighting alter ego, but as a scientist studying the neurophysiology of vision.[4] She knows everything there is to know about the physical processes involved in sight, from the physics of photons to the wavelength associated with the term "maroon," from the anatomy of the retina to the particular chemical processes involved in conveying visual information in the brain. Strangely, Barbara has spent her whole life in a room absolutely devoid of color and has experienced the world beyond her room only through a black-and-white television monitor. So while Barbara has a fully functional set of visual hardware from cornea to occipital lobe, she has never seen a field of yellow daisies, oranges at the grocers, or bronzed lifeguards in a blue ocean.

Now suppose that while she slept, you slipped a shiny ripe tomato onto Barbara's nightstand. Even with her complete knowledge of the physical processes necessary for vision, when she sees the tomato in the morning, should we expect her experience of "redness" to be just like yours or mine? It seems unlikely, given the innumerable places, times, and hues of "redness" that you and I have experienced in the past relative to her single encounter. If this difference holds between Barbara Gordon's experience of redness and ours, it seems reasonable to expect that for you to know what it's like to be Batman, would require you to have had formative experiences similar to his. Given that Batman and the Joker were transformed into the creatures they are now under similar rare and horrific conditions, and given that each has attempted to make sense of the world through this shared and fractured lens, I suspect that if anyone besides Batman could know what it's like to be Batman, that person would be the Joker.

Freedom and Conflict

> At every opportunity, the truth comes to light, the truth of life and death, of my solitude and my bond with the world . . . of the insignificance and the sovereign importance of each man and all men. . . . Let us try to assume our fundamental ambiguity. It is in the knowledge of the genuine conditions of our life that we must draw our strength to live and our reason for acting.
>
> —Simone de Beauvoir[5]

Now we switch gears a bit, from discussing phenomena and consciousness to discussing situated freedom and identity, but for a very good reason. Just as you and the color-deprived Barbara Gordon experience the redness of the tomato differently despite both having the capacity to see red, Batman and the Joker find their lives built upon similar foundations, which result in very different narratives bringing each man to his current place in life.

At base, both Batman's and the Joker's self-identities—and with them their conceptions of duty and right—are firmly anchored in *situated freedom*, a concept developed by Simone de Beauvoir (1908–1986).[6] Situated freedom refers to the idea that our capacity to act and make sense of the world is always constrained by our lived experience of the world. In other words, there are objective conditions under which we live, and these conditions open some options to us while closing others. Thus, while a Neanderthal-era Batman would likely live in a Batcave, he would never strap into the Batmobile or understand the Joker as in need of anything less than a good beating. Similarly, it is difficult to imagine an Elizabethan Batgirl who could appear in public without the corset and petticoats of her contemporaries, or who had the opportunity to develop the martial skills of Barbara Gordon or Cassandra Cain.

The "freedom" part of situated freedom means that the individual is constantly in a position to make meaningful choices that manipulate the world, choices that in turn alter the options available later. Given that we are social beings with our futures open in this way, a choice made by one person may well change the options available to another. So, even the smallest of our decisions carries with it some moral weight.

For example, your decision to sign on as the Penguin's henchman simultaneously expands and restricts your future opportunities. You'll meet people and visit places you likely wouldn't have otherwise, while at the same time sacrificing any chance you may have had to attend the police academy. Your decision also ripples through the futures available to those around you: the wealth and influence that come with being the Penguin's enforcer may have gotten your child into the exclusive Brentwood Academy with Tim Drake and the other scions of Gotham's upper crust; similarly, a shopkeeper late with one of Mr. Cobblepot's payments may never be able to play the violin because of your enthusiastic, crowbar-wielding reminder.

To say that this freedom is "situated" is to acknowledge that we're all born into a world already brimming with buildings, ideology, poems, commerce, dental hygienists, mythology, bacteria, and hats. The world didn't start anew with our birth, but rather is an independent and complex product of the past in which we must learn to navigate. As such, there are facts about our existence over which we have little or no control, from our gender, poor eyesight, and strawberry allergy to when, where, and to whom we were born. Obviously, at least some such contingencies can affect future options available to us.

To recognize that freedom is situated is to also recognize that the future is unwritten, as well as that we are always teetering at the edge of violence. While we all share the desire to live a life that is as fully human as possible, decisions made by people grounded in different situations will necessarily neither open nor close off the same future options. Since all possible futures cannot simultaneously come to fruition, we inevitably come into conflict with one another. Violence is thus a constant presence lurking about the edges of human freedom.

One Bad Day

All it takes is one bad day to reduce the sanest man alive to lunacy. . . . You had a bad day, and it drove you as crazy as everybody else—only you won't admit it!

> You have to keep pretending that life makes sense,
> that there's some point to all this struggling!
>
> God you make me want to puke.
>
> —The Joker, *The Killing Joke*

Batman and the Joker were each born in violence, each the product of an ordinary person who was fundamentally transformed on "one bad day." Their strange intimacy is the madness shared by two angels of death debating conditions necessary for human freedom.

Batman's story is well known. Young Bruce Wayne witnesses the senseless murder of his parents by a small-time crook. Despite their cooperation, the mugger loses his nerve and shoots the pair. In that instant, Bruce loses not only his parents, but also his illusory understanding of the world. Suddenly, he realizes that not all people are decent and that not everyone cares about his happiness; that some problems can't be resolved by a generous dip into a bottomless bank account; that visceral hate and explosive violence can be liberating; and that the polished world of Wayne Enterprises is built upon a sunless foundation in which suffering and want are not isolated occurrences.

The Joker's "one bad day" is less well known: An unremarkable chemical engineer has quit his job and failed at his dream of being a stand-up comedian; he loses his pregnant wife in a fluke accident, is forced into a bungled robbery of his former employer, and plummets into a tank of noxious waste while fleeing the police.[7] It is a baptism from which emerges the Joker: green hair, pallid skin, and insane. Recognizing Batman's similar experience of destruction and rebirth, the Joker is stunned by Batman's commitment to fight chaos:

> When I saw what a black, awful joke the world was,
> I went crazy as a coot! I admit it! Why can't you? I mean,

you're not unintelligent! You must see the reality of the situation. . . . It's all a joke! Everything anybody ever valued or struggled for—it's all a monstrous, demented gag! So why can't you see the funny side? Why aren't you laughing?[8]

For both Batman and the Joker, violence overthrew a coherent picture of the world without installing a replacement; they share this realization and are bound together in an effort to make sense of it. Like violators of the tabernacle or visitors in Oz, each has glimpsed behind the curtain of appearances—that is, beyond the "merely" phenomenal world. Recognizing that what we call "the world" is just an appearance cobbled together by our minds from sense data, is also to admit that there is a world "out there" unmediated by our sight or touch. This other world that exists behind the appearances—what Immanuel Kant (1724–1804) called the *noumenal world*—is terrifying.[9] It serves as the armature upon which our knowledge is organized; and yet, we can know next to nothing about it apart from what might be inferred from those illusory appearances.

This experience of becoming disillusioned and of catching this glimpse of secret knowledge binds Batman and the Joker, though neither is quite sure what was revealed about how the world "really is." While they have different hopes regarding the nature of that world behind the appearances, they have only one another with whom to commiserate regarding the terrifying recognition that this world—our world of cops and robbers, joy-buzzers and cemeteries—for them doesn't exist.

Even acknowledging that this phenomenal world is one of appearance, Batman and the Joker, at least in regard to each other, behave as if the world matters. Batman has ended more than a few story arcs by returning the killer clown to Arkham Asylum—something one might not expect given the Joker's body count and the numerous opportunities Batman has had to offer Gotham City "a more permanent solution" to its recurring Joker problem.[10] Yet as he reveals to Mr. Zsasz, the serial killer who commemorates each kill with a tally mark carved into his own body, Batman needs to continue his relationship with those he fights. It is in their struggle that he gains recognition as something apart from the world of appearance: "Do you want to know what power is? Real power? It's not ending a life, it's saving it. It's looking in someone's eyes and seeing that spark of recognition that instant, they realize something they'll never forget."[11]

The Joker, too, recognizes this reciprocal relationship with Batman, a relationship without which each one would cease to be who he now is. As he explains it to Batman, "You can't kill me without becoming like me. I can't kill you without losing the only human being who can keep up with me. Isn't that ironic?!"[12] For the Joker, behind the façade that dissolved in the tank of chemical slop, there is only chaos. While literally nonsensical, chaos is also wholly liberating—in chaos, there is no fear to restrain you and no conditions that might limit your choices. According to his therapist at Arkham Asylum, the Joker "creates himself each day. He sees himself as the Lord of Misrule and the world as a theater of the absurd."[13] For Batman, this world beneath the appearances is one of order, though not a predetermined order one might read about in that copy of *Metaphysics for Dummies* you picked up from the discount table at your local bookstore. Rather, it is a *moral* order that must be wrestled into existence by recognizing the effect of one's choices on our shared future.

What It Is Like to Be Out of the Asylum

Yet, for all of the shared events, nonsense, chaos, tragedies, and victories that Batman and the Joker have experienced, they do not—and *can* not—know what it's like to be in one another's shoes. Batman's phenomenal experience and situated freedom is wholly his own; the Joker's phenomenal experience and situated freedom is wholly *his* own; and each is unable to experience the world in any other way. Yet, both Batman and the Joker are committed to the absurd yet serious task of seeing the world as it truly is. Each seems to grasp that this requires a sort of testing, and thus the other's participation, despite that other person's literal inability to experience the world in the same way.

With this in mind, consider the joke the Clown Prince tells Batman at the end of *The Killing Joke* as they wait for the police to arrive. Two inmates decide that they should escape the lunatic asylum together. They scramble to the top of the asylum's wall and gaze upon the world spread before them in the moonlight. Just one hop to a nearby roof and they're free—out of the asylum and into the world. The first jumps across and then turns to see his partner frozen on the far side. As the Joker puts it, "His friend darednt make the leap, y'see. Y'see, he's afraid of falling." The inmates stand there, freedom waiting in any direction if only the second man would leap over what his companion sees as a little gap but which he perceives as a deadly abyss. The first man proposes a solution:

> He says, "Hey! I have my flashlight with me. I'll shine it across the gap between the buildings. You can walk along the beam and join me."

> But the second guy just shakes his head. He says . . . he says, "What do you think I am crazy? You'd turn it off when I was half way across!"

As it begins to rain and the police lights appear in the distance, the Joker and Batman laugh. Their snickers build to doubled-over roars, overcome by the absurdity of their shared secret. The first unable to know what it is like to be Batman; the second unable to know what it is like to be the Joker.

NOTES

1. Thomas Nagel, "What Is It Like to Be a Bat?" *Philosophical Review* 83 no. 4 (October 1974): 435–450. The article has since been reproduced in many anthologies concerned with the philosophy of mind, such as *The Mind's I: Fantasies and Reflections on Self and Soul*, ed. Douglas R. Hofstadter and Daniel C. Dennett (Basic Books: New York, 1981).

2. Nagel, "What Is It Like," 436.

3. Nagel does not specify any particulars about his bat beyond the capacity for echolocation. But the Joker, having stumbled upon the Batcave, used its computer to help determine the taxonomical classification for Batman. Deciding that "obviously he's from the ghost-faced family," the Joker cannot restrain his giggling at the genus name *mormoops* (Alex Irvine's novel *Inferno* [New York: Del Rey Books, 2006], 73).

4. This scenario is a variation on a much-discussed thought experiment developed by philosopher Frank Jackson in "Epiphenomenal Qualia," *Philosophical Quarterly* 32 no. 127 (1982): 127–136); and "What Mary Didn't Know," *Journal of Philosophy* 83 no. 5 (1986): 291–295).

5. Simone de Beauvoir, *The Ethics of Ambiguity*, trans. Bernard Frechtman (Secaucus: Citadel Press, 1948).

6. See Simone de Beauvoir, *The Second Sex*, trans. H. M. Parshley (1949; repr., New York: Penguin, 1972), for de Beauvoir's fullest treatment of "situated freedom."

7. This version of the Joker's origin—and there have been many—is revealed in flashbacks throughout *The Killing Joke* (1988).

8. Ibid.

9. The terms "phenomena" and "noumena" are technical terms used by Immanuel Kant in his 1781 opus *Critique of Pure Reason*, trans. Norman Kemp Smith (New York: St. Martin's Press, 1929), 9.

10. See Mark D. White's essay in this book for more on why Batman has never ended the Joker's life.

11. "Scars,"*Batman: Black & White*, vol. 2 (1996).

12. *Batman* #663.

13. *Arkham Asylum* (1989).

PART FIVE

BEING THE BAT: INSIGHTS FROM EXISTENTIALISM AND TAOISM

ALFRED, THE DARK KNIGHT OF FAITH: BATMAN AND KIERKEGAARD

Christopher M. Drohan

The Saint

Alfred Pennyworth is a man of exceptional character. As butler to the illustrious Bruce Wayne, Alfred single-handedly manages all of Bruce's domestic affairs. He also serves as Bruce Wayne's confidant, and perhaps the closest thing that he has to a father. Ever since young Bruce saw his parents gunned down before his eyes, Alfred has been there to care for him. Only Alfred is privy to the horrific nightmares that haunt Bruce Wayne, and to the alter ego of Batman that they spawned.

Accordingly, Alfred bears another set of duties paralleling his work as a housekeeper. At a very different level, we must consider the role that Alfred plays knowing that Bruce Wayne is also Batman, for it is Alfred who mends his costumes, mans his digital networks, attends to the mechanics of his many "toys," and carefully stitches Batman up every time he's beaten to a pulp. When Batman is in the field, it's Alfred who waits up all night for him, patiently watching Batman's cameras and computers, ready to help him in any way that he can. On top of this, Alfred personally guards the security of the Batcave and the manor above it, going so far as to wrestle intruders to the ground.[1]

Alfred performs his tasks with prodigious energy, both physical and spiritual. His devotion to Wayne reveals his belief in a higher duty, an ethical obligation to serve another to the best of one's ability. It nurtures his soul; after all, how else could he accomplish so much in so little time, and with such disregard for his own health, safety, and personal gain? Alfred was willing to lose his mind and even die for Batman.[2] Why, he even claims to have been kidnapped twenty-seven times in his service![3] Taking no part in the notoriety of Bruce Wayne or Batman, Alfred certainly doesn't do it for the fame. Rather, we're astounded at his humility, for although Alfred is surely aware of the vital role he plays in the Dark Knight's forays, he asks for no praise. Instead, he remains so humble that on the same day that he changes the tires on the Batmobile, programs Wayne Manor's security systems, and reinvents Batman's utility belt, he'll happily clean toilets, as if there were no difference between the tasks.[4]

Through it all, Alfred exudes a level of commitment and faith that is reminiscent of mythical heroes: knights-errant, martyrs, or even saints. However, there is nothing quixotic about his mission, and at no point do we think of him as some kind of naive disciple of the cult of the bat. Alfred is too confident and self-assured to be that kind of man. In fact, he spends most of his time chastising Bruce for his recklessness, showing that his only concern is for his master's well-being. While Alfred is obviously worried about Batman's methods, his devotion to him nonetheless reveals that he ultimately believes in Batman's conviction that justice can be realized concretely, and that Gotham can someday be a peaceful place.

In this chapter, the great Danish philosopher and theologian Søren Kierkegaard (1813–1855) will help us understand Alfred's loyalty to Batman. In particular, we will focus on Kierkegaard's work *Fear and Trembling*, in which he compares two fundamentally different ethical orders. On the one hand, there are those like Batman, who champion infinite justice as their ethical ideal, while on the other, there are those like Alfred, who champion personal love, devotion, and faithfulness as the moral high ground. Although both ethics are noble in their own ways, in the end we'll see that Alfred's justice is superior, for, as Kierkegaard points out, "Faith is a miracle, and yet no man is excluded from it; for that in which all human life is unified is passion, and faith is a passion."[5] Whereas humanity may never realize infinite justice, we are all capable of being faithful to each other. Accordingly, Alfred, like Kierkegaard before him, understands that peace begins on an individual basis and that justice is served only when we treat each other with respect.

Justice: Law and Fairness versus Love and Devotion

For Batman, justice is first and foremost sociopolitical. Justice is served when life and liberty are protected, namely by the laws and legal institutions founded in justice's name. These structures set clear boundaries for people's behavior and stop them if they overstep these limits. Accordingly, Batman works hand and hand with the police and the justice system, the sworn protectors of law and order, because ultimately they're the ones responsible for defending its justice.

However, Batman is the first to break the law if he deems it unjust, and the first to work against the police if they overstep the boundaries of either law or justice. Batman realizes that justice is something concrete that no legal system could ever completely capture. There are always situations that exceed abstract legal codes and precedents, moments when the laws are either too broad or too narrow. For example, few people would argue that stealing food to feed a starving family or jaywalking is morally reprehensible. Yet they are *illegal*, and subject to the full punishment of the law.

Considering that the law gets its power from justice, Batman's ethical obligation belongs primarily to that very justice. Batman knows (like any juror, judge, or police officer) that every crime involves variables that our abstract laws cannot account for, and that the law must be interpreted so as to preserve its just mandate. When the law fails justice, as it sometimes does, Batman is forced to supersede it so as to restore the balance between justice and law, crime and punishment.

Like Batman, Alfred also believes in a concrete and non-abstract form of justice. For Alfred, justice isn't so much a matter of social structure, but a personal matter of treating people with respect, kindness, and love. Alfred's actions reflect his intrinsic belief that people are duty-bound to each other, and that justice occurs when one serves another to the best of one's ability. But Alfred also views justice as duty, whereby he honors his promises, cares for those he is responsible for, and values the work he has chosen. Thus when Alfred agreed to serve the Wayne family, the commitment was a blood oath, a lifelong obligation to be broken only by dismissal or death.

Although we could say the difference between Batman and Alfred is the difference between social justice and personal justice, this would actually miss the point entirely. Whereas Batman shows us justice as law, peace, and fair institutions, Alfred shows us a much higher justice, that of justice as love and devotion. This kind of justice is inherently *unfair*, because there's never a guarantee that one's kind deed will be reciprocated. In fact, for Alfred, that's rarely the case. Although Bruce Wayne treats Alfred with respect, he will never attend to Alfred like Alfred does him. Instead, Alfred passively accepts that his life is but a means to Wayne's ends, and that his justice has been subordinated to Batman's quest for social order.

The Absurdity of It All

And yet paradoxically, Alfred must willingly give himself and his justice over to Batman so that his own justice can be realized. The situation is entirely *absurd*! Alfred often feels that Batman's justice is a misguided one, though in order for him to teach the young Bruce Wayne how to channel it positively, Alfred must follow Wayne's orders so that this most stubborn student doesn't abandon him entirely. In actuality, though, Alfred is only superficially led by Wayne. Tacitly he not only remains Wayne's moral compass, but also his physical protector, feeding, clothing, and caring for him like one would a child.

Despite the absurdity of this situation, Alfred nevertheless retains his faith in Master Bruce, knowing that Wayne's education will be a lifelong process. As his teacher, Alfred possesses a superior wisdom that only comes with age, and so his judgment is always ahead of Wayne's, guiding his young apprentice toward a kindred inner peace. No matter how Bruce reciprocates his love and support, Alfred gives it unconditionally, never for a moment believing that he will not succeed in helping him calm his inner demons. Faith against all odds and faith amidst the absurd—this is Alfred's *existential condition*.

Many philosophers have tried to describe our "existential condition." It was Kierkegaard who observed that from the moment we are born, "man is not yet a self":[6] we each struggle to discover who we are and our relation to the world around us. Building on this idea, Heidegger (1889–1976) noticed that our existential condition is therefore a matter of "Being-in-the-world," which "is as it is."[7] Regardless of whether we are born into a life of privilege and luxury, or one of pain and misery, we are all "thrown" into the world and must make of it whatever we can. This "thrownness" constitutes a perpetual state of anxiety for us, as we try to define ourselves distinctly from our environment and from the mass of other people surrounding us. This is what Kierkegaard called our "Sickness Unto Death," a term borrowed from the Gospel of John 11:4. We "despair" at the absurd paradox of trying to constitute a unique identity amidst places and histories that existed before us, and despite the opinions and identities that others impose upon us.[8] And yet the moment we define ourselves for others is the moment we succumb to *their* histories and definitions, never really arriving at our own individuality. Thus, "an existing individual is constantly in process of becoming," says Kierkegaard.[9]

Jean-Paul Sartre (1905–1980) interpreted this idea positively. Being born without identity, we are therefore free to choose to become whatever or whomever we want: "First of all, man exists, turns up, appears on the scene, and, only afterwards, defines himself. If man, as the existential conceives him, is indefinable, it is because at first he is nothing. Only afterward will he be something, and he himself will have made what he will be."[10] "Sickness" or "despair" at life arises from the fact that we are all "condemned to be free."[11] However, being free, we then become completely responsible for choosing the ethic that will guide our lives, a choice that always involves a certain degree of absurdity. For instance, it is absurd that we will never really know the full impact of our ethical decisions, and how much or how little they affect others. It is absurd that our existence changes as we go through life, and that we constantly face new ethical decisions, while being haunted by those we've made in the past. It is absurd that someday we will die, and that all our ethical decisions may be in vain. And it is absurd that we exist with the faith that our life has meaning, without ever knowing what that meaning ultimately is.

Like Alfred, Bruce Wayne grapples with his own absurd existential predicament. To start with, imagine how the young Bruce felt as his parents were gunned down in front of him by

Joe Chill. As his parents bled to death at his feet, we can imagine the child's worldview shattering. Thereafter, he would seem to be damned to a life of grief. We wonder how it was that someone so traumatized could then find it within himself to dedicate his life to the pursuit of justice, a justice that he can never share in. When he finally meets Chill and has a chance to kill him, he instead takes pity on the man, realizing that Chill is a pathetic sot whose whole life is already a damnation.[12] Batman must face the fact that killing Chill will neither absolve him of his past, nor bring the kind of justice he's looking for. This realization becomes all the more absurd when Batman is forced to ally himself with Chill in order to stop the Reaper, inadvertently making Chill a tool of the same justice that Batman seeks.[13] Furthermore, Chill's mother, Mrs. Chilton, may have even helped raise Bruce Wayne, leaving us to wonder whether caring for Bruce caused her to neglect raising her own son, and if this could have, ironically, led to Joe's life of crime.[14] Regardless of all these twists of fate, Batman trudges on toward justice, desperately trying to make some good of his tragic life, so that his parents' deaths were not in vain.

Absurdity, Irony, and Faith

The absurdity and irony that both Alfred and Batman face, and the way in which they both use their personal faith and belief to overcome them, remind us of the biblical character Abraham, whom Kierkegaard once used as a philosophical model of the perfect man of faith. As the story goes, Abraham and his wife Sarah had been trying for many years to have a baby, so that they would have an heir to their family name and fortune. With both of them nearing old age, it seemed impossible that Sarah would ever bear a child. However, the Bible tells us that as a reward for upholding his covenant to God, and for worshipping no other, Abraham and Sarah were finally blessed by Him with a son, Isaac.

After so many years trying, the couple was astounded at this gift of life, and loved Isaac dearly. However, unbeknownst to Abraham, God had another test of faith in store for him. One day he called to Abraham, saying, "Take your son Isaac, your only one, whom you love, and go to the land of Moriah. There you shall offer him up as a holocaust on a height that I will point out to you" (Genesis 22:2). Abraham was astounded, for God was asking him to sacrifice the very gift He had given him, his only son, whom he loved more than anyone else on Earth. And yet despite the absurdity of the request, Abraham submitted to God's task.

Kierkegaard remarks on this moment in Abraham's life, saying: "He believed by virtue of the absurd; for there could be no question of human calculation, and it was indeed the absurd that God who required it of him should the next instant recall the requirement. He climbed the mountain, even at the instant when the knife glittered he believed . . . that God would not require Isaac."[15] When Kierkegaard tells us that it was by "virtue of the absurd" that Abraham believed, he means that Abraham was able to trust God because what he was being asked to do was unfathomable. That he could find no reason for God to give him such an impossible task did not dissuade him; instead, it actually made him believe in its necessity. Rather than speculate at God's motives, Abraham instead simply trusted in God, for God had never let him down and had never betrayed his blind obedience.

Batman, the Knight of the Infinite Resignation

Just like Abraham resigned his will to the dreadful task that God asked of him, Batman, too, "believe[s] by virtue of the absurd."[16] The pain of his parents' death could have destroyed him, for "sorrow can derange a man's mind," yet he managed, like Abraham, to find a "strength of will which is able to haul up so exceedingly close to the wind that it saves [his] reason, even though he remains a little queer."[17] Psychologically, Bruce Wayne is scarred and somewhat neurotic, though he takes his trauma and reshapes it. His neuroses are transformed into weapons, as he uses what would otherwise defeat his will as a means to propel it. By allying himself with his fears, Batman allows them to pass from his heart into the hearts of his enemies. Accordingly we must look at the suit, the car, the bat-signal, and so on as artistic and therapeutic creations whereby Bruce Wayne converts his internal fears into external objects, so that those who oppose justice can see the terror they truly inspire, ironically making these villains suffer the same violent trauma they try to inflict upon others.

Externalizing and organizing his pain in this way, Bruce Wayne is able to again carry himself self-assuredly. In the face of the absurd, he has confidence in a more infinite justice, to which he resigns himself. Kierkegaard tells us that "resignation [is] the surrogate for faith,"[18] for as a person resigns himself to what is infinitely just, that justice becomes the crux of his very existence, and the ground for his faith. At once he feels that his life has meaning, and he looks beyond his own pain and suffering toward easing the pain and suffering of others. Bruce Wayne regains his confidence precisely at the moment he devotes himself to helping others, realizing that if only people were more inclined toward protecting and enforcing justice, perhaps the tragedy of his parents' death might not have occurred.

Once people have gained such confidence in the meaning of their lives, they take on a certain air. No longer are they content to passively participate in the world; instead they strive to take control of their life, using it as a means toward something greater. In this way, Kierkegaard says that these confident souls are more like knights, unwavering in their mission and completely devoted to their just cause. Batman is one of these "knights of infinite resignation," for he has dedicated his life toward sowing infinite justice. His poise discloses his calling: "The knights of the infinite resignation are easily recognized: their gait is gliding and assured."[19] Having found a higher reason for living, these knights glide toward it like bats in the night soaring from one rooftop to another, plunging at it blindly, but without fear, for they are not afraid to die in the name of what is glorious. Their life is now but a means to an infinite end, an end that surpasses all other concerns, including self-preservation.

Alfred, the Knight of Faith

In contrast, Alfred Pennyworth is a knight of a different breed. He is not devoted to some infinite and ideal virtue, but to a humble trade. He strives not to make the infinite real, but to preserve only one man: Bruce Wayne. Why? Because in doing so he serves two purposes. First, so long as Bruce Wayne and Batman are preserved, so is their justice. Thus Alfred realizes the same justice as Batman does, but does so vicariously. Second, he then surpasses this justice by simultaneously realizing love, which is to say a justice made tangible in the instant. Whereas Batman's infinite justice is never complete, and always something to come or some future state of order and peace to be attained, Alfred's loving justice is always at hand, and made real in the moment. *Justice as love* fulfills itself in the very movement in which it is made: the smile that follows a touch; the comfort of knowing that someone else is there for you; or the confidence that comes from having people around you that you can trust. Accordingly, Alfred sees justice in everything he does: how he can ease Batman's pain with a little medical care; how he can calm Batman's tortured soul with a few nice words and a homemade sandwich; or in any one of his witty remarks, which help to ground Batman and remind him of his tendency to overreact.

The paradox of this higher ethic is that on the surface it looks so ordinary, so banal. Whereas the knights of infinite resignation look confident and self-assured, "those on the other hand who carry the jewel of faith are likely to be delusive, because their outward appearance bears a striking resemblance to that which both the infinite resignation and faith profoundly despise . . . to Philistinism."[20] Oddly enough, the knights of faith give no sign of their ethical bent, nor do they express any of the panache found in the knight of infinite resignation. Rather, they look and act like ordinary and unenlightened people—Philistines. Kierkegaard describes the typical knight of faith, saying:

> The moment I set eyes on him I instantly push him from me, I myself leap backwards, I clasp my hands and say half aloud, "Good lord, is this the man? Is it really he? Why, he looks like a tax-collector!" . . . I examine his figure from tip to toe to see if there might not be a cranny through which the infinite was peeping. No! He is solid through and through. His tread? It is vigorous, belonging entirely to finiteness; no smartly dressed townsman who walks but to Fresberg on a Sunday afternoon treads the ground more firmly, he belongs entirely to the world, no Philistine more so. One can discover nothing of that aloof and superior nature whereby one recognizes the knight of the infinite. He takes delight in everything, and whenever one sees him taking part in a particular pleasure, he does it with the persistence which is the mark of the earthly man whose soul is absorbed in such things. He tends to his work. So when one looks at him one might suppose that he was a clerk who had lost his soul in an intricate system of book-keeping, so precise is he. He takes a holiday on Sunday. He goes to church.[21]

The knight of faith looks like a tax collector, a clerk, or in this case a butler, dressing as plain as any, and carrying on with the daily grind. Alfred dresses conservatively, keeps a pleasant demeanor, and is meticulously organized, just like Kierkegaard's man of faith.

In contrast, the knights of infinite resignation are spectacular, their armor matching their self-assurance, and their deeds expressing infinite flair. Batman's costume and his toys announce his heroic presence as much as they proclaim the metaphysical justice he stands for—some final kingdom of peace on Earth. While his work is nothing short of magnificent, epic in all its dimensions, how meager the knights of faith seem in the shadow of such an idol! Their dress is nothing special; their deeds are routine.

The real difference between these two, however, has nothing to do with the attention they draw to themselves. While the knights of infinite resignation are always waiting for some future ideal state, the knights of faith have found it, and are living it presently. Their eternity is not to come, but is found in the moment, as they realize that in loving and serving others they exercise the kind of fellowship that will infinitely sustain humanity. For them, peace on earth must be made with every gesture and every action. And it starts by committing ourselves to another person and by helping that person in every way that we can.

Alfred knows that if we all treated others in this way there would be no need for Batman, or for any type of coercive justice for that matter. And so he acts as a model for Batman, like some sage who follows Bruce Wayne around, if only to remind him of the true face of a justice here and now, and not a justice to come. This is why Alfred's solitude never brings him malaise, and why he "takes delight in everything."[22] Every little deed he does for Bruce Wayne reinforces his faith, for he not only helps him survive, but also subtly inspires Wayne by his good example.

Like Kierkegaard's knight of faith, "[he] is no fool,"[23] for he chooses his profession so as to serve a misguided although otherwise good man. If anyone, Batman is the fool, recklessly chasing criminals to the point where he nearly gets killed. Alfred, on the other hand, is realistic about the type of justice he can accomplish with his life; as Kierkegaard writes:

> Fools and young men prate about everything being possible for a man. That, however, is a great error. Spiritually speaking, everything is possible, but in this world of the finite there is much which is not possible. This impossible, however, the knight makes possible by expressing it spiritually, but he expresses it spiritually by waiving his claim to it.[24]

Unlike Batman, Alfred does not foolishly seek out some type of justice for all, but only justice for the one person he cares for, Bruce Wayne. He waves his claim to the type of lofty justice that Batman is committed to, knowing that he is incapable of fighting crimes like Batman. Instead of combating felons on the street, he chooses to fight the tyranny of the soul that has made Bruce Wayne so cynical, and shattered his faith in humanity.

Toward this end, Alfred commits his whole life and the entirety of his faith, his honor coming from his vow. Alfred remains a knight because he never wavers from his commitment to help Batman. Were he to do so, he would abandon moral duty in favor of moral speculation. Batman's life would henceforth become a means to Alfred's own happiness, instead of an end in itself. Serving Batman unconditionally, though, Alfred avoids this moral contradiction. In remaining faithful to Batman, Alfred remains faithful to himself, to his past oath of duty, and to his ethical belief. And this, Kierkegaard tells us, ultimately is "Love."[25] By sacrificing his own life for the betterment of Bruce Wayne's, Alfred demonstrates that he truly loves Bruce Wayne in the most selfless way possible. This is the kind of love that has "assumed a religious character," a creed of love, whereby he dutifully cares for Bruce with all his heart, will, and effort.[26]

Paradox and Peace

Never for a second does Alfred stop remembering the commitment he made to the young Bruce Wayne the night his parents died, and how he made a secret oath there and then to stand by the suffering boy until Bruce became a whole person again. This oath and this remembrance are a constant pain for Alfred, for he is the one who must stand by and watch Batman struggle to attain his faith, a faith that Batman remains ignorant of because of his complete resignation to an infinite and ideal (and therefore impossible) justice. Alfred's pain is like that of a father watching his child grow, of seeing the naiveté and idealism of youth and hoping that someday it will take on more realistic proportions. With the same love and affection that a father would give, Alfred relentlessly tries to teach Bruce Wayne justice as love, hoping beyond hope that he can lead him toward his own work of faith someday.

In the end, the story of Batman and Alfred, like the story of Abraham and the ethic of Kierkegaard, is analogous with our own personal struggles to find purpose and meaning in life. It is a story of struggling against impossible odds, of faith despite suffering and tragedy, and the wholehearted belief that our lives can make a real difference in the world. We must aspire to become "knights of faith," whose sanguine devotion approaches religiosity, leading us to an ethic of hope and cheerfulness: "Faith therefore is not an aesthetic emotion but something far higher, precisely because it has resignation as its presupposition; it is not an immediate instinct of the heart, but is the paradox of life and existence."[27]

Abraham's paradox is that of a completely altruistic father, who loves his child despite knowing that his son may be destined to suffer from forces he can never protect the boy from. Batman's paradox is that he has resigned his life to an impractical justice, a completely ideal justice, that no one person could ever possibly instantiate on their own, while Alfred's paradox is the paradox of concrete faith, of loving and believing in Bruce Wayne despite his faults, hoping that someday soon the both of them will be at peace, and that Batman will find the justice he seeks.

NOTES

1. See *Batman* #16 (April–May 1943), which is also Alfred's first appearance.

2. Alfred saves Batman and Robin by pushing them out of the way of a falling boulder in *Detective Comics* #328 (June 1964), and he is revived by a mad scientist in *Detective Comics* #356 (Oct. 1966).

3. See *Batman: Gotham Adventures* #16 (Sept. 1999).

4. See the interview with Bat-Tzu in chapter 20 of this book for more about Alfred's humility.

5. Søren Kierkegaard, *Fear and Trembling and the Sickness Unto Death* (Princeton, NJ: Princeton Univ. Press, 1970), 77.

6. Ibid., 146.

7. Martin Heidegger, *Being and Time* (San Francisco: HarperSanFrancisco, 1962), 84.

8. Kierkegaard, *Fear and Trembling*, 146.

9. Søren Kierkegaard, *Concluding Unscientific Postscript* (Princeton, NJ: Princeton Univ. Press, 1941), 176.

10. Jean-Paul Sartre, *Existentialism* (New York: Philosophical Library, 1947), 18.

11. Jean-Paul Sartre, *Being and Nothingness* (New York: Gramercy Books, 1956), 439.

12. *The Dark Knight Returns* (1986).

13. *Batman: Year Two* (1987).

14. *The Untold Legend of the Batman* #1 (July 1980).

15. Kierkegaard, *Fear and Trembling*, 47.

16. Ibid.

17. Ibid.

18. Ibid., 46.

19. Ibid., 49.

20. Ibid., 49.

21. Ibid., 48–49.

22. Ibid., 49.

23. Ibid., 52.

24. Ibid., 47.

25. Ibid.

26. Ibid., 54.

27. Ibid., 58.

DARK NIGHTS AND THE CALL OF CONSCIENCE

Jason J. Howard

Does Batman Have a Conscience?

Not many things I was interested in as a teenager continue to appeal to me with the same intensity as the Batman. He is the modern Dracula, a wraith, a dark knight, and an avenging spirit, someone you would sooner find in a Greek tragedy than in a comic book. Batman's method is to terrify his enemies almost to the point of madness, and in terrifying them he forces them to confront who they have become. The central question for me has always been how the Batman, who uses the very fear tactics and subterfuges employed by his enemies, and who himself is damaged goods, can remain the hero without becoming the villain. His quest to purge Gotham of crime and avenge his parents' death is played out on the moral equivalent of a razor's edge. (To see just how sharp this edge can be check out Frank Miller's *The Dark Knight Returns*, from 1986.) What enables Batman to walk this edge, look into the abyss of men's souls, and continue on? The best way to answer this question is to find out whether Batman has a conscience.

The problem of conscience—where it comes from, how it justifies moral behavior, and whether it even exists—has been debated in moral philosophy for over two thousand years. To appreciate how Batman fits into this debate, however, we need to go beyond the typical line of moral reasoning, which would focus on the nobility of his intentions and his moral authority as a "superhero." These questions certainly bring out the complexity of Batman's behavior, but they are of limited use in clarifying the underlying origin and legitimacy of conscience as a form of motivation. Rather we need to see these questions against the larger backdrop of Batman's struggle to lead an "authentic existence." Just as most of our moral choices are determined, at least in part, by who we are as individuals, Batman's choices also flow from his deeper *existential struggle* to lead an authentic life. Because Batman is very much aware of the complexity of his dual life and the questionable character of his own choices, his life is an existential struggle. How he contends with these issues can not only explain the difference between an authentic and an inauthentic conscience, it can also help account for his continuing appeal as a superhero.

Conscience and Authority

This idea of leading an authentic life, as well as having an authentic conscience, is a philosophical theme that was introduced with the trial and execution of Socrates (470–399 BCE). But it was with twentieth-century existentialism that authenticity was defined in its full glory. *Existentialism* is a prominent school of philosophy that emphasizes the ambiguity and absurdity of human existence. It focuses its attention on the alienation that underscores much of everyday life, while largely rejecting any straightforward universal explanation of human behavior, whether religious, economic, political, or moral.

It may seem strange to turn to the Batman to gain some clarity on the meaning of authentic conscience. Certainly a man hiding behind a mask and prowling around at night seems inauthentic to say the least! Yet if we understand the term in its existential sense as developed by Martin Heidegger (1889–1976), the notion of authenticity is entirely appropriate. To say someone is authentic means at least two things: First, they are honest with themselves about what is and is not in their control, especially when it comes to the inevitability of death. Second, they take full responsibility for the direction of their lives and try to make transparent the meaning and purpose of what they do. Batman manages to live up to both these standards, despite serious emotional, psychological, and physical challenges.

People constantly make appeals to their conscience. Whether it is Martin Luther King Jr. or Osama bin Laden, there is a widespread belief that somewhere deep within everybody, if only we take the time to listen, we will discover an unfailing moral compass. This mainstream view endorses an "authoritarian" or "essentialist" form of conscience, where our most important moral duty is to follow through on our moral convictions. There have been many different philosophical advocates of this view, most notably Jean-Jacques Rousseau (1712–1778) in his *Emile or On Education*.[1] If this innate view of conscience were the one embraced by the Batman, where moral goodness consists of listening to one's heart, there would be little to be learned from him. But Batman is not Superman, and as an expert on criminal psychology, he is far too experienced to embrace such a simplistic view of moral behavior. That does not mean Batman has no moral stance, but only that this stance is not founded upon some "a priori" (timeless and universal) moral sense. Instead, Batman's moral stance stems from an appreciation for the complexity of human behavior and the extreme forms such behavior can take.

For Heidegger, as well as for other existentialist thinkers like Jean-Paul Sartre (1905–1980) and Albert Camus (1913–1960), life is what you make of it.[2] Each of us as individuals defines the meaning of our own existence through the choices we make and the stances we take. We cannot avoid this burden if we want to appreciate the reality of human freedom and its connection to moral integrity. Yet how does this struggle for authenticity relate to the Batman?

The young Bruce Wayne was disillusioned and unsure of himself before he discovered the symbol of the Bat, traveling the world to perfect his detective skills with little more than vengeance on his mind. But if the symbol of the Bat was more than just an invention to cope with the grief over his parents' death, what did it promise young Bruce that he did not already have? The persona of the Batman completes the identity of Bruce Wayne by instilling in him a new sense of authentic conscience, one that is not clouded by revenge, burdened by the expectations of others, or anchored in any single all-embracing moral vision, but rather speaks to the actualization of freedom and human potential. (I think that's enough, don't you?)

Money, Hot Tubs, and Life's Tough Decisions

One of the central concepts of Heidegger's philosophy, developed in his masterpiece *Being and Time* (1927), is the notion of "fallenness." According to Heidegger, it is inevitable that people take on the expectations and concerns of other people. But when this happens, we often become so wrapped up in these concerns that we lose ourselves in the lifestyle and the views of the majority. This is especially true when it comes to other people's opinions on moral matters. In this state of "fallenness," as he calls it, we give up our own authentic potential to be ourselves, because others have decided upon the very meaning of our existence, and so we simply act out our part in life.

For Heidegger, as for most other existentialists, human life is constantly open to reinterpretation. To emphasize the interpretive character of human existence Heidegger employs the German word *Dasein* when discussing human beings. In using this term, Heidegger draws our attention to the unique way in which human beings are aware of their own "Being" (*Sein*) as always "there" (*da*) in some specific place, and engaged in some specific project. It is precisely because *Dasein* (aka human beings) can be aware of not only practical projects (like building bridges and making money), but also of what it is to exist, that conscience is possible.

Because we are *Dasein*, the meaning of our being is never settled. However, society functions on the premise that existence is settled, and that the purpose of life is to be a doctor, make lots of money, have a family, or some other host of clichés. As Heidegger explains: "The Self of everyday Dasein is the *they-self*, which we distinguish from the *authentic Self*—that is, from the Self that has been taken hold of in its own way."[3] You're probably familiar with the "they-self" from such bits of conventional wisdom as "They say you shouldn't wear white after Labor Day" and "They say you shouldn't swim until twenty minutes after eating." When we follow the "they-self," we don't think or act for ourselves. Instead we just accept what the anonymous "they" of society has to say. In many ways the life of the young Bruce Wayne exemplifies the experience of fallenness and the difficulty one can have in affirming one's own unique identity. (We are all in search of role models, and the death of Bruce's parents would have made this search especially painful and confusing, though Alfred made for an excellent surrogate.)

But life as just Bruce Wayne would not have been so bad, right? Blessed with an ungodly fortune and good looks, he could have made a name for himself in countless ways. And the irony is that if his sole purpose in life was to do something with his life that his parents would recognize as noble, he would have been better off as just Bruce Wayne, running Wayne Enterprises full-time as a charity organization.[4] But regardless of how much good Bruce Wayne could have done, his life would not have been free, because the choice to run Wayne Enterprises would not have been his own authentic choice. Moreover, his parents' death would have become just one more statistic, and Bruce just one more anonymous CEO. Rather than resign himself to the world of the "they" and their expectations, Bruce Wayne decided to struggle against that world to accommodate the pangs of his own conscience. In doing so, Bruce confronted not only the meaning of his own existence, but also the deeper meaning of his parents' death.

Seeing Things Clearly with Better Bat-Vision

The conventional wisdom among Batman fans is that the tragic death of his parents transformed Bruce Wayne into the Batman. For Heidegger, Sartre, and Camus, all meaningful transformations and changes in people's lives come from the realization that we *interpret* existence. The meaning of life and death is never settled and finished, like some equation that can simply be memorized and parroted. In Batman's case, although there is little doubt that the murder of his parents was the catalyst for change, it is the act of interpreting the *meaning* of their deaths that initiated the existential transformation from Bruce Wayne into the Batman. Following Heidegger's insight on this score, we can say that it is through "wanting to have a conscience" that any substantial insight into the meaning of existence is gained.[5] And it is the unique combination of wanting to have a conscience while facing up to the full meaning of his parents' death that initiated his metamorphosis from a bloodthirsty young man to a caped crusader.

But what does it mean to want to have a conscience? According to Heidegger, much of what passes for human behavior is motivated by self-deception, both intentional and unintentional. People are constantly fleeing from their own possibilities, their past, and the inevitability of their own death, toward what is familiar and comforting. This state of fleeing is the defining characteristic of fallenness. We want existence to be something settled, to know we had no real choice in our failures or misfortunes, and that life has a clear-cut purpose we just need to find. As a result, much of social life ends up being an elaborate diversion to avoid contemplating the reality of our own mortality. As Heidegger sees it, we cannot authentically desire to have a conscience as long as we buy into a world in which everything in life is settled and death is some vague and distant event, since the only purpose that conscience can have under these conditions is censoring our individuality.

The common view of conscience that is epitomized by the anger and guilt of young Bruce Wayne is not the "authentic" conscience, but an internalization of familiar reactions and expectations. This internalization, although a common expression of conscience, ends up dictating how we should act and feel, making any personal resolve or insight we may have into the meaning of existence redundant. Appreciating the distinction between these two ways of experiencing conscience—authentic and inauthentic—can be difficult. On the one hand, we have the authentic sense of conscience that affirms individuality, while on the other, we have the inauthentic sense of conscience that denies any role for personal insight and ingenuity. What makes the Batman such an intriguing character is that despite being a superhero, he demonstrates the distinction between these two senses of conscience in a very instructive way.

Batman: Year One (1987) makes it quite clear that despite his many years of training, Bruce Wayne was largely a failure as a crime fighter without the persona of the Batman to guide him. But the interesting question here is: why? It's not as if his training substantially improved once he put on the costume, or that his identity could be sufficiently hidden only through cape and cowl. As he states himself, commenting on his first few months as a crime fighter: "I have the means, the skill—but not the method . . . no. That's not true. I have hundreds of methods. But something's missing. Something isn't right. I have to wait." Certainly Bruce is not waiting for someone or something in the usual sense, nor is he expecting something to happen, so what exactly is he waiting for?

As Heidegger explains, "Conscience summons *Dasein's* Self from its lostness in the 'they.'"[6] This "summons" is not expressed in words, or moral commands—if so, conscience would just be another incentive to live up to other people's expectations. On the contrary, conscience "individuates" people by pulling them away from the world of others by making them confront their own unique possibilities. The crucial point here is that the experience of authentic conscience is one of intense individuation, wherein we realize that at the end of the day no one can share the event of our death, nor prevent it. Just as we must own up to the inevitability of our own death, so we must take direct responsibility for the "meaning" of our own lives.

On that fateful night when a lone bat flew through the window of Wayne Manor, answering Bruce Wayne's search for a new identity, he had what Heidegger calls a "moment of vision." This moment of vision is distinctive in that it is not the expression of some religious command, or a simple moral ideal. Neither is it the answer to all of life's problems. Rather, it is in this moment of vision that we experience the full meaning of conscience, which "calls us forth into a situation" by disclosing the deepest riddle of our own Being, revealing that who we are is perpetually an "issue" for each one of us.[7]

Through appropriating the symbol of the Bat "for himself" Bruce discloses his own anxiety and stands up to his own unique calling. As suggested in *Legends of the Dark Knight* #1 (November 1989), the Bat is recognized as Bruce Wayne's totem, yet we miss the full significance of this totem if we look to give it some specific content or message. This would be to reduce Bruce Wayne's discovery to that of the "public

conscience." Recognizing the Bat as Bruce Wayne's totem discloses his authentic conscience in a moment of vision, in which
Bruce confronts the power of possibility. Consider the following description from "The Man Who Falls," which comments
on Bruce's realization of the Bat as his elemental symbol: "He
knew. In that single instant, he understood what his direction had been all those years, what was possible to him—what
he had to be. For a moment, he quietly savored a new emotion.
For a moment he was happy."[8]

Feeling Guilty (or "How to Battle the Blues")

Batman's existence is a continual attempt to locate and reaffirm
the meaning of his own rebellion. Rather than deny the madness of his parents' death and his own futile efforts to thwart
crime in Gotham, Batman affirms the absurdity of his predicament as his own unique possibility. For when viewed in terms
of overall success, Batman's career as a crime fighter is surely
questionable. Crime in Gotham never really decreases, and
every major villain he puts away just ends up escaping again.
Moreover, as the early issues of the *Legends of the Dark Knight*
show, Batman's exploits bring out copycat "vigilantes" who
cause havoc for the general public.[9] Beyond that, Batman's
very presence in Gotham acts as a beacon for every would-be
lunatic in the area. The only explicit moral codes that Batman
follows are his refusal to spill the blood of an innocent and his
vow to never intentionally take another's life, yet even these
stances have been compromised on rare occasions. Yet if it is
true that Batman's success as a crime fighter is questionable
given the collateral damage his very presence creates, what
kind of guidance or wisdom is gained from having an authentic
conscience?

Batman's existence is his liberation and his torture, and it is
the way he affirms both while acknowledging the larger futility

of his quest that keeps him honest and authentic. Unlike many other heroes, Batman has no illusions about the questionable character of what he is doing.[10] In early issues of *Legends of the Dark Knight* he repeatedly considers retiring the cape. What's more, in *The Dark Knight Returns*, it is the summons of his truest possibility, the Batman, that after ten years of retirement calls him back from his *fallen* state of alcoholism. As Heidegger clarifies, the summons of authentic conscience "constitutes the *loyalty* of existence to its own Self."[11] Yet this true self is not some timeless person or voice deep within us, which is the common view of conscience, but the resolute desire to distinguish what is trivial and accidental in life from what is inevitable and truly one's own. This struggle to unearth our deepest commitments and motivations can be seen in the way Bruce Wayne comes to terms with the fact of his parents' death.

His transformation into the Batman occurs when Bruce confronts his guilty conscience over his parents' death by grasping the meaning of his guilt in a different way, which is what Heidegger claims distinguishes the "moment of vision" as a form of awakening. Bruce's personal guilt, which is experienced as suffocating and confusing, is disclosed at a more basic level of existence as the guilt of Being. Here the issue is not primarily one of "indebtedness" or "duty," but the awareness of one's own "nullity" or negativity.[12] This means that one owns up to the fragility that limits life while also recognizing that this very fragility holds the power to transform life. The guilt shifts from one of simple blame to the realization that everyone is guilty to the extent we all must take a stand on who we are and how we should live.

In choosing to free himself from the typical response to his tragedy, that of blind rage and vengeance, Bruce interprets the event of his parents' murder as a calling to rebel against a life of victimization, complacency, and cynicism. In so doing Bruce redeems a senseless tragedy by confronting the senselessness of violence itself. With this the guilt that originally condemned him is experienced as a summons to be himself, and so Batman becomes the authentic conscience of Bruce Wayne. Taking on the persona of the Dark Knight enables Bruce to confront the absurdity of his parents' death by disclosing another way of experiencing guilt, through recognition of one's own mortality. It is in the acceptance of this and what it means for the legitimacy of his choices that gives Batman the courage to see the inevitability of his own death as a challenge "to be."

Dark Nights and the Call of Authentic Conscience

Batman is ready to die. He has come to terms with the inevitability of death, yet this alone does not make him authentic; many people are ready to die for a cause. So what can Batman, a "mere" comic book character, teach us about being authentic? One of the crucial points to keep in mind is that Batman's choice to risk his freedom on an impossible cause is not an escape from the reality of the world, but an affirmation of it. Batman does not seek to convert people to his cause, nor does he begrudge those who choose to fight crime in other, more traditional ways. Likewise, there is no completion to his quest, no proper ending, and no salvation, but only a continual reappraisal of his own choices. In accepting his choices in life as his own unique fate, Batman reveals himself as someone who has accepted the world for what it is, with all its absurdity and sorrow, while nonetheless remaining tolerant and compassionate toward everyone except those whose actions end in senseless violence.[13]

Batman does not stand against this onslaught of senseless violence on the basis of an explicit moral code or religious creed, but rather from the resolute acknowledgment of his own freedom to accept death, which is the authentic conscience. It is this freedom to accept life in all its perplexing ambiguity, and to decide for himself how to deal with it, that makes Batman who he is, not his costume. Batman lives in his decision "to be," acknowledging the reality of his own anxiety while anticipating the nothingness that haunts each of us:

> Anticipation allows *Dasein* to understand that that potentiality-for-being in which its ownmost Being is an issue, must be taken over by *Dasein* alone. . . . *Dasein* can be *authentically itself* only if it makes this possible for itself of its own accord. . . . When, by anticipation, one becomes free for one's own death, one is liberated from one's lostness in those possibilities which may accidentally thrust themselves upon one; and one is liberated in such a way that for the first time one can choose among the factical possibilities lying ahead.[14]

This "freedom towards death," as Heidegger calls it, is the distinguishing feature of the authentic conscience. To say someone is free to anticipate their own death does not imply a death wish, nor is it some morbid fixation on "the end." It is the penetrating realization that the point of existence is something each of us must come to grips with as individuals by continually reaffirming the meaning of our own mortality. It is this attitude of authenticity that ensures that our lives are as transparent as possible in terms of who we are, freeing us from the "illusions of the 'they'" and their obsession with familiarity, tranquility, and distraction.[15] This is not easy. It requires that we admit our own vulnerability, along with rejecting any kind of fatalistic determinism or escapism, accepting that "to be" is to be anxious about who we are.

If we assume people are simply "born" with a conscience, rather than struggling to have one, as Heidegger explains, then there is no room for people to exercise their freedom to authentically make their own decisions in life. This does not mean that having an authentic conscience entails abandoning morality. On the contrary, it prevents morality from becoming another kind of conformism where the exercise of free and spontaneous moral judgment is exchanged for blind commitment and intolerance.

Of course, Batman is not the only example of an authentic conscience, but he is certainly an instructive one. Moreover, what makes him so instructive is the existential complexity of his identity, and not simply the fact that he is a superhero. It is his willingness to come to grips with his past, his rejection of all facile excuses, and his passion to deal with reality on its own terms that distinguish Batman from the moral fanatic, and that make his type of heroism so significant. As Batman himself puts it, "You play the hand you're dealt. . . . What I am, I am of my own choice. I don't know if I'm happy, but I'm content."[16]

Conclusions, Capes, and Cowls

The choice to lead an authentic life brings with it some dark nights, yet this is the price we have to pay to lead a life without delusion. Batman's acceptance of this sustains his heroism. He relies on his own will to have an authentic conscience, not some superhuman power. Consequently, the purpose of his cape and cowl is not to hide who he is. Rather, it stands as testament to the choices he has made and the man he has become. Although we cannot literally emulate the Batman and the risks he takes—after all, he is a comic book hero—his internal battles are by no means alien to most of us. He is a person struggling to affirm the weight of his own choices and lead an authentic existence. In a world where mindless conformism is rampant, ignorance is the order of the day, and fear is our greatest taskmaster, Batman's call to conscience is an example of how our willingness to confront the meaning of our own existence can also be the path to personal liberation.[17]

NOTES

1. Jean-Jacques Rousseau (1762), *Emile or On Education*, trans. Alan Bloom (London: Penguin Books Ltd., 1991). Other notable examples are St. Thomas Aquinas (1225–1274) and Bishop Butler (1692–1752).

2. A good introduction to Sartre is *Existentialism Is a Humanism* (New Haven, CT: Yale Univ. Press, 2007), while a good introduction to Camus is *The Myth of Sisyphus and Other Essays* (New York: Vintage, 1991).

3. Martin Heidegger, *Being and Time*, trans. John Macquarrie and Edward Robinson (New York: Harper & Row, 1962), 167.

4. See the essay by Mahesh Ananth and Ben Dixon in chapter 8 of this book for the ethics of young Bruce's decision to become the Batman.

5. Heidegger, *Being and Time*, 342.

6. Ibid., 319.

7. Ibid., 347.

8. "The Man Who Falls," from *Secret Origins* (1989 trade paperback), reprinted in *Batman Begins: The Movie and Other Tales of the Dark Knight* (2005).

9. For instance, see "Prey" (*Legends of the Dark Knight* #11–15, 1990) and "Faith" (#21–23, 1991).

10. Consider Batman's testimony before the government subcommittee on the issue of superheroes: "Sure we're criminals . . . we've always been criminals. We have to be criminals" (*The Dark Knight Returns*).

11. Heidegger, *Being and Time*, 443.

12. Ibid., 332.

13. For examples of this compassion, consider his complex relationships with Two-Face and Catwoman.

14. Heidegger, *Being and Time*, 308.

15. Ibid., 311.

16. *Legends of the Dark Knight* #23, 26 (October, 1991).

17. My thanks to Rolf Samuels and Ken Lee for looking over earlier versions of this paper.

BATMAN'S CONFRONTATION WITH DEATH, ANGST, AND FREEDOM

David M. Hart

A Determined Batman?

In the pantheon of comic book superheroes, few characters are more focused and determined than Batman. Superman makes time for a relationship with Lois Lane, Spider-Man worries about Aunt May and his job at the *Daily Bugle*, and the Fantastic Four are constantly preoccupied by their family squabbles. But Batman seems to devote every moment of his life to his personal war on crime, an endeavor that he takes to be his very reason for being. Even on the few occasions when he makes choices that might seem to give him something resembling a "normal" social life, like attending a Wayne Enterprises fund-raiser, invariably with a beautiful woman as his date, Batman always seems to justify those actions in terms of his mission. Being seen with a supermodel, for instance, helps keep up his playboy reputation and wards off suspicion that Bruce Wayne might be Batman. And going to a public event as Bruce Wayne gives him the chance to gather inside information and hear rumors. Relating every action back to his own personal war gives Batman's life project a cohesive unity; everything he does is done to serve a single, greater purpose.

But the tricky thing about a character who is so deeply committed to one goal is that "excessive" passion can sometimes seem a little crazy. Indeed, since the mid-1980s, many writers have opted to push Batman's single-minded dedication to such an extreme that the character often comes off as borderline psychopathic, driven not by an altruistic intention to create a better world, but rather by an irresistible compulsion induced by childhood trauma. In recent years, fans seem to have tired of this interpretation, and DC Comics has responded by focusing on a "kinder, gentler" version of the character. The new consensus among creators and fans seems to be that making Batman's vigilantism no more than the simple product of a damaged psyche might have compromised the character's heroism. The "grim and gritty" version of Batman appeared to be endlessly seeking vengeance rather than justice—and, at least in our current culture, being motivated by vengeance doesn't seem all that superheroic.

The editorial decision to exorcise some of Batman's psychological demons—literally, in *52* #30 (November 29, 2006)—and return him to a more traditionally heroic characterization raises some important philosophical questions concerning the problem of human freedom. For example, does Batman do what he does because he has chosen a path that he believes to be right, or does he do it because he feels like he simply can't do anything else? Putting this question in philosophical terms, we might ask whether Batman's behavior is completely determined by his past, or if there is a sense in which we can say that his choices are made freely. Furthermore, if his

actions aren't wholly determined by his past, can we explain
Batman's dedication to his mission in any way other than by
a mechanistic law of psychological cause and effect, in which
his childhood trauma leads inevitably to a need to punish bad
guys? And can such an alternate explanation allow us to retain
the notion of self-determination that seems to be tied to a
hero's nobility?

This chapter will offer some possible answers to these
questions using the philosophy of Martin Heidegger (1889–
1976), and along the way, we'll explore a classic philosophical
problem known as the "free will versus determinism debate."
By examining Batman's motivations and actions through one
of the major figures in recent philosophy, we'll shed a little
light on the way the Dark Knight made his choice of a life (if,
indeed, he even had a choice).

Alfred and Appearance

Heidegger sets himself apart from his predecessors by overcoming the philosophical distinction between appearances and
that which is said to "truly" exist. This distinction, which had
dominated philosophical discourse since its earliest beginnings, is usually expressed in more recent philosophy in terms
of a "subject-object dualism." In everyday life, we use these
categories when we say that an opinion is "merely subjective,"
in contrast to the presumed objectivity of empirical science.

At the heart of this distinction is a conception of the human
being as an autonomous subject, who exists in a sort of "inner
world" of the mind, which is held to be completely separate
from the external world of objects. The problem with this
position is that drawing a firm line between the inner world
of that which appears to the subject, and the world that objectively exists outside of us, results in a radical disconnection. It
becomes seemingly impossible to establish that the appearances in our minds actually correspond to anything outside

ourselves in the "objective" world. If we follow this line of reasoning through, it then seems to be possible (in theory) that the way the world appears to us could be no more real than the hallucinations Batman has when he's hit with the Scarecrow's fear gas!

In the absolutely radical response to the subject/object, inner/outer world problem that is developed in his major book *Being and Time*, Heidegger's fundamental claim is that there simply is no meaningful inner/outer world distinction for human existence.[1] On the contrary, Heidegger argues that human existence (to which he gives the technical name *Dasein*, German for "existence" or, more literally, "being there") is fundamentally always already "out there," in the world, among things, and outside of itself.

How can he make such a claim? Obviously, from a scientific perspective, we exist in and through our bodies; if Killer Croc takes a massive chomp out of our brains, we can no longer exist. But Heidegger's response to that line of reasoning would be that a medical approach is guided by the same technical interpretation of being that led philosophers to the subject-object distinction. While it may be valid and good for its own purposes (for medical science or for the design of Croc-resistant Bat-cowls), thinking of the brain as an inner world in opposition to an external world doesn't really get at the core of what it is like to be human. Instead, Heidegger's analysis of human existence claims that our particular kind of being is fundamentally "in the world," not simply in the sense of being within an area of space, but also in the sense of being always involved with or engaged in a world.

To clarify Heidegger's claim that human existence is always "being-in-the-world" and thus always outside of itself, let's consider Alfred's way of being. As someone who has been a butler for many years, Alfred has a particular kind of existence, and accordingly, his world exists in a very particular way. When he glances around a room in Wayne Manor, Alfred doesn't just see an "objective" collection of matter, mere atoms taking various forms. Rather, he sees the grandfather clock that needs to be dusted, the dust cloth he'll use on the grandfather clock, the silver tray he uses to carry tea to Master Bruce, and so on. That is, he sees the world in terms that are not scientifically objective but are instead specific to his own existence. Moreover, according to Heidegger's argument, insofar as these things "really are" anything, they really are just as Alfred understands them according to his own interpretive horizon. If we ask him, "What is a silver tray?" an entirely appropriate response would be, "A device used to carry Master Bruce's tea." For Heidegger, the scientific perspective, according to which a silver tray might be defined as "a polished silver instrument of such and such dimensions," is only one possible interpretive horizon among many; while it is useful in terms of its own goals, it is still no more absolutely valid than Alfred's perspective (or anyone else's).

The major conclusion we can draw from this position is that for Heidegger, the most basic answer to the question of the meaning of being is that being *is* appearing. Particular beings in the world really are what they show themselves to be in appearances, so that Alfred's silver tray can exist as both an instrument for transporting tea *and* as an object of scientific study, depending on one's interpretive horizon; neither interpretation is more absolutely true than the other. And, to bring us back to the subject-object problem, if being is appearance, this also means that there simply is no purely "objective" world for us to be separated from. Rather than an inner world of the subject that might be cut off from the external world, Heidegger argues that we are fundamentally always out in the world, engaged with things as they show themselves (which is to say, exist) through our interpretive horizons; humans exist as beings who are always concerned with (and thus related to) things, and things exist in and through their appearances.

However, thinking further about Alfred's existence leads us to what Heidegger argues is an even more fundamental way in which human existence is always outside of itself. We said that things show themselves to Alfred in terms of his own interpretive horizon, but what determines this interpretive horizon? In Alfred's case, the answer lies in his being a butler. Batman doesn't see the dust on the grandfather clock as something he needs to worry about; he probably doesn't notice it at all. But because Alfred has chosen to live his life as a butler, dust is an issue for him; it's something he has to concern himself with. In Heidegger's terminology, being a butler is a project for Alfred, a way of living that determines not only how the world at hand appears to him, but also how he relates to his own future. Because Alfred has taken up this project, the clock *is* something that ought to be dusted immediately, dinner *is* something that should be prepared by the time Master Bruce comes home, and living as Batman's faithful assistant *is* what he plans to do for the rest of his life.

Thrown into Our Worlds

Like all of us, Alfred is always related to his own future in terms of the life he has chosen for himself, the projects he has taken on. Furthermore, this means he's also always related to his own past. At some point in his life, Alfred made a choice between the possibilities available to him and decided to become a butler. This is why Heidegger characterizes human existence as a "thrown-project." Finding ourselves always already "thrown" into a world, various concrete possibilities have always already presented themselves to us. For example, Alfred, as a young man, might have had the opportunity to become a professional actor or a career man in the British military. Becoming a butler was a choice he made from among the possibilities that he found available to him as a person thrown into that particular situation. Having made his choice of a life, he now relates to his own future in a way that is appropriate to (and determined by) that choice. It is in this sense that Heidegger makes the claim that human existence is temporally ecstatic ("ecstatic" being derived from a Greek term meaning "standing out"). Humans live as always outside of ourselves in time, projected toward the future so that we're always, in a sense, ahead of ourselves through the plans we make and, at the same time, thrown into our present from out of a particular past.

More important for our purpose, the temporally ecstatic way in which humans exist means for Heidegger that we fundamentally *are* our own possibilities. The possibilities we've chosen in the past determine the concrete possibilities that are available to us in the present and the way they appear to us, while our being projected into the future determines how we'll relate to those present possibilities. To continue our example, having at one time chosen to be a butler, Alfred now finds himself having the possibilities of either dusting the clock or starting dinner early. Because he wants to continue effectively serving Batman well into the future, Alfred will choose whichever of these possibilities he thinks will best bring about that future for himself.

Alternatively, we can imagine an Elseworlds story in which Alfred gets sick of faithful servitude and decides that he wants to spend the rest of his life in peace and quiet without having to worry about whether his employer is going to survive another night of crime fighting. In this case, the decision of whether to dust or cook first would cease to have any importance to Alfred ("Batman can dust his own clocks, for all I care!"), and other possibilities would present themselves instead (such as whether or not to move to a less dangerous city). Ultimately, Heidegger's point is that what and where a person is at any given instant is far less important to understanding human existence than that person's past and their plans for the future. A scientific study of Alfred can tell us that he's balding and has a mustache, but we can never understand who he really is without knowing the choices he's made for himself and the way he wants things to be tomorrow, next month, and ten years from now. For Heidegger, understanding those things demands an understanding of one's existence as the various possibilities that one has chosen and the possibilities that emerge from a projected future.

Death and the Dark Knight

So what is Heidegger's connection to Batman's mission? In a word: death. As even the most casual Bat-fan knows, Batman's experiences with death play a major role in making him who he is. Every retelling of Batman's origin includes the scene in which a very young Bruce Wayne witnesses the tragic murder of his parents, and we readers are to understand that this traumatic experience set him on the path to becoming Batman. But the comics (and films) don't tell us exactly how this experience shapes the way Batman chooses to lead his life. If we discard the notion of Batman as compulsively driven and obsessed with vengeance (as the editors at DC have promised to do), then what exactly is the impact on Bruce Wayne of witnessing his parents' murders? And just how does this experience lead him to take up his mission?

This is where Heidegger's analysis of human existence comes in. For Heidegger, human existence fundamentally consists of its own possibilities, and, of course, death would be the limit of those possibilities. But for Heidegger, the significance of death is not that it is a literal end to one's life, like a sort of end point on a line, but rather that it makes human beings aware of the fact that their own lives, their own possibilities, have a limit. That is, although we exist in a temporally ecstatic way, we are also temporally finite (limited), and what's more, we know it. As Heidegger would say, "Initially and for the most part," humans don't think about our own deaths; we find

ways to cover over death and avoid it. We busy ourselves with
our projects, with our entanglements in the things at hand,
and generally think of death as something that happens to
other people. Admitting to ourselves that "people die" is easy
enough, but there's something unnerving about thinking "*I* will
die." Heidegger terms the uncomfortable feeling of authentically confronting the certain possibility of one's own death
Angst, and although we fans are quite familiar with "angsty"
superhero comics, Heidegger has a very specific meaning for
this word.

In the experience of *Angst*, Heidegger argues that death
appears as what it really is: the possibility of my own impossibility. Once I die, I will no longer have my possibilities. After
death, all my choices will have been made already, and the
story of who I am will be complete. This is why Heidegger
claims that the authentic confrontation with death in *Angst*
individuates human existence. When I confront my own death,
I see that it is something that no one else can do for me, something I will have to face myself. This in turn casts my whole life
in a new light. Recognizing my death as the unavoidable end
to my own life shows me that my existence is mine and mine
alone. The completed story of my life will be the result of the
possibilities I chose for myself from out of the situation into
which I was thrown at birth. I alone will have been responsible for whoever I was. Beyond that, in *Angst*, the meanings
of all the ordinary things of the world slip away, such that
things in the world are no longer relevant at all. If we imagine
Alfred in *Angst*, the silver tray and grandfather clock would no
longer be things of concern to him. In the authentic relation to
his own death, such things would be, quite simply, nothing.

Why should this be the case? Because confronting my
own death puts all of my projects in question. Things show
themselves to us in terms of their relevance to our projects,
but in the consideration of one's life as a whole that *Angst*
brings about, our projects themselves appear to us as what they

really are: possibilities we have chosen for ourselves. In our average, everyday way of existing, people don't often deeply question the choices they have made for their lives. Alfred doesn't lie in bed every morning wondering if he has any real reason to get up because most of the time, he simply thinks of himself as being a butler, and butlers get up in the morning to do their jobs. However, in *Angst*, being a butler would appear as a choice Alfred has made for himself, and in showing itself as a possibility, being a butler would appear as something changeable. In other words, it's not written in stone that Alfred has to be a butler for the rest of his life; he could choose otherwise and begin a wholly different life. In short, *Angst* lets the world as it is fall away, bringing one's projects into question by showing them as possibilities, and allowing one the freedom to choose a life (and thus a world) for oneself.

I Shall Become a Bat

Mindful of his own mortality, Batman is able to maintain a single-minded determination about his mission, seeing his life and his world exclusively in terms of the singular project he's chosen for himself. Instead of being driven by guilt over his parents' death (an event he really had no control over) or by a violent need to exact vengeance for that traumatic loss from criminals who had nothing to do with it, perhaps the real impact of that fateful night was instilling in young Bruce Wayne an authentic understanding of his own life as finite and limited. If Heidegger's claims about our relation to death are right, then the consideration of his own death in *Angst* would have allowed Bruce to decide on a life for himself without any regard for the expectations of so-called normal society. Free to organize his entire existence around a mission of his own choosing, and limited only by the possibilities into which he finds himself thrown (which aren't very limiting when you're an heir to billions), an authentic recognition of his own inevitable death could have allowed Bruce Wayne to become Batman purely out of a sense of responsibility for his own existence.

To some extent, this Heideggerian interpretation of Batman is supported by the comics. The end of the first chapter of Frank Miller's *Batman: Year One* (1987) beautifully illustrates the idea of *Angst* as giving one the freedom to choose a life. Having completed his years of training abroad, Bruce Wayne returns to Gotham. Although he wants to somehow take a stand against the criminals and corruption in his city, he has yet to find the right means to accomplish his goal. After a botched attempt to help out an underage prostitute, Bruce sits alone in the dark, bleeding profusely, having an imaginary dialogue with his father. Although he realizes that his wounds are severe enough that he could die, he doesn't seem very concerned about them. Rather, he is concerned with the possibility that he may never find a way to do what he feels he should. He thinks to himself, "If I ring the bell, Alfred will come. He can stop the bleeding in time," but having lost patience with waiting for the right solution to appear to him, Bruce would rather die now than continue living a life that doesn't fulfill the expectations he has for himself.

Physically confronted with his own death and remembering the night his parents died, Bruce recounts all the possibilities he could take advantage of, if only he had a project to organize them: "I have wealth. The family manor rests above a huge cave that will be the perfect headquarters . . . even a butler with training in combat medicine." Yet none of that matters without a concrete project to take make use of it; as Bruce says, it's been eighteen years "since all sense," all meaning, left his life, and he's become absolutely desperate for a project that will once again give his world significance. Then, without warning, a bat crashes through the window, and everything falls into place. The possibility of a project that will give meaning to his life suddenly shows itself, making itself available for him to choose. At the moment when Bruce says to himself, "I shall become a bat," the whole of his new existence, his new world, comes into view, and from that point on, his every action will be determined from out of this one, authentic choice of a life.

Determinism and the Dark Knight

If we return now to the debate between free will and determinism in light of this example, it should be easy enough to see why neither of these categories can sufficiently encompass Heidegger's analysis of human freedom. In the first place, the free will–determinism distinction is grounded in the same subject-object dualism that Heidegger is so intent on critiquing and overcoming. Theories of free will rely on a notion of the human subject as radically disconnected from the "external" world, so that one's choices may be determined by nothing outside of oneself.[2]

On the other hand, psychological and scientific understandings of determinism interpret human existence in the same terms we apply to objects that can be present at hand, such that human choices are in no way exempt from the regime of cause and effect. As nothing more than moments in a great chain of causation, determinism treats human choices as a mere illusion of self-determination. As we have seen, Heidegger's thinking deeply complicates this simple, binary division between human existence and the world by reinterpreting the concept of "world" itself. When Bruce authentically confronts his own finitude in *Angst*, the world that had existed for him drifts away, leaving his choices radically undetermined.

Simultaneously, though, his choices are limited by the concrete possibilities that are available to him and that now appear to him as pure possibilities. Had the bat never crashed through the window, Bruce might never have had the idea to become Batman, yet at the same time, neither that event nor the death of his parents forces him to carry out his mission in the way that he does. Indeed, the experience of *Angst* lets all of his possibilities show themselves as they are. This means that the possibility of taking on responsibility for his own life appears right alongside the possibilities that would allow him to run away from that responsibility. The experience of death in *Angst* could always end with a flight from one's own finitude and the responsibility that it entails. Bruce could easily have buried his experience of *Angst* by living the hedonistic life expected of a billionaire playboy. And perhaps it is just this choice, this refusal to flee from himself, that makes Batman such a great hero. When he could have taken the easy way out and when nothing forced him to do otherwise, Bruce Wayne authentically took up the choice of his life as a whole. He chose to become Batman when nothing demanded that he must.

NOTES

1. Martin Heidegger, *Being and Time*, trans. Joan Stambaugh (Albany: SUNY Press, 1996); also see the articles in *The Cambridge Companion to Heidegger*, ed. Charles Guignon (Cambridge: Cambridge Univ. Press, 1993).

2. See, for example, the articles in *The Oxford Handbook of Free Will*, ed. Robert Kane (Oxford: Oxford Univ. Press, 2004).

PART SIX

FRIEND, FATHER, . . . RIVAL? THE MANY ROLES OF THE BAT

WHY BATMAN IS BETTER THAN SUPERMAN

Galen Foresman

Backstory: Bat-fans' Bane

A classic staple of discussion in the world of comics is the comparison of two great superheroes, and perhaps the most famous of all comparisons is that between Batman and Superman. Unfortunately, all too often Batman is summarily dismissed for lacking any superpowers, leaving Bat-fans crying foul. This chapter—like a great hero—comes to the aid of those Bat-fans by giving a brief introduction to value theory, specifically the notion of "better than."

Donning the Philosophical Persona

As shown in *Batman: Year One* (1987), Batman's first night out on the streets of Gotham ended disastrously. Bruce Wayne entered the fray unprepared. True, he did have years of martial arts training, but no matter what the movies show, if enough guys attack at once, all that training won't be enough. Bruce learned from that little adventure, and from it he developed his Batman persona. We can learn from that little adventure, too, by making sure we don't jump into a dispute with Super-fans without adopting a persona of our own.

Bruce knew that criminals were a superstitious and cowardly lot, and that the best way to catch them off guard—and ultimately be more effective—was to be scary. Childhood experience in a well (that would later become the Batcave), and a random run-in with a bat in his sitting room at home, convinced Bruce to don his famous cape and cowl.

In the realm of arguments and disputes, there is no better persona than the philosopher. It certainly isn't as scary as a man parading as a bat—in many cases philosophers are quite laughable—but philosophers are specially trained to argue. When you need to strike fear in an opponent, be like a bat—dark, elusive, and scary. But when you need to change a person's mind about something, be like a philosopher—careful, quizzical, and tenacious. More specifically, if you're trying to convince someone that something is "better than" another thing, then be like a value theorist.

Value theory is the area of philosophy that is primarily concerned with the study of value and evaluation. *Evaluation* is the process of determining how good or bad something is, and *value* is what makes that thing good. For example, we might suppose that "being cool" is one of the properties that makes something good. In a way, then, being cool is a sort of value to us. When we are evaluating something that's cool, like the Batmobile, then we count that value of being cool as one of the reasons the Batmobile is so good. Unfortunately, it isn't so obvious what values really are. "Coolness factor" is just an example of what values are like, but it isn't likely to be an actual candidate for real value.

Most of value theory is devoted to figuring out what values boil down to, and among other things, value theorists try to figure out what the difference is between something valuable and something that isn't valuable. Value theorists are also particularly interested in how something can be "better than" or "worse than" another thing. In our case, we want to be like value theorists, because we want to know what it is that makes Batman better than Superman.

Donning now our philosophical persona as value theorists, we can continue our quest. The first step is to prepare our utility belts with a little vocabulary that will help us on our way. When we say that Batman is better than Superman, we are making an *evaluative comparison*. Comparisons are pretty common in our everyday lives, but many of them are not necessarily evaluative. Sometimes we're just trying to explain how two things are alike or different without saying that one is better than the other. We'll call these *descriptive comparisons*. An example of a descriptive comparison could be noting that one car is black and another is blue. If our only aim is to explain how the two cars are different, then we aren't making an evaluative comparison.

An evaluative comparison relies on our evaluation of several things, and basically, evaluations tell us how good or how bad something is. Thus an evaluative comparison occurs when we take our evaluation of one thing and compare it with our evaluation of another thing. For example, if we evaluate the black car and determine that it is really good, and we evaluate the blue car and determine that it is really bad, then we can compare these evaluations and conclude that the black car is better than the blue car. In so doing, we will have made an evaluative comparison.

This vocabulary that we've added to our utility belt helps us describe our quest. The battle that rages between Bat-fans and Super-fans is a dispute over an evaluative comparison. Bat-fans think Batman is really good and Superman is not so good, and so they conclude that Batman is better than Superman. Bat-fans are just comparing their evaluations of these two superheroes. Whether their judgment is correct hinges crucially on whether their evaluations of these two great superheroes are correct. We can't, however, solve this puzzle without doing a little background detective work.

The Origin Story: How We Make Evaluative Comparisons

The evaluative comparison of Batman and Superman is much like any evaluative comparison we've made in our lives, and so there's something to learn by examining how we've made these evaluations in the past. For example, evaluative comparisons we once made as children do not always come out the same when we make the comparisons as adults. If we're honest with ourselves, when we Bat-fans were young and immature, we too may have really liked Superman and all his superpowers. What's more, we may have a difficult time explaining why we changed our minds. When Batman fights crime, we all know why he does it. We're all familiar with what Joe Chill did to his parents. Batman's origin story helps explain why he does what he does as an adult, and in similar fashion, we have origin stories, too. So let's take a moment to explore our own origin stories to see how it is that we came to make evaluative comparisons in the way that we do. In doing this, we may be able to put our finger on why it's so difficult to justify our evaluative comparison that Batman is better than Superman.

When many of us were young, evaluative comparisons of ice cream primarily revolved around the amount of ice cream we were going to get. In other words, the bigger the bowl of ice cream, the better it was, and between two bowls of ice cream, the bigger bowl was the best. We'll call this simplistic way of making evaluative comparisons the *quantitative* method. Quantitative evaluations are evaluations based on the amount or number of something there is. When we move to comparing those evaluations based solely on differences in amount or number, we are making quantitative evaluative comparisons.

As we grew up and became more sophisticated in our tastes, the mere amount of ice cream simply wasn't enough to persuade us. We began to prefer things like chocolate to vanilla, and so our evaluative comparisons took on new and more complicated aspects. Quantitative evaluations would take us only so far, because now we began to recognize that *qualitative* differences in things sometimes made smaller amounts better than larger amounts. Suppose you think chocolate is better than vanilla. If you had to evaluate and compare a bowl of chocolate ice cream to a bowl of vanilla ice cream, then the chocolate ice cream is probably going to be better to you. We'll call this sort of evaluative comparison a qualitative evaluative comparison.

Our evaluations and comparisons become the most difficult to make when we blend quantitative and qualitative aspects of things together. If, for example, you need to evaluate a large bowl of vanilla ice cream against a spoonful of chocolate, then you run into the difficult challenge of determining which bowl of ice cream is better than the other by mixing quantitative and qualitative evaluation. If you really hate vanilla, then no amount of it is going to be good to you. But what if you think vanilla ice cream is okay? Is a lot of okay-tasting ice cream really better than a spoonful that tastes really good?

By now I suspect most Super-fans have tired of reading about evaluation, comparison, and ice cream. Their origin stories still have them thinking quantitatively: more power is better. This explains why they've probably moved on to something that doesn't take as much intellectual fortitude. Bat-fans' efforts, on the other hand, have been rewarded by learning what makes the comparison of Batman to Superman so difficult. And if we've learned anything from Batman, it's that knowing and understanding the problem is essential to solving it. (This is why we think villains are so stupid for sharing their evil schemes with heroes once they've been captured.) We can sum up the problem like this: comparing Batman and

Superman is like comparing two bowls of ice cream that have many good qualities in various amounts. Knowing that it's sometimes hard to make a simple comparison of ice cream helps us to see it's exponentially more difficult to compare two great superheroes. But I am confident that Bat-fans are like their fearless (and smart) hero, and so they're up to the challenge. (Don't let me down!)

Lurking Villainy: Begging the Question

We've come a long way, Bat-fans, but before moving further into the heart of this debate, it will be useful to note an important error that people tend to make when evaluating and comparing. This error is the lurking villainy in most evaluative comparison disputes like those over Batman and Superman, and it is particularly important to take note of it so as to not employ it ourselves. The error I'm referring to is a general argumentative strategy called "begging the question." It's a subtle and fallacious—in other words, bogus—style of argument that can be employed in virtually any argument. It's relevant to the Batman and Superman dispute because it is commonly employed when we make lists of pros and cons to make difficult evaluative comparisons.

"Question-begging" is an abused term these days. We often hear people say things like "This begs the question" when what people really mean is "This *raises* the question." What philosophers mean when they say something begs the question is that an argument assumes the truth of the conclusion in its premises, whereas a good argument will support its conclusion with evidence or reasons that people can agree on apart from the conclusion.

For example, suppose you and I are arguing over whether or not vanilla is a better flavor than chocolate. I think vanilla is better than chocolate, and in order to convince you that I'm correct in thinking this, I formulate the following argument:

"Vanilla is better than chocolate, because vanilla is the best flavor in the world." The conclusion is that vanilla is better than chocolate, and the reasoning for this conclusion follows from the fact that vanilla is the best flavor in the world. When we examine this argument, we can see that if vanilla really is the best flavor in the world, then it has to be better than chocolate. The problem, however, is that if you don't think vanilla is better than chocolate, then you aren't going to be convinced by my reason that vanilla is the best flavor in the world. For vanilla to be the best flavor in the world, vanilla must be better than chocolate. Unfortunately, our original argument assumes that vanilla is the best flavor in the world and so it assumes that the conclusion is true as well. Therefore, it begs the question.

In the dispute over Batman and Superman, we run into the very same begging-the-question problem. In these arguments, Superman's amazing powers come up time and time again as the reason Superman is better than Batman. But just as in the chocolate and vanilla dispute, unless you already agree that superpowers make for the best superhero, then you aren't going to agree with the Super-fans' conclusion. For decades now, the Super-fans have been using this bogus argument to undermine Batman's primacy, and that's an insidious villainy we must put a stop to. (To the philosophy-mobile!)

As we all know, in stopping any villain, it is of supreme importance to avoid stooping to the level of the villain. In this particular case this means avoiding begging the question against Super-fans. To avoid the Super-fans' mistake and to help them see the error of their ways, we need to once again discover the source of their mistake. When we were exploring our origin story, we noticed that it is extremely difficult to justify an evaluative comparison when mixing quantitative and qualitative evaluations, which we're doing when we claim that Batman is better than Superman. One of the most common ways to overcome these difficulties is to list the pros and cons of the things you are comparing. It is, however, this very method of deciding between two possibly good options that causes us to beg the question.

When we make a list of pros and cons, we are making assumptions about what should count as a pro and a con. This means that you are not providing a reason for why something goes on the pro side of the list or the con side of the list. You are simply assuming that particular attributes are pros while others are cons. If you did something similar with Batman and Superman, your lists of pros and cons for each superhero would consist solely of the attributes the superheroes have that you assume are good and bad. Problematically, this provides fertile ground for begging the question in a dispute.

When a Super-fan makes their list of pros, it's probably chock-full of things like X-ray vision, superstrength, and the ability to fly. When the very same Super-fan makes a list for Batman, they probably cite Batman's *lack of* X-ray vision, super-strength, and the ability to fly as cons for Batman. But this is clearly an unjustified evaluation of Batman, since Batman does not need these features to be great. And it begs the question against Batman's greatness when Super-fans assume that Batman needs these features to be the better superhero.

Bat-fans, on the other hand, must also avoid making lists based on the assumption that only the features that Batman has are good. I hesitate to point out the number of times Bat-fans have said that Batman is better because he is smarter. While certainly true, it, too, runs the very same question-begging problem. What makes us Bat-fans think that being smart is so great? We need to have a good reason for thinking this that is independent of our evaluation of Batman, before we can use it as a reason to justify Batman's greatness. To empha-size the error that is being committed when Bat-fans assume this, let's take a look at a similar argument.

Suppose we made a list of pros and cons for Batman. Batman has a lot of cool gadgetry. He needs it. Which column would cool gadgetry go into, pro or con? I'd put it down as a pro, as I suspect many other Bat-fans would. But for what reason? Here is one reason we cannot use: Batman is great and so his gadgetry must be a pro. Of course, this would beg the question, since we are trying to figure out why Batman is so great. If you think about this argument, it would go like this: Batman is great because he has awesome gadgetry, and his awesome gadgetry is great because he's Batman, and Batman is great. This argument travels in a circle. To avoid begging the question, we need to straighten that circle out. To do this, we need to justify the greatness of Batman independently of how we already feel about Batman.

So here's the task for the Bat-fan: explain why Batman is better than Superman in such a way that doesn't already assume all the things about Batman are better than features possessed by Superman. If we think about how we got to this point in the discussion, we can see where some of the major errors in reasoning have occurred. In particular, think about making lists of pros and cons. Such lists start by assuming some things are good and some things are bad, even though they don't tell us why we think they're good and bad. To avoid begging the question when comparing Batman and Superman, we need to decide first what makes a superhero great and then see whether Batman or Superman has those features. In other words, figure out what sorts of things belong on the list of pros and cons before evaluating the individual superheroes.

Justice Restored: Superheroes and Bravery

No doubt the last section ended with a difficult task, but this is no time to despair. We have discovered a great weakness in these nefarious argumentative strategies, and now it's time to bring them to justice. To accomplish this difficult task, we need to decide on some essential features of a superhero. We can then use these essential features to make a list of pros and cons for both Batman and Superman that doesn't beg the question in favor of one or the other. These lists will, however, tell us who turns out to be the best superhero of the two.

Our list of essential features will have to be brief, since it would take an entire book to cover the issue thoroughly. The motivation is for you to get an idea of how to start thinking about solving this comparison between Batman and Superman. I will offer one possible argument. It is not watertight, but it may kick off a more fruitful debate about what it is to be a great superhero, and why Batman better fits that mold than Superman.

Before diving into the argument—because we know that usually turns out badly—here's my plan of attack. Good superheroes must be heroic, and to be heroic a person must be courageous or brave. Batman is more courageous and brave than Superman, and so he is more heroic. The more heroic a superhero, the better that superhero is, and since Batman is more heroic than Superman, we can conclude that Batman is a better superhero than Superman. To see how this argument works, let's make up a superhero to see how he compares to these greats.

Imagine, for a moment, a superhero who has the ability to make socks appear on people's feet by clapping his hands. And these socks are extremely comfortable and durable. Every time this superhero does this, however, he gets a small headache. He likes to help people, and so he often endures the headache to provide socks for hundreds of thousands of people around the globe. He can do something that ordinary people cannot do, and he makes a personal sacrifice to help people every time he endures his headaches. This is a superhero, and we, of course, are interested in determining how great this "Argyled Avenger" really is.

I've suggested that one thing that separates great superheroes from the not-so-great is bravery. There are, of course, other factors like the greatness of their goals, and for this argument we'll assume that Batman and Superman are basically tied on that score. The Argyled Avenger is a superhero as well, but he's not so great since his heroism comes from putting socks on people's feet at the cost of suffering a small headache. If he were somehow risking his life to do this great service, then we'd probably speak more highly of him as a superhero, even though his goals are still not as lofty as those of Batman and Superman. Bravery, then, is fundamental to evaluating a superhero. If a superhero is not all that brave, then he is not all that great.

What does it take to be brave or courageous? Enduring a headache doesn't seem to be very brave, even if it is making a sacrifice to help others. But why is it that enduring a headache doesn't seem all that brave? One reason is that we don't think that enduring pain automatically qualifies as doing something dangerous, and we do think that doing dangerous things can mean a person is brave. Going to work can give most people a headache, but we aren't going to be handing out certificates of valor to those with good attendance. On the other hand, when someone confronts something dangerous to help others, then we usually say that person is brave.

It's also important that the heroic person knows that what they're doing is dangerous in order for us to think of them as brave and courageous. For example, there is a big difference between the person who runs into a burning building to save children when he knows it could collapse at any moment, and the person who runs in thinking that the fire is small and unlikely to harm them. A brave person understands what he's doing is dangerous and confronts it anyway.

Return now to Batman and Superman. They both have the lofty goals of saving lives and maintaining justice, but only one of them faces danger on a regular basis and knows it. Only one of them is consistently brave and courageous, while the other is a lot like the Argyled Avenger. (Three guesses as to which one . . .)

Batman has no superpowers. He is not bulletproof. He cannot fly. He cannot look through walls to see what's coming.

What's more, he is smart enough to know that he is constantly putting himself in danger to help others. So Batman is braver and more courageous than Superman. In other words, Batman takes bigger risks to help people than Superman. In this respect, Batman is better than Superman, which means that on the list of pros and cons, Batman is a better superhero than Superman on a very important score.

To our credit, we came to this conclusion without begging the question against Superman. We didn't have to stoop to the Super-fans' level. Our goal was accomplished by thinking about what makes superheroes great before we applied our criteria to our evaluation, and our comic relief—the Argyled Avenger—was a useful foil for helping us in the evaluation of all superheroes. (See—he was useful after all!)

To Be Continued . . .

This does not, of course, end the debate. I suspect some Super-fans who got bored learning how to reason fairly opted to just skip to the end of this chapter to see the conclusion, and in so doing have had time to think of many objections to my claims about Superman's bravery. It's true that Superman is, on occasion, brave, and it's also true that on occasion Batman is not brave. After all, sometimes his gadgetry stops bullets or helps him fly, but the simple quantitative comparison here is that more often than not, Batman is more heroic than Superman. The great irony in all this is that the things so many Super-fans like about Superman, his superpowers, are the very things that prevent him from being better than Batman. After all, isn't Superman at his most heroic when kryptonite or magic is around? It's just too bad for Super-fans that it isn't around more often![1]

NOTE

1. I'd like to give a special thanks to Chris Metivier and John Ridgway for inspiring critical thoughts in this chapter.

WORLD'S FINEST . . . FRIENDS? BATMAN, SUPERMAN, AND THE NATURE OF FRIENDSHIP

Daniel P. Malloy

No one would choose to live without friends even if he had all other goods.

—Aristotle, *Nicomachean Ethics*

I teach you not the neighbor, but the friend. The friend should be the festival of the earth to you and an anticipation of the overman.

—Nietzsche, *Thus Spoke Zarathustra*

World's Finest

There is no superhero duo more emblematic of the extremes in comics than Batman and Superman, the world's finest team. One is the pinnacle of human perfection and will, an ordinary man who made an extraordinary promise the night his parents were murdered before his eyes and who has dedicated every waking moment since to fulfilling it. The other is the last son of a dying race, sent out in an act of desperation, adopted by a childless farm couple, raised as their own with their traditional values. But he was blessed by his alien DNA with powers and abilities far beyond those of mortal men.

Beyond the differences in their origins and abilities, there are also fundamental differences in their methods. Just compare their costumes: Batman's dark, cowled figure stands in stark contrast to Superman's maskless, bright uniform. Superman inspires hope and trust, while Batman relies on fear and superstition. It is extraordinary that such extremes can exist in a single universe, but there is something even more amazing about these two remarkable beings—their friendship.

What makes their friendship especially noteworthy is that Batman and Superman, who agree on very little, disagree even on the nature of friendship itself. At first this may sound strange. Everyone knows what friendship is, right? And everyone agrees about its nature, right? Wrong, on both counts. Philosophers have been debating the nature of friendship since Plato, and they still haven't been able to agree on it. When you think about it, it's obvious that there are various degrees and kinds of friendship. You have a certain sort of friendship with the neighbor you say hello to every morning, but the friendship you share with the people you grew up with is different from that, in both degree and kind.

Similarly, with Batman and Superman, each calls the other his friend, but each means something entirely different when he says that. Just consider the other people they associate with. Superman has Lois Lane, both his friend and his wife; his pal Jimmy Olsen; and many of the other heroes in the DC Universe. Batman, on the other hand, has no other friends. To be sure, he has acquaintances and comrades-in-arms—Alfred, Robin, Nightwing, Oracle, Huntress, and so on. The "Bat-Family," as Batman's inner circle has been called, is indeed large. But, with the possible exception of Catwoman (whose relationship with Batman is never clear), none of them are friends. They are an odd combination of family members and soldiers in his war, but only Superman is a true friend in Batman's world.

While Superman and Batman are definitely friends, their friendships with one another have different meanings. Superman's concept of friendship can be traced to the philosopher Aristotle (384–322 BCE), while Batman's concept has its origins in a very different philosopher, Nietzsche (1844–1900).

That Superman—What a Guy!

So is Superman a superfriend? It's easy to see that ol' Kal-El is quite the friendly guy. In either his street duds or his world-saving red and blues, Superman is the kind of guy you want to have around. He may be a little naïve and old-fashioned for some, but let's face it: can you think of anyone better to turn to when you need a helping hand?

How great would it be to have Superman as a friend? Can you think of anyone you'd rather have to help you move? He'd be finished in six seconds, with a coffee break. Or how about a cookout? Heat vision to light the grill, microscopic vision to make sure all the nasty little things in the meat are dead, superbreath to keep the cold drinks cold? He's a one-man barbecue! And those are just his physical attributes; let's not forget the personal attributes of Superman. It's not for nothing that he's been called the world's oldest Boy Scout—he's trustworthy, loyal, helpful, courteous, kind, cheerful, and brave. Sure, he may not be cool, or particularly fun, but he's reliable and good-natured, and every group of friends needs at least one doormat. It doesn't hurt to have a superpowered, demigod-like doormat.

So it's easy to see why anyone would want to have Superman as a friend. But this review of Superman's personality traits does raise a question—given his overall friendliness and his positive, optimistic attitude toward the world and everyone in it, why does a ray of sunshine like Superman choose to pal around with Batman, the original Captain Bring-Down? Think about it: Batman's greatest nemesis is the embodiment of levity (a dark and twisted levity, it's true), the Clown Prince of Crime himself, the Joker. At one point, Superman, with a kryptonite bullet lodged near his heart, asks Batman to do them both a favor and buy a sense of humor.[1] The only time Batman has any fun is when he's hurting people—people who deserve it, that is. This duo is like the captain of the football team hanging out with the creepy Goth kid. So why does Superman count Batman as a friend, never mind a close friend?

On the one hand, we could say that it's just because of Superman's general friendliness. This is the kind of guy who would try to make friends with a shark—and probably succeed. But there's something more going on in his relationship with Batman. Big Blue isn't just being friendly; he genuinely trusts Batman. He even likes him, proving that he truly is a super man—even Batman's nearest and dearest don't particularly like him. But what's important here is the trust factor. Superman famously can only be harmed by one substance: kryptonite. And he has a small sample of kryptonite shaped as a ring—a ring he entrusted to Batman.

So why is Superman so close to Batman? Why trust him above everyone else? Why not leave the ring with Aquaman? Or Wonder Woman? The answer goes back to Superman's understanding of friendship, and why he is closer to Batman than anyone else in the superhero community.

Superman the Aristotelian

Philosophically, Superman's understanding of friendship comes closest to Aristotle's conception of the highest type of friendship. Friendship plays a key role in Aristotle's ethical theory.[2]

Naturally, we have neither the time nor the space to go into all the details of Aristotle's theory of friendship. Happily, we don't need to, because the word that is translated as "friendship" from Aristotle's Greek has a much broader meaning. That word is *philia*, and it is used by Aristotle to indicate a broader range of relationships than "friendship," which is why we can focus solely on Aristotle's highest type of friendship.

In the books of the *Nicomachean Ethics* that deal with *philia*, Aristotle discusses virtually every type of human relationship, from familial bonds to the relationship between a buyer and a seller. Most of these relationships obviously have little or nothing to do with "friendship" as we understand the term. Aristotle does, however, discuss at length something akin to the modern understanding of friendship. Bear in mind that Aristotle's theory is proposed as part of an overall ethical theory. Given that, it should come as no surprise that the highest friendship, and the type most deserving of the name, is the friendship between two good men.

There are a few reasons for this. First, only good people can love each other purely and simply for who they are—for their characters. For this same reason, this type of friendship lasts the longest. A true friend loves the character of his friend—something that changes very little over time. Other friends, friends for pleasure or for utility, are friends only for as long as they can get pleasure or utility from one another. Many of us have experienced these types of friendship—the girl down the block you played with only because she had the coolest toys, the guy in college you talked to only because he had a car, that kind of thing. These friendships, of course, tend to be short-lived. The highest type of friendship not only tends to last longer, it encourages us to be better.

Superman's friendships tend to be of the highest types. He simply does not have shady friends. Lois Lane, Jimmy Olsen, Perry White—they're all good people. And Superman's superhuman friends are all heroes, and they all look up to him. Superman once confessed to the Flash that he finds all the adulation from younger heroes humbling, and he isn't sure he can live up to his reputation.[3] (Interestingly, later in the same story, Supes goes toe-to-toe with an angel!)

This also applies to Superman's friendship with Batman. Batman may be dark, and he may employ methods based on fear, but underneath it all, he is a good man in Superman's mind. Of all of Superman's friends, Batman is easily the most calculating and ruthless. Should the need arise, he may be the only one willing to use the kryptonite ring against Superman. But when would the need arise? The kryptonite ring is to be used, and has been used, in the eventuality that Superman himself goes rogue. So, in a certain sense, the ring is a testament to this aspect of their friendship—it exists to keep Superman a good person.

But that isn't enough to explain the close bond between Big Blue and the Dark Knight. For that explanation we must turn to Aristotle, who tells us that your friend is another self. This means, among other things, that you want the same things for your friend that you want for yourself. But it also means that your friend is a kind of mirror. Now, Superman has lots of mirrors in this sense, but none so good as Batman. Why? For all of their differences, Batman and Superman share the same morals, broadly speaking. Also, Batman and Superman are both pinnacles of achievement. Of all the heroes in the DC Universe, Batman is one of the few who weren't inspired by Superman. As such, he, unlike other superheroes, can stand on equal footing with Superman. Equality, after all, is central to this highest type of friendship. Other heroes are not really equal to Superman. Too many of them follow his lead. Aristotle says that friendship of a type is possible between unequals, but it can never be the highest friendship.

Don't think so? Let's suppose you have a rich man and a poor man who share common interests, values, and goals. Can they be friends? Our egalitarian consciences will want to scream "Yes, of course they can." But they can't, not really.

Their concerns are too different, and the friendship will rapidly deteriorate. The same is true, although in a less dramatic way, in Superman's relationships with other heroes. He is their hero, and as such, is not allowed to fail. This is dramatized when Superman and Batman reveal their secret identities to fellow members of the Justice League of America—one of them announces that he didn't think Superman even had another identity![4] After all, how could Superman be just a man?

What Kind of Friend Is Batman—or Bruce Wayne?

So we've seen what kind of friend Superman is. What about Batman? In asking this question, we face a problem that we didn't have to deal with in the discussion of Superman: the question of identity. Because, while there is some distance between the personalities of Superman and Clark Kent, it isn't much: they have the same values, drives, and so on. The only real difference is that Superman displays more grace and confidence—oh, and superpowers. But between Batman and his alter ego, Bruce Wayne, the differences are pronounced. We won't go very far into this question of identity, but we should note the differences between the two faces of the Batman, because you might want one of them as a friend and not the other.

Bruce Wayne would make an excellent friend in a number of ways. The man's got more money than God, throws a great party, loves sharing the wealth, and has connections that world leaders would kill for. Never mind the fact that he's smooth, sophisticated, and handsome. Who wouldn't want to count Bruce as a friend? Sure, Superman's a one-man barbecue—but Bruce can supply the meat and the kinds of guests you wouldn't mind spending some time with. Of course, you would never be his "close" friend; he's too flighty for that. But if you're looking for a friendship of utility or pleasure, you would be hard-pressed to do better than Mr. Wayne.

The Batman, on the other hand, is not nearly so flighty as his alter ego. If you could get close to him, you would find a loyal friend. On the other hand, unlike his alter ego, Batman is not a good friend for pleasure or utility. He's not exactly a party guy or a people person. How much fun can you have with a guy whose primary activity is brooding and who gives demons nightmares? The only time he smiles is when he's inflicting pain or planning to inflict pain. And those are just the surface problems! When it comes to the idea of a friendship of utility with the Dark Knight, there is one major drawback: he's smarter than you, and he has plans of his own. Batman is driven and, in some ways, utterly Machiavellian in his war on crime. He manipulates everyone around him, and no one ever knows exactly what's going on in his head.

There have been several excellent storylines in recent years exploring this aspect of the Batman. First, in the JLA trade paperback *Tower of Babel* (2001), it was revealed that Batman has developed plans to neutralize his superpowered teammates in the Justice League. His "friends," as it were. Would you like a friend secretly scheming to neutralize you? In another storyline, a crossover of the Batman-related comics titled "Bruce Wayne: Fugitive," Batman abandoned the identity of Bruce Wayne as well as his inner circle, because he felt they had become hindrances to his work.[5] Just like that, he turned his back on the closest thing he's had to a family since his parents were murdered. Finally, in the lead-up to DC's recent *Infinite Crisis* storyline, it was revealed that Batman had developed and deployed a satellite, Brother Eye, to spy on all of Earth's meta-humans, including his fellow heroes.[6] In each case, the people who were closest to Batman, who counted him among their friends, discovered that they had been manipulated or betrayed (or both).

Through all of this, however, Batman has continued to count Superman as his friend. For instance, after his countermeasures to the Justice League were stolen and used by Ra's al Ghul, Batman was voted out of the League—with Superman casting the deciding vote. Batman didn't mind the other Leaguers voting against him, even Plastic Man (whom Batman brought into the League), but Superman's vote felt like a betrayal. What does that mean? It certainly means something different and something more than it does in Superman's case, because Batman does not make friends easily, and he does not trust easily. Like Superman, Batman has a close circle, but they are not his friends. He associates with superheroes, but they are not friends.

Superman's vote was a betrayal of their friendship, while the votes of Plastic Man, Wonder Woman, and Aquaman were not, because the latter three are not Batman's friends. Why not? What does Batman share with Superman that he doesn't with other superheroes? Most important for us, Batman considers Superman his equal. This is key in both Superman's and Batman's conceptions of friendship, but they have different ideas of equality. Superman's notion of equality is something akin to moral equality. All of us, by virtue of being moral agents, are the equal of Superman and, therefore, potential friends. To Batman, on the other hand, being a moral agent does not qualify a person as his equal. If it did, then all the members of his inner circle could be his friends, rather than the bizarre mix of family members and aides-de-camp that they are, as could his fellow Justice Leaguers. Superman is Batman's friend because Batman sees him as an equal, not in terms of being a moral agent, but in terms of his abilities and character. Superman's nigh-incalculable power makes him the equal of Batman, with his ingenuity and drive. Equality in Batman's friendships means an equality of power. In keeping with his aristocratic heritage and upbringing, not all people are created equal in the Batman's mind.

Batman the Nietzschean

To understand Batman's friendship with Superman, we have to turn to a different philosopher.[7] Nietzsche's conception of friendship is a bit harder to explain than Aristotle's, in large part because it has to be pieced together from some passing comments. However, the general connection between Batman and Nietzsche has been made before, that Batman represents the *Übermensch*, or "overman."[8] And there is a connection between the overman and Nietzsche's concept of friendship. In *Thus Spoke Zarathustra* Nietzsche writes, "In your friend you shall love the overman as your cause."[9] Interestingly enough, in early translations of Nietzsche, *Übermensch* is often rendered as "superman." Superman represents to Batman something that humans could be, not in terms of his powers and abilities, obviously, but in terms of his values and virtues. In truth, Superman is something that Batman would like to be, but can't.

This is not to imply that Batman wants to be Superman—not in every aspect, at least. Batman doesn't want powers. In fact, during one adventure his consciousness was placed in Superman's body. He described the experience as exhilarating and dangerous—the temptation, he said, was not to rely on his wits, and to fall back on the sheer power.[10] So, unlike everyone else on the planet, Batman doesn't want Superman's powers. Instead, Batman would like to mimic his friend in terms of his character. Batman wishes he could be as trusting and optimistic as Superman is. It's not the "super" bit that Batman wants, but the "man." For Batman, Superman serves as a living monument of what a man can be.

Think about it like this: Superman is a demigod trying to earn people's trust. As such, in his dealings with the public, he has to downplay his distance from them. Therefore, he acts like the Boy Scout, and everyone (with a few notable exceptions) loves him. Batman, on the other hand, is an ordinary human trying to do extraordinary things. He has to create a myth around himself that serves as part of his armor. We all know the famous line "Criminals are a superstitious and cowardly lot." But in order to use that superstition and cowardice against the criminal element, Batman must likewise distance himself from the citizens he protects. It's not enough for criminals to find Batman mysterious—everyone has to, or the jig is up. Naturally, this creates a lonely, isolated life that is in large part self-imposed.

This monumental appreciation does not go just one way, though. So far, what we have is a kind of familiar hero worship—the kind of relationship that Superman has with most of the other superheroes in the DC Universe. In order for their relationship to be a friendship, in Nietzsche's sense, there must be reciprocity and equality. For instance, Superman is an ideal for Batman, but at the same time, Batman believes that Superman has a great deal to learn. Why? For all of his powers and virtues, Kal-El is far from perfect—far from being Nietzsche's *Übermensch*. Big Blue's powers make him vulnerable—precisely insofar as he believes himself to be invulnerable. He forgets—despite his "death"—that he is still mortal, and also that his rosy image of human beings is entirely inaccurate. It is Batman's contribution to their friendship to try to teach Superman all of the lessons that his parents' killer, his years of training, and his complete awareness of his own and others' vulnerabilities have taught him so harshly. Batman is a hard teacher, as Nightwing, Robin, and Oracle can attest, and he does his best teaching in combat—never is he a friend to Superman as well as when these two come to blows.

When Friends Fall Out: Batman versus Superman

The differences in how these two pillars of the DC Universe approach their friendship become most clear when their friendship is stretched and strained. Fights aren't pleasant to begin with, and then there's the added factor of fighting a friend. But as most of us learn sooner or later, we can't always avoid unpleasant situations. Neither, it seems, can superheroes, because Batman and Superman always find themselves pitted against each other.

It's a perennial game among geeks of every stripe to ask who would win in a fight between X and Y. What if Spider-Man fought Darth Vader? What if He-Man took on the Hulk? Who would win between Galactus and the Anti-Monitor? One of the oldest of these arguments is what if Batman fought Superman—who would win? The commonsense answer is Superman. Superhuman strength, speed, and senses, flight, heat vision, X-ray vision, and superbreath? No contest, right? Wrong. Batman wins. Hands down. Every time. Why? Because he's Batman. He's ruthless, he's intelligent, and he's always prepared. Oh, and he has access to kryptonite. Every time Big Blue and the Dark Knight go toe to toe, Batman wins.

In large part, Batman's string of upsets against Superman is due to the way that the two of them approach the fight and each other. Superman views Batman as a friend in a conventional sense. He trusts Batman and believes (incorrectly) that he would never harm a friend. As Batman himself once described their differences, "Deep down, Clark's essentially a good person. And deep down, I'm *not*."[11] Superman approaches confrontations with the Dark Knight with kid gloves. He pulls punches, leaves himself open. He expects Batman to fight honorably, which he does to an extent. More important, Superman understands what he could do to Batman if he wanted to. The power he wields makes it all the more important for him to restrain himself. So even in the heat of battle, he doesn't use every advantage against Batman. He doesn't use his speed or ability to fly; he tries not to use his heat vision or his arctic breath. Essentially, Superman wants to come as close to fighting fair as he can.

That's why he loses—Batman doesn't fight fair. He's not in the same fight as Superman. He knows very well that Superman has all the advantages in a fair fight—so why bother fighting fair? In all of their battles, whether in Gotham or Metropolis or the depths of space, Batman uses the environment to his advantage. Sometimes that means using the city's entire power grid to stun Big Blue, as he did in *Hush*. (That's right: to *stun* him. Absorbing enough electricity to power one New York–sized city won't hurt Superman, but it will give him pause.) Sometimes that means setting things up well in advance—things like hunter missiles activated by X-ray vision, or charges that will drop ninety tons of rock onto Superman on cue. Any advantage, however small, is worth using.

That also means taking advantage of Superman's weaknesses. That's right: weakness*es* (plural). The obvious one, and one that Batman always uses, is kryptonite. But Superman has another weakness stemming from the power difference between himself and Batman—or, really, himself and everyone else. In Superman's mind, he's so much more powerful than . . . well, almost everybody, that he has to be careful not to cause permanent damage. Batman may be the most dangerous man on the planet, as Supes once called him, but he's still just flesh and bone, like all the rest. From Batman's perspective, Superman is cocky and arrogant—and foolishly underestimates his opponent. His reliance on his powers means that he has never learned to think strategically—an art that the Dark Knight had to master long ago.

Perhaps the best way to explain how Batman approaches Superman is by thinking about the term "respect." Respect has any number of meanings, many of them morally important. For instance, one can speak of the sort of respect that every human being owes every other by virtue of the fact that both are moral agents. Then there are the kinds of respect reserved for friends, for colleagues, and for those whose example one would like to follow. These are all a part of how Batman deals with Big Blue. But another kind of respect also comes into play—the respect that one owes a rival. This is a key difference between Batman and Superman: Supes doesn't view Batman as a rival, but Batman does. They are in competition, whether actively or not. Thus, when they are pitted against one another, as occasionally happens, Batman is prepared for it.

BSFs: Best Superfriends Forever?

What lessons can we draw from the friendship of Batman and Superman? One that springs to mind, and is perhaps somewhat trite, is that fights do not have to end friendships. But most of us know this by the age of six, so let's move on to something a bit more important: fundamental disagreements, even about the nature of friendship itself, don't have to end friendships. Even the inability to understand one another is not an obstacle to friendship. Superman knows that he will never fully understand what drives his darkest friend, just as Batman acknowledges (with some frustration) that he will never get Superman's apparent naiveté. They know that they view the world, and each other, in incompatible ways, but that does not destroy their friendship—it makes it and them stronger. The differences and misunderstandings between the Caped Crusader and the world's oldest Boy Scout strengthen their friendship by providing something for them to work through. Certainly this process is aided by the common ground they share: their common goals, and distinct methods, keep the world's finest friends linked to one another—protecting and correcting each other. These differences, along with their desire and ability to work together in spite of them, make each of our heroes all that much better at what they do.

NOTES

1. *Superman/Batman* #1 (August 2003).

2. He spends fully a fifth of his *Nicomachean Ethics* discussing the types and attributes of friendship. Aristotle, *Nicomachean Ethics*, trans. Terence Irwin (Indianapolis: Hackett, 1999), 119–153.

3. *JLA* #7 (July 1997).

4. *JLA* #48 (January 2001).

5. *Bruce Wayne: Fugitive*, vols. 1–3 (2002–2003).

6. *The OMAC Project* (2005).

7. For an excellent analysis of Batman's relationship from an Aristotelian point of view, and to see why the highest type of friendship is not possible for Batman, see

Matt Morris, "Batman and Friends: Aristotle and the Dark Knight's Inner Circle," *Superheroes and Philosophy*, ed. Tom Morris and Matt Morris (Chicago: Open Court Press, 2005) 102–117.

8. C. K. Robertson, "The True *Übermensch*: Batman as Humanistic Myth," in *The Gospel According to Superheroes*, ed. B. J. Oropeza (New York: Peter Lang, 2005).

9. Friedrich Nietzsche, *Thus Spoke Zarathustra*, trans. Walter Kaufmann (New York: Penguin, 1978), 62.

10. *JLA: Foreign Bodies* (November 2000).

11. *Batman: Hush*, vol. 1 (2004).

LEAVING THE SHADOW OF THE BAT: ARISTOTLE, KANT, AND DICK GRAYSON ON MORAL EDUCATION

Carsten Fogh Nielsen

A Superhero without Superpowers

Batman is a superhero without superpowers. He's a very different character from, for instance, Superman, whose powers and abilities exceed and surpass those of any mere mortal. No amount of training or preparation could ever turn a human being into Superman.

But no supernatural or highly implausible scientific gimmicks are needed for someone to acquire Batman's powers and abilities. This may be the reason Batman has inspired and attracted a number of pupils and apprentices: Nightwing, Robin (or Robins), Oracle, and Huntress, to mention but a few. For various reasons these characters have all devoted their lives to the continuing fight against crime, and they have all chosen Batman as their mentor. Why? Because Batman's powers, as opposed to Superman's, Wonder Woman's, or Spider-Man's, are recognizably *human* powers. What Batman is, what he has become, is not the result of an unexplained natural phenomenon or a mysterious, scientific accident. Batman's "powers" are the result of a dedicated (and arguably obsessive) human pursuit of physical, mental, and moral perfection. It may be far-fetched, but it is possible, at least in principle, that an ordinary human being, by devoting his or her life to a program of relentless exercise and study, could attain the same level of physical, mental, and moral excellence as Batman.

Aristotle and Learning-by-Doing

The idea that you can learn to be a good or virtuous human being by emulating or imitating a morally exemplary person is a very old idea. The Greek philosopher Aristotle (384–322 BCE) argued for precisely this idea almost 2,500 years ago in his book the *Nicomachean Ethics*. Aristotle asked a very basic and very simple question: How do we become good human beings? His answer was equally simple: We become good human beings in the same way that we become good at most other things, namely through practice and repetition. As he wrote, "Anything that we have to learn to do we learn by the actual doing of it: people become builders by building and instrumentalists by playing instruments. Similarly we become just by performing just acts, temperate by performing temperate ones, brave by performing brave ones."[1]

At first glance this might seem mere common sense. How else could we learn anything except by actually doing it, or at least attempting to do it? It is how we learn to do math, drive a car, throw a Batarang, and so on. But there seems to be a problem with Aristotle's idea. It seems easy enough to distinguish and recognize the activities and actions involved in, say, building a house or playing an instrument, but how do we know which acts are just, temperate, and brave? How do we determine whether any particular action embodies the virtues that we are trying to acquire and develop?

Luckily Aristotle had an answer to this problem: if we want to know what it means to be just or temperate or brave, we should study those persons to whom we attribute these virtues.[2] A just person, after all, is a person who regularly and reliably performs just actions; a temperate person is a person who can be relied on to not overindulge; and a brave person is a person who faces dangers without backing down. So, if we want to learn about justice, temperance, or bravery, we should look to those morally exemplary persons who we think actually *are* just, temperate, or brave.

However, if we want to be just, temperate, or brave, we should not merely study the actions of people who are just, temperate, and brave. We should also try to imitate the actions of such people, in the hope that we might in the process acquire their admirable moral qualities or virtues. If we want to become brave, we should perform actions similar to those a brave man would perform; if we want to become temperate, we should perform actions similar to those a temperate man would perform; and so on.

Is Batman a Morally Exemplary Human Being?

Consider the relationship between Batman and Robin. Batman not only teaches Robin certain particular skills, like how to use the Batarang or the best way to disarm a robber. By his very actions Batman also provides Robin with certain moral standards and norms; for example, the idea that criminals should be pursued relentlessly, that dangers should be faced without flinching, and that one should attempt to make the world a better place. By following the example set by Batman, by attempting to act as Batman acts, Robin gradually acquires not only certain practical skills and abilities, but also a moral outlook and a number of virtues (like courage and a sense of justice) related to this outlook.

Batman thus seems to be a good example of what Aristotle had in mind when he suggested that we look to the virtuous person for guidance about how to become morally better persons. In Gotham City, in the DC Universe in general, and even in our own mundane reality, many people regard Batman as a morally exemplary human being. And, it would seem, with good reason: Batman is without a doubt courageous and intelligent. He has a strong sense of justice, is capable of keeping his head cool even in the midst of battle, and is willing to sacrifice his own life and happiness to make the world a better place. These all appear to be desirable and valuable qualities, which we would like more people to possess. So, following Aristotle's suggestion, we should all perhaps attempt to be more like Batman, to act as he would act, in the hope that we can gradually acquire some of the virtues he has. Nightwing, Robin, Oracle, and the other masked heroes who have chosen Batman as the ideal by which to model and structure their lives thus seem to be following sound Aristotelian advice. They have chosen to emulate the actions and behavior of a morally exemplary person in order to acquire and develop the morally desirable qualities he seems to possess.[3]

Authority Shmauthority!

There are several problems with Aristotle's account, however. He may very well be correct that we acquire our very first understanding of right and wrong by following the example of people we regard as morally exemplary. In practice, the people whom children regard as morally exemplary will, more often than not, be people in a position of authority—their parents, their teachers, and so on. So it's not surprising that Robin regards Batman as a person worth following and imitating. Both the first and the second Robins, Dick Grayson and Jason Todd, regard Batman as a kind of father figure. Bruce Wayne took Dick Grayson in as his legal ward after his parents were killed, and he adopted Jason Todd after having surprised him trying to steal the tires off the Batmobile.[4]

But people should not be regarded as morally exemplary persons merely because they are in positions of authority; they should be regarded as morally exemplary because they *are* morally exemplary. Batman should not be considered a person who embodies many valuable virtues simply because he is Batman, but because he actually *embodies* these virtues. And children should choose to admire and emulate people who actually *are* morally admirable, not simply people who happen to be authority figures. Parents and teachers are not necessarily morally admirable persons, and the fact that children often admire and imitate their parents does not mean that their parents are, in fact, worth admiring and imitating. Just imagine what would have happened if the Joker, not Batman, had taken in Dick Grayson.

Let's Call This the "Gordon-Yindel Disagreement"

So how do we know that the people we *regard* as morally virtuous actually *are* morally virtuous? Most of the people in Gotham City, as well as most of us here in the real world, may very well think that Batman is courageous, intelligent, just, strong, and so on. But not everyone thinks so. Some people believe that Batman is a dangerous vigilante, whose deliberate disrespect for the law constitutes a far greater threat to society than do the actions of criminals he puts behind bars.

The question of whether Batman is a hero or a villain is a very important theme in Frank Miller's *The Dark Knight Returns* (1986).[5] When James Gordon resigns as police commissioner of Gotham City, his last request is to ask his successor, Ellen Yindel, to take note of, and learn from, Batman. But instead, Yindel's very first action as the new head of the police department is to denounce Batman as a masked vigilante and to sign a warrant for his immediate arrest. Yindel later regrets this decision, and toward the end of *The Dark Knight Returns* she actually seems to support Batman's actions. But her initial reaction, and one shared by many of the characters appearing in Miller's tale, is a clear rejection of the very idea of Batman's being a morally laudable person.

The disagreement about Batman's moral status reveals that merely *regarding* someone as morally virtuous and worth emulating does not mean that they actually *are* morally virtuous and worth emulating. But how should we decide whether someone actually is morally virtuous? We cannot simply rely on popular opinion or the advice of others, since popular opinion can be divided and people can disagree. Both James Gordon and Ellen Yindel are highly intelligent people who live in the same country, indeed the same city, and who share many of the same moral beliefs and values. And yet they disagree strongly about Batman's moral status. Both Gordon and Yindel cannot be right at the same time, so how do we decide who *is* right? And, more important, if we have no clear and unanimous conception of who is, and who is not, morally virtuous, then how do we go about becoming morally better persons? Aristotle's notion of moral education seems to be in trouble.

And in the Other Corner . . . Kant!

These objections to the Aristotelian account of moral education can be traced back to the German philosopher Immanuel Kant (1724–1804). In his influential book *Groundwork of the Metaphysics of Morals* (1785), Kant thus criticized the idea that we can use morally exemplary human beings to determine what to do, how to act, and whether a particular action is right or wrong. "For, every example . . . represented to me must itself first be appraised in accordance with principles of morality, as to whether it is also worthy to serve as an original example, that is, as a model."[6] Kant claimed that this is true even for Jesus, and he would presumably have said the same about Batman as well. Whether Batman actually is a morally exemplary human being, worthy of admiration and imitation, cannot be determined simply by appealing to the fact that most people think he is, or to his apparent authority. We need to directly ask whether Batman embodies the fundamental norms and requirements of morality.

For Kant the most fundamental feature of human existence, and therefore the most important moral value, is freedom. In the *Groundwork* Kant argued that the defining feature of human beings is their ability to direct their lives in accordance with rational, universal principles or laws, which they themselves had chosen. Kant named this ability *autonomy*, and claimed that being autonomous, being able to direct one's own life in accordance with self-chosen or self-legislated universal principles, is what human freedom is: "What, then, can freedom of the will be other than autonomy, that is, the will's property of being a law to itself?"[7]

According to Kant, every human being has the capacity to act autonomously insofar as they are rational.[8] But not everyone actually uses or realizes this capacity. Some people live their lives not in accordance with principles they have chosen themselves, but by how others think they should live. Kant calls the condition of letting your life and your actions be determined by external authorities or forces *heteronomy*.[9] In *What Is Enlightenment?* Kant gives the following description of what it means to be in the condition of heteronomy and explains why many people never leave this condition: "It is so comfortable to be a minor! If I have a book that understands for me, a spiritual advisor who has a conscience for me, a doctor who decides upon a regimen for me, and so forth, I need not trouble myself at all. I need not think if only I can pay; others will readily undertake the irksome business for me."[10]

Throughout history, Kant claims, heteronomy has been the default option for most people. Gods, priests, kings, doctors, and politicians have all been busy deciding how human beings should live and have spared little thought for those individuals' own capacity for autonomy. And most people have not protested. Why? Because it is easy and comfortable to let others decide what to think and how to act. For Kant the primary purpose of moral education is to bring people from this comfortable condition of heteronomy to a point where they can effectively exert their capacity for autonomy. And this, Kant thinks, is somewhat at odds with the Aristotelian idea of moral education as primarily a process of imitation and emulation of other people. "The imitator (in moral matters) is without character, for character consists precisely in originality in thinking," as Kant put it.[11] The problem with Aristotle's idea is that by letting the actions of someone else (like Batman for instance) determine how I should act, I seem to submit myself to an external authority: I relegate the responsibility for my own life to someone else and refuse to accept the burden of deciding for myself how to live and what kind of person to be.

The famous (or perhaps infamous) Batman TV series from the 1960s provides an extreme example of what Kant has in mind. One of the most irritating features of this show, even for fans, is the way Robin (played by Burt Ward) always comes off as a cheap copy of Batman (Adam West). Batman has all the bright ideas—Robin merely follows in his wake. Whenever the villain of the week manages to trap Batman and Robin in his surefire, "they'll never get out of here alive" trap, it's always Batman—never Robin—who finds the only, and often implausible, way to escape. Whenever the Dynamic Duo has to figure out some mysterious clue, it's always Batman—never Robin—who manages to decipher it. It's not because Robin does not *try*; the problem is rather that whenever he tries to show initiative, to think on his own, he fails because he has not acquired an independent frame of mind. He has merely adopted Batman's way of thinking.

Dick Grayson and How to Become an Autonomous Human Being (or Your Money Back!)

So we have a problem. On the one hand, Aristotle's account of how human beings acquire and develop a moral outlook seems quite convincing; we imitate and emulate those we regard as morally admirable, and through our attempts to follow their example, we gradually acquire certain values, norms, and virtues. On the other hand, Kant also seems to be right in insisting that autonomy, the capacity to determine for oneself the principles and norms by which one's life should be structured, is a crucial feature of what it means to be human. The problem is that these two ideas seem to pull in different directions. Aristotle thinks that examples set by other people play an important role in moral education; Kant believes that relying on the actions and conduct of other people to tell us what to do amounts to a denial of autonomy. Who's right?

Perhaps they are both right, or at least partly right. It seems obvious that most children are not able to consciously direct their own lives in accordance with universal principles, which they themselves have chosen. They simply do not possess the ability to do so. If we take Kant seriously, then one of the most important tasks of moral education must be to provide immature human beings with these capacities. But one way in which human beings acquire the capacities required for full-blown autonomy might very well be by imitating and emulating other persons, in particular, persons who seem to embody important moral virtues. If so, then both Aristotle and Kant may very well be right: Aristotle describes the initial stages in the process of moral education, whereas Kant focuses on the aim, or end, of this process. Neither Kant nor Aristotle would probably agree with this, but if we accept that they both seem to have gotten something right, then this is perhaps the price we have to pay. In philosophy, as in life, you cannot assume that because someone is right about one thing he or she is also right about everything else.

Once again the Batman-Robin relationship can be used to sharpen our understanding. One difference between the Robin of the 1960s TV series and Robin as portrayed in the comic books is that the former never manages to develop an independent personality and frame of mind (he remains in a condition of heteronomy), whereas the latter does. In the comics, Dick Grayson, the first Robin, gradually develops a life separate from and independent of Batman. He graduates from high school (no mean feat when simultaneously battling supervillains and crime lords next to Batman), leaves Gotham City for college, and cofounds and leads several versions of the Teen Titans. And, at the perhaps defining moment of his career, Dick Grayson actually gives up his identity as Robin and instead assumes a new superhero persona, Nightwing. In at least some versions of the story, this latter decision leads to a heated encounter with Batman, who initially refuses to accept that Dick Grayson/Robin will no longer act as his sidekick. However, Nightwing perseveres and goes on to become the champion of his own city, Blüdhaven.

Dick Grayson doesn't just free himself from Batman's influence and become a respected crime fighter in his own right, he does so using the very abilities and character traits he has acquired and learned from Batman. Most obviously, Nightwing uses the detective skills he has been taught by Batman, and the physical and mental abilities he has developed through their mutual collaboration, in his own war against crime. Equally important, but not nearly as obvious, is the way Nightwing employs the courage, intelligence, and integrity that Batman has helped instill in him, to liberate himself from Batman's influence.

It takes guts to stand up to Batman, as most villains (and many superheroes) will testify, but Nightwing manages to do so and even gets Batman to accept his decision to quit being Robin. And he is able to do this largely because of the moral character he has acquired through his relationship with Batman.

Dick Grayson thus appears to have acquired and developed the capacities needed for him to become an autonomous human being, mainly by imitating and emulating a morally exemplary person, Batman. If this is right, then there is no necessary opposition between Aristotle and Kant. Or at least there is no necessary opposition between the Aristotelian idea that moral education involves learning from and emulating other people and the Kantian insistence on the importance of autonomy, the capacity to direct one's life in accordance with self-chosen or self-legislated universal principles.

This also answers another question, namely how we determine whether a person whom we regard as morally admirable and worthy of emulation actually *is* morally exemplary. Remember that Kant believed that in order for someone to qualify as a morally exemplary person, he would have to "first be appraised in accordance with principles of morality."[12] For Kant, autonomy, the human capacity to direct one's life and actions in accordance with self-determined principles, is the most important moral value. Using the Kantian notion of autonomy, we can now say that a person is morally exemplary if emulating her actions and behavior helps people develop the abilities and competencies needed to become autonomous human beings. If what we said about Nightwing is true, then Batman can truly be considered a morally exemplary person.

Leaving the Shadow of the Bat

Dick Grayson's moral development has shown us that Aristotle and Kant can be reconciled. The virtues and abilities we acquire by emulating other people can be a (perhaps necessary) step on the way toward becoming autonomous human beings who are able to take responsibility for our own lives.

As Kant noted, it is easy and comfortable being in the state of heteronomy, being a person who has relegated the responsibility for her own life to kings, priests, and parents. Taking responsibility for one's own life is not easy, and to be able to do so is an achievement, not something that simply happens. Other people can offer help and guidance, and their lives and actions can inspire us to better ourselves, to become the sort of person we ought to be. But at some point we have to stop being guided by others; we have to stop living our lives through examples set by other people, and start deciding for ourselves what to do, how to act, and what kind of person we ought to be. Batman can inspire us, but in the end we, like Dick Grayson, have to take charge of our own lives and give up the comfort of living in the shadow of the Bat.

NOTES

1. Aristotle, *Nicomachean Ethics*, rev. ed., trans. J. A. K. Thomson (London: Penguin Classics, 1976), 1103b2–5. The numbers refer to marginal page numbers that are the same in any edition of this work.

2. Ibid., 1140a24–25.

3. For further discussion of Aristotle's idea of moral education, see the essay by David Kyle Johnson and Ryan Indy Rhodes in chapter 9 of this book.

4. Tim Drake, the third Robin, is a somewhat different case. Tim had a family of his own when he joined Batman; he voluntarily chose to seek out Batman and become his sidekick; and he was only recently adopted by Bruce. Tim has relied much less on Batman as a father figure than the previous Robins did, which is probably why he was never as intimidated by him as Dick and Jason were.

5. Incidentally, the problem of vigilantism was also important at the very beginning of Batman's career. In the very early stories Batman showed a far greater disrespect for the law than later in his career, a characteristic quickly removed by his editors. See Will Brooker's insightful discussion of the origin of the Batman-mythos in chapter 1 of *Batman Unmasked: Analysing a Cultural Icon* (London: Continuum International Publishing Group, 2000).

6. Immanuel Kant, *Groundwork of the Metaphysics of Morals*, trans. Mary Gregor, in the *Practical Philosophy* volume of *The Cambridge Edition of the Works of Immanuel Kant* (Cambridge: Cambridge University Press, 1999), 408. All subsequent references to

Kant's writings are to standard marginal page numbers that are found in all decent editions of his texts.

7. Ibid., 446–447.

8. Ibid., 440.

9. Ibid., 433, 441.

10. Kant, *What Is Enlightenment?* trans. Mary Gregor, in the *Practical Philosophy* volume of *The Cambridge Edition of the Works of Immanuel Kant* (Cambridge: Cambridge University Press, 1999), 36.

11. Kant, *Anthropology from a Pragmatic Point of View*, trans. Robert Louden (Cambridge: Cambridge University Press, 2006), 293.

12. Kant, *Groundwork*, 408.

THE TAO OF THE BAT

Bat-Tzu (as interviewed by Mark D. White)

Master Bat-Tzu, I thank you for granting me this interview, especially since you have never spoken to anyone of your unique relationship with Bruce Wayne, also known to some as the Batman.

You're most welcome. If my humble words can be of any help to anyone, I am glad to do it. Yes, as you say, I have known Bruce Wayne since he was a little boy. I was a friend of his parents, you know, particularly his father, Dr. Thomas Wayne. Good man, Dr. Wayne—I think of him often, as well as his lovely wife. So, of course, does Bruce.

I have tried to be a friend to Bruce since the untimely death of his parents. I hoped to guide him to a more harmonious place, but he chose a different path, what he has called the "way of the bat."[1] Even though I disagreed with his choice, I have tried to provide counsel when I could.

Why did you disagree with his choice?

Please don't misunderstand—he does an immeasurable amount of good as the Batman. But his life as the Batman is a life without balance, and balance is necessary for all things, especially people. The importance of balance is one of the central teachings of the Taoist masters, such as Lao-Tzu and Chuang-Tzu, and through their writings they have been my teachers, as I have been Bruce's.[2]

Taoist masters?

Yes, Taoism is an ancient Eastern philosophy, dating at least as far back as Lao-Tzu's time, which focuses on the natural flow of the universe. The Chinese called this *tao*, or "the Way," for lack of a better name. Lao-Tzu actually says that the way is that which cannot be named.[3] Taoists try to align themselves with the Way by balancing the opposing forces within themselves, the light and the dark, the feminine and the masculine, the soft and the hard—what the Taoists called *yin* and *yang*.

Like the popular black-and-white, circular symbol?

Correct—that symbol is a representation of the balance between opposing forces that defines everything about the world we live in. *Yang* (the white part) represents the masculine, the hard, the unyielding, while *yin* (the black part) represents the feminine, the soft, the nurturing. The way that the two sides look like snakes chasing each other's tails shows that both sides flow into each other and ultimately define each other. This is also shown by the black dot in the white area, and the white dot in the black area—they tell us that the root of each side lies in the other.

Since that horrible day, I'm afraid that Bruce has let his *yang* dominate, believing it necessary to rid his beloved Gotham City of the criminals that infest it, but he has forgotten that he must still embrace his *yin*.

So he does have yin?

Yes, everybody does, and he is no exception—you can see it in the less tense moments, especially with Dick and Tim. . . .

The original and current Robins.

Correct—Bruce was often very hard on them, very demanding, in accordance with his *yang*, but he has had tender moments with them as well (though few and far between).

Didn't he recently go on some sort of "spiritual quest" with Dick and Tim? Do you think that shows some striving for balance?

Yes, the year he spent traveling around the world, after that horrible mess with Brother Eye and Alex Luthor, when Dick was almost killed.[4] I think he realized then that his *yang* had dominated for too long, and he had become bitter, cold, paranoid—even for Bruce. Lao-Tzu wrote that "sages remove extremes, remove extravagance, remove arrogance."[5] I think that is what he has started to do. Indeed, since he returned, I have seen changes in him—for instance, he decided to adopt Tim shortly after their return. And he has shown such tenderness toward Selina Kyle's beautiful newborn child, Helena—I even heard he took her a teddy bear, in his Batman costume no less![6]

Why, he has even forgiven the magician, what is her name . . .

Zatanna? For the mind-wipe, you mean?

Yes, that's right, Zatanna—lovely girl, though very hard to understand sometimes.

Ha!

Even I was surprised when I heard about that—I thought Bruce would never forgive her for violating his mind like she did.[7] But you see, that's his *yin*—warm, soft, accepting of others' flaws—and it has begun to manifest itself more since his return. Of course, he still needs his *yang*, not only to perform as Batman, but to be a complete person, in harmony with the world and the Tao. All of us need that balance between the hard and soft, masculine and feminine.

Why is that? One of the key traits of the Batman is his single-minded devotion to the cause of fighting crime.

But a person with no balance is not in harmony—"knowing harmony is called constancy, knowing constancy is called clarity."[8] Many of Bruce's teachers taught him this, not just me.[9] The world is defined by dualities of opposing forces that must be held in balance to be effective—this is the meaning of the black and white intermingling in the *yin-yang* symbol. Lao-Tzu wrote, "Being and nonbeing produce each other: difficulty and ease complement each other, long and short shape each other, high and low contrast with each other, voice and echoes conform to each other, before and after go along with each other."[10] Without the repulsive, we would not know the beautiful; without the dark, there could be no light. We need the bad to highlight the good—how else would we know what the good is?

Look at Bruce, for example—he is defined by many dualities. Publicly, he lives in spacious, palatial Wayne Manor, but he spends most of his time in a dank, dreary cave covered in bat guano (dreadful stuff). He is one of wealthiest people in the world, a captain of industry, but he spends much of his fortune to support numerous charitable causes, as well as financing his crime-fighting activities. He could easily live a life of pampered leisure, but instead he has devoted himself to a thankless task, fighting crime, every day fighting exhaustion and injury that would fell a normal person. He is one of the most intelligent, learned people in the world, as well as a physical specimen of human perfection, yet he does not take pride in these things but rather uses his abilities for the good of mankind, claiming no credit for his accomplishments.

Think about this, my friend—for all of his physical prowess, his dark, frightening costume, and his formidable size and presence, the Batman's most intimidating feature is that which is not even there—his shadow! As Lao-Tzu wrote, "The use of the pot is precisely where there is nothing. When you open doors and windows for a room, it is where there is nothing that they are useful to the room."[11] Nothingness can be more important than substance, which Bruce uses to "strike fear into the hearts of criminals," as he likes to say (endlessly, I'm afraid).

Now what was I saying—oh yes, he can be single-minded, as you say. If I had but a penny for every time I've implored him to take a night off, enjoy the company of one of the beautiful, intelligent women he's seen over the years, I could melt them down and make a second giant penny, like the one he keeps in his cave. But he usually relents only when doing so would serve the greater mission against crime—silly man.

[Laughs.] The giant penny, yes—that reminds me of a story. Did you know that once, Bruce was so lonely he asked that Aquaman fellow—not that new, young one, but the one from the old Justice League days—to help retrieve that horrid museum piece from the crevice it fell into during the earthquake that struck Gotham City? He couldn't bring himself to ask his colleague to visit but instead had to concoct a ruse to lure him here. Insufferable man, so afraid to share his feelings, to admit his emptiness, even with those closest to him.[12]

Have Dick and Tim inherited Bruce's imbalance?

Oh, thankfully no. Take Dick, for instance—despite all of his soul-searching, he is a young man who keeps his *yin* and *yang* in balance. Ever since he was a young boy, newly in our charge . . .

You were involved in raising Dick?

What? No . . . no, of course not, though I saw him quite a bit while visiting Bruce over the years. As I was saying, despite being struck by the early, violent death of his parents, as was Bruce, Dick managed to maintain a basic lightheartedness about him, light to balance the dark.

He had to—he couldn't exactly be sullen in green Speedos and pixie shoes!

Oh! Don't remind me. . . . [Laughs.] Sorry. . . . You've distracted me again. Stop that.

You know, I've heard that Dick, in his adult role as Nightwing, is often said to be "the Batman with a feminine side," which is precisely my point. He cares about his friends—not just as his responsibility, as Bruce does, but truly cares about them and for them. Just think about his recent tenure with the Outsiders, which was supposed to be a working group of heroes, rather than a family like the Titans, his former allies. But he found he couldn't do it—he found it impossible *not* to care about his colleagues, who truly became his friends, and he could no longer tolerate leading them into danger. Of course, who did he hand the group off to? Bruce, who was more than happy to assemble a group of heroes who would follow his commands to march into the flames of hell.[13]

What about Tim, the current Robin?

Oh, Tim is the one I fear for. He has lost so much since he began his crime-fighting career alongside Bruce—first his mother, early on, and more recently his father; his girlfriend, Stephanie Brown, who fought crime as the Spoiler (and Robin, for a brief time while Tim was "retired"); and two of his best friends, Conner Kent and Bart Allen.[14] And all of them died at the hands of criminals, just like Bruce's parents did. If anyone has a right to sink into despair and lose his soft, compassionate nature in strict devotion to his hard, retributive side, it's Tim. In fact, he told me once that when his mother died and his father lay paralyzed in a hospital bed, he stared "into the dark side," and felt "the night-demon's cowl . . . sucking me into a lifetime in hell."[15]

But in the end I think Tim realized this danger; he is a very self-aware young man. As Lao-Tzu wrote, "Those who know others are wise; those who know themselves are enlightened."[16]

He's seen what loss has done to Bruce—you know, when Tim originally came to us . . .

"To us"?

Sorry, I did it again—when Tim came to Bruce, after deducing his secret identity, he said that Batman needed a Robin, that Batman had sunken too far within himself after the death of the second Robin, Jason Todd. He had become too hard and angry, again allowing his *yang* to rule over his *yin*. I suppose, in a way, that Robin has always been the *yin* to Batman's *yang*, the light to balance the Dark Knight.

I suppose so. I had also never realized the role that death has played in many of Batman's inner circle, including Dick. . . .

Certainly, Dick has shouldered his share of loss—his own parents, of course, and more recently his adopted town of Blüdhaven, including many of his close friends. But perhaps he understands the nature of death, and hopefully he can help Tim (and, perhaps, even Bruce).

What do you mean by "the nature of death"?

Death is just part of a natural cycle and should be accepted as part as the path that we all take. Chuang-Tzu wrote well on this subject: "If you are at peace in your time and live harmoniously, sadness and happiness cannot affect you."[17] He questioned the preference for life over death: "How can I know that wanting to live is not delusion? How can I know that aversion to death is not like a homeless waif who does not know where to return? . . . How do I know the dead do not regret having longed for life at first?"[18]

I suppose the resurrection of Jason Todd would be a good example of that?

Yes—who is to say that he is happier now than in his previous state?

Oh, poor Jason—he was so angry, so wild, so uncontrollable—everything that Bruce could be if he doesn't maintain a constant check on his rage. Lao-Tzu wrote, "When beings climax in power, they wane; this is called being unguided. The unguided die early."[19] Jason needed to learn control; we all tried to teach him that. Unfortunately, his mysterious return doesn't seem to have taught him much either. Chuang-Tzu wrote that "the perfection of virtue is to take care of your own mind in such a way that emotions cannot affect you when you already know nothing can be done, and are at peace with what is, with the decree of fate."[20] But his fate remains to be seen, and I can only hope he can learn to accept what he cannot change; Bruce must learn this too, of course.

Of course, we can't discuss Jason without bringing up his murderer, the Joker.

The Joker . . . well, the less said about him, the better, I think. I'm sure others have much more to say about him than I could offer.[21] But interestingly enough, I do remember, once Bruce said that Dick told him that "the Joker exists because of me. How I represent the order that is necessary to live in Gotham City and the Joker is the chaos that disrupts that order."[22] That's another example of how members of a duality support each other (and of Dick's budding wisdom, I daresay).

I notice you haven't mentioned Alfred yet.

Oh, I haven't? Well, there's . . . I suppose there's really not much to say about Mr. Pennyworth, except that he's a loyal servant, a trusted advisor—a paragon of humility. "Sages take care of themselves, but do not exalt themselves."[23]

A bit like you, Master . . .

Oh, I suppose, yes. Actually, I've always regarded Alfred as quite the epitome of the wise man, or sage, of Taoist thought. After all, Lao-Tzu wrote that "sages manage effortless service and carry out unspoken guidance."[24] That suits Alfred very well, I should think. Of course, he has put Bruce in his place on many an occasion, I should say.

Indeed.
Pardon me?

I'm sorry, just something caught in my throat.
Can I get you some water?

No, thank you.
Now that I think about it more, it seems to me that Alfred embodies a very important concept of the Tao, that of *wei-wu-wei*, or "action without action." Lao-Tzu wrote, "Do nondoing, strive for nonstriving."[25] The wise man knows when to do nothing, and by doing so, does something. Alfred is of inestimable aid to the Batman, but does so by simply seeing a clue that Bruce did not notice, a possibility he did not imagine, or some valuable insight that escaped him. Alfred's mind is open, and so he sees all at once. Chuang-Tzu told a story of a butcher who was so skilled he had never sharpened his blade in nineteen years. The butcher said that when he cuts up an ox, "the joints have spaces in between, whereas the edge of the cleaver blade has no thickness. When that which has no thickness is put into that which has no space, there is ample room for moving the blade."[26] Alfred is like that butcher, seeing what is there, and also what is not, which is often more important.

"Sages never do great things; that is why they can fulfill their greatness."[27] Alfred is not the Batman, but Bruce would not be the Batman without him. Chuang-Tzu wrote, "Sages harmonize right and wrong, leaving them to the balance of nature."[28] Alfred must balance the right and wrong within Bruce, tending to his health and his injuries, his joy and his sadness, his calm and his rage, trying to align them with the natural balance of things, the Tao.

It is a very difficult task that he has assumed, but that is Alfred's way, and he chooses to go with it, not against it. He reminds me of what Lao-Tzu wrote about water: "Nothing in the world is more flexible and yielding than water. Yet when it attacks the firm and the strong, nothing can withstand it, because they have no way to change it. So the flexible overcome the adamant, the yielding overcome the forceful."[29] Water runs gently through your fingers but over time can carve mountains. It is patient, as is Alfred—yet another lesson Bruce could learn from him. As you know, many of the martial arts that Bruce has mastered over the years are grounded in basic Taoist principles such as flexibility and yielding—for instance, they teach one to use an opponent's size and energy against him. Would that Bruce took those lessons to heart in other aspects of his life!

You know, Lao-Tzu wrote, "I have three treasures that I keep and hold: one is mercy, the second is frugality, the third is not presuming to be at the head of the world."[30] I can imagine Alfred saying that too.

It's almost like he just did. . . .
    Pardon?

Nothing, nothing . . .
    Do you have something to say, young man?

No, Master, it's just interesting how you've gushed about Alfred, especially since a few minutes ago you "didn't have much to say" about him.
    (Silence.)

Okay . . . well . . . thank you again, Master. It has been a most . . . illuminating discussion.
    You're very welcome. Now, if you'll excuse me, I have some cleaning to do . . .

NOTES

1. *Shadow of the Bat Annual* #3 (1995).

2. The exact details of Lao-Tzu's and Chuang-Tzu's lives, including their true identities (sound familiar?), are a mystery. The *Tao Te Ching* is widely believed to have been compiled from various sources around 500 BCE, and Chuang-Tzu's primary writings date back to around 300 BCE.

3. Lao-Tzu, *Tao Te Ching*, chapters 1, 25, and 32. All quotations from this masterpiece are translated by Thomas Cleary and can be found in *The Taoist Classics: Volume One* (Boston: Shambhala Publications, 1994), 12–47.

4. See *Infinite Crisis* #7 (June 2006); the yearlong travels occurred during the *52* series (2006–2007), but were explicitly shown only occasionally.

5. Lao-Tzu, *Tao Te Ching*, chapter 29.

6. *Catwoman* #53 (Mar. 2006), reprinted in *Catwoman: The Replacements* (2007).

7. The mind-wipe was revealed in flashback in *Identity Crisis* (2005); Bruce forgave her in *Detective Comics* #834 (September 2007).

8. Lao-Tzu, *Tao Te Ching*, chapter 55.

9. "In my teachings I had many masters, each with his own singular philosophy. My masters agreed on one point only: to be a warrior requires balance" (Batman, in *Batman Confidential* #8, October 2007).

10. Lao-Tzu, *Tao Te Ching*, chapter 2.

11. Ibid., chapter 11.

12. The giant penny was lost during *Catalysm* (1998); the Aquaman episode occurred in *Gotham Knights* #18 (August 2001).

13. See *Outsiders* #49 (September 2007).

14. Tim's mother died in "Rite of Passage" (*Detective Comics* #618–621, 1990); his father in *Identity Crisis* (2005); Stephanie in *Batman* #633 (December 2004), reprinted in *War Games Act Three* (2005); Conner in *Infinite Crisis* (2006); and Bart in *The Flash: The Fastest Man Alive* #13 (June 2007).

15. *Detective Comics* #621 (September 1990); see also the last three pages of *Robin* #167 (December 2007) with regard to the death of Tim's father.

16. Lao-Tzu, *Tao Te Ching*, chapter 33.

17. Chuang-Tzu, *Chuang-Tzu*, chapter 3, p. 68. The "Inner Chapters" of Chuang-Tzu are included in *The Taoist Classics Volume One*, 51–100, from which the translations I quote are drawn, again translated by Thomas Cleary. These chapters are the most widely known and are the only ones attributable to the master himself. The unabridged *Chuang-Tzu*, including material appended by later scholars, can be found in *The Texts of Taoism*, vols. 1 and 2 (Mineola, NY: Dover, 1962).

18. Chuang-Tzu, *Chuang-Tzu*, chapter 2, p. 64.

19. Lao-Tzu, *Tao Te Ching*, chapter 35.

20. Chuang-Tzu, *Chuang-Tzu*, chapter 4, p. 73.

21. Indeed, see the essays in this book by Robichaud, and Donovan and Richardson.

22. *Batman* #614 (June 2003), included in *Hush Volume Two* (2003).

23. Lao-Tzu, *Tao Te Ching*, chapter 72.

24. Ibid., chapter 2.

25. Ibid., chapter 63.

26. *Chuang-Tzu*, chapter 3, 66–67.

27. Lao-Tzu, *Tao Te Ching*, chapter 63.

28. *Chuang-Tzu*, chapter 2, 60.

29. Lao-Tzu, *Tao Te Ching*, chapter 78.

30. Ibid., chapter 67.

CONTRIBUTORS

The Clown Princes (and Princess) of Casuistry
and Categorical Imperatives

Mahesh Ananth is assistant professor of philosophy at Indiana University–South Bend. His primary areas of study and teaching include ancient Greek philosophy, medical ethics, philosophy of biology, and philosophy of mind. He is the author of *In Defense of an Evolutionary Concept of Health: Nature, Norms, and Human Biology* (Ashgate, 2008) and "Spock's Vulcan Mind-Meld: A Primer for the Philosophy of Mind" in *Star Trek and Philosophy* (Open Court, 2008). Mahesh secretly hopes to be Batman upon Bruce Wayne's retirement, but he realizes that this is mostly wishful thinking in light of his present figure and the requirement of those damn tights!

Sam Cowling is a Ph.D. student in the Department of Philosophy at the University of Massachusetts–Amherst. When he's not writing a dissertation on metaphysics and epistemology, he spends his time anxiously awaiting the publication of *Man-Bat and Philosophy*.

James DiGiovanna is a substitute professor of philosophy at John Jay College of Criminal Justice/CUNY and an award-winning film critic for the *Tucson Weekly*. He has written on the aesthetics of fictional worlds, the ethics of neural implant technology, and the possibilities for self-creation in virtual space. He has also published a number of short stories, and was the codirector and cowriter of the award-winning underground feature film *Forked World*. Most importantly, he would like it to be known that his relationship with Robin is purely professional and that the Batman's jealous assertions to the contrary are both unfounded and rather frightening.

Ben Dixon holds the William Lyon Visiting Chair in Professional Ethics at the United States Air Force Academy. Previously he taught at the University of Maryland, Baltimore County. Professor Dixon has published articles on the topics of moral progress and the idea of human dignity. When not instructing college students or doing his own research, he volunteers at Arkham Asylum, teaching an "Introduction to Moral Reasoning" course. Continuously shocked by the number of A's he gives the inmates' papers, he is starting to suspect that some of them may be capable of cheating.

Sarah K. Donovan is an assistant professor in the Department of Philosophy and Religious Studies at Wagner College. Her teaching and research interests include feminist, social, moral, and continental philosophy. She hopes one day to found a college for superheroes and villains (hey, you need a degree to get a job these days).

Christopher M. Drohan earned his Ph.D. in the philosophy of media and communication in May 2007 from the European Graduate School, Saas-Fee, Switzerland. Currently, Dr. Drohan is assistant director for the European Graduate School's Canadian Division, in addition to occasionally acting as an associate professor for the school. An active writer and editor, he has published several scholastic works on philosophy, semiotics, and cultural theory. In his free time, Dr. Drohan puts on various costumes and prances about in the night.

Galen Foresman is a lecturer in the Department of Philosophy at the University of North Carolina at Greensboro. He teaches courses on contemporary moral problems, aesthetics, and logic. He has a personal vendetta against fallacious arguments and is convinced that Michael Keaton was the best Batman.

David M. Hart is a graduate student in the Philosophy Department of DePaul University in Chicago. His research focuses on the intersections between phenomenology, ethics, and politics, particularly as they occur in the thought of Martin Heidegger, Emmanuel Levinas, and Jean-Paul Sartre. He hopes his contribution to this volume will help justify all the long boxes of Batman comics that are still taking up space at his mom's house.

Jason J. Howard is assistant professor of philosophy at Viterbo University, where he specializes in nineteenth- and twentieth-century European philosophy and ethics. He has published articles in the areas of moral psychology, philosophy for children, and social/political philosophy. At the moment Jason is applying to become a stunt double for Christian Bale in his third Batman movie; so far, no interviews.

Randall M. Jensen is associate professor of philosophy at Northwestern College in Orange City, Iowa. His philosophical interests include ethics, ancient Greek philosophy, and philosophy of religion. He has recently contributed chapters to *South Park and Philosophy*, *24 and Philosophy*, *Battlestar Galactica and Philosophy*, and *The Office and Philosophy*. He's convinced that Batman can rid Gotham City of evil only if he at last completes his training by following Plato's teachings and becoming the world's greatest philosopher-king.

David Kyle Johnson is currently an assistant professor of philosophy at King's College in Wilkes-Barre, Pennsylvania. His philosophical specializations include philosophy of religion, logic, and metaphysics. He has also written chapters on *South Park*, *Family Guy*, *The Office*, *Battlestar Galactica*, Quentin Tarantino, and Johnny Cash and will edit the forthcoming Blackwell Philosophy and Pop Culture series book on *Heroes*. He has taught many classes that focus on the relevance of philosophy to pop culture, including a course devoted to *South Park*. Kyle would also like to point out that the only true Catwoman is Julie Newmar, Lee Meriwether, or Eartha Kitt. In addition, Adam West did not need molded plastic to improve his physique . . . pure West (tap your chest with two fingers when you say that). And how come Batman doesn't dance anymore? Remember the Bat-tu-see?

Stephen Kershnar is a professor in the Department of Philosophy at the State University of New York College at Fredonia. He has written two books: *Desert, Retribution, and Torture* (University Press of America, 2001) and *Justice for the Past* (SUNY Press, 2004), and a number of articles on sex, violence, and racism. Psychiatrists have recently judged him to be more psychopathic than Harvey Dent and more fun than the Joker.

Daniel P. Malloy is an adjunct assistant professor of philosophy at Appalachian State University in Boone, North Carolina. His research focuses on twentieth-century critical theory (particularly that of Herbert Marcuse) and its application to contemporary issues such as biotechnology and terrorism. Daniel frequently employs Scarecrow's fear toxins in his classes, particularly on exam days.

Carsten Fogh Nielsen is a Ph.D. student at the Institute of Philosophy and History of Ideas at the University of Aarhus, Denmark. His main interests are the philosophy of Immanuel Kant, moral philosophy, and the philosophy of popular culture, and he has published articles in Danish on all of these topics. He spends much of his time trying to convince other philosophers that comic books are cool, but despairs when having to explain "who that Frank Miller guy is."

Ron Novy teaches courses in ethics, metaphysics, and philosophy of mind in the Philosophy and Religion Department at the University of Central Arkansas. It is unlikely he will ever convince his wife that they should get a pet hyena named Giggles.

Brett Chandler Patterson teaches theology and ethics at Anderson University in South Carolina. He has written articles analyzing moral responsibility in the Spider-Man universe, utilitarian logic in *24*, and images of redemption in *Lost* (also published by Blackwell). His current research analyzes the fantasies of Lewis, Tolkien, Wolfe, and Card. He wishes to be considered, if Christian Bale were to drop out, for the Bruce Wayne role in the next Batman film.

Chris Ragg is a Ph.D. student in the department of philosophy at the University of Massachusetts–Amherst. He is also one of the Joker's henchmen—or at least looks the part.

Ryan Indy Rhodes is a visiting lecturer at Stephen F. Austin State University in Nacogdoches, Texas, while completing his dissertation for the University of Oklahoma. His research interests include ethics, warrior codes, and honor. A long-time Batman fan, Indy is thrilled to see his first publication combine two of his favorite subjects. He is still waiting to hear a public apology for the movie *Batman and Robin*.

Nicholas Richardson is an associate professor in the Department of Physical Sciences at Wagner College in New York City, where he teaches general, advanced inorganic, and medicinal chemistry. When not teaching, he spends his time at work in the lab designing new chemicals for Batman's utility belt.

Christopher Robichaud is an instructor in public policy at the John F. Kennedy School of Government at Harvard University. He is currently finishing his Ph.D. in philosophy at MIT. When not teaching folks about the many moral issues surrounding the political life, or writing about whether properties have essences, he's busy looking for a way into Emperor Joker's world. He'd like to pay a visit to his favorite supervillain, though he reluctantly acknowledges that it's probably not the best place to live.

Jason Southworth is currently completing a Ph.D. in philosophy at the University of Oklahoma, in Norman, Oklahoma, and is also an adjunct instructor for Fort Hays State University, in Hays, Kansas. He would like the world's greatest detective to figure out whose idea it was to have cute additions at the ends of our bios.

Tony Spanakos is a mild-mannered assistant professor of political science and law at Montclair State University and an adjunct assistant professor of politics at NYU. He has written many articles and book chapters on political economy, democracy, and citizenship in Latin America and coedited the book *Reforming Brazil* (Lexington Books, 2004). He has been a Fulbright Visiting Professor at the University of Brasilia (2002) and is currently a Fulbright Visiting Professor at the Institute for Advanced Policy Studies in Caracas, Venezuela. Local police in Latin America all agree that "he is always the first one to respond when we flash the Bat-signal."

Mark D. White is associate professor in the Department of Political Science, Economics, and Philosophy at the College of Staten Island/CUNY, where he teaches courses combining economics, philosophy, and law. He has written many articles and book chapters in these fields; contributed chapters to other books in the present series dealing with Metallica, *South Park*, *Family Guy*, and *The Office*; and coedited *Economics and the Mind* (Routledge, 2007). He is waiting for the "goddamn Batman" to kick New Earth Batman's ass (and good).

INDEX

Abraham (biblical), 189–190, 196
abstract objects, 153, 155
absurdity, 177, 178, 187, 188, 189–190,
    191, 199, 206, 208
act-focused ethics. *See* deontology;
    utilitarianism
actions, 29–32
    free will and, 72, 74–79
    moral responsibility for, 72–80
    Taoist concept of, 275
    utilitarian view of, 106
    See also moral actions
Adams, Ruth, 134–135
addiction, 78, 79
Aftershock, 42–43
After Virtue (MacIntyre), 23
agent-neutral/agent-specific rules,
    9–10, 12
Alice's Adventures in Wonderland
    (Carroll), 135
alienation, 199
Allen, Bart, 272
alternate Earths, 97–98, 123, 145,
    146–148, 152, 154, 160
ambiguity, 199
anarchy, 42, 48–54, 58, 63–64
Anarky, 63–64
Angst, 220–224
Aparo, Jim, 153
appearances and reality, 176, 177,
    214, 216
a priori moral sense, 200
Aquaman, 246, 271

argument from prevention, 104–105
Aristotle, 23, 29–31, 95–96, 97
    friendship concept of, 239, 241,
        242–243, 244, 247
    moral education and, 255–256, 257,
        259, 261, 262–263, 264
Arkham, Amadeus, 135–136,
    138–140
Arkham Asylum, 129, 132, 134–140
authenticity, 199–210, 220, 221, 223
authority, 199–201, 257–258.
        See also state
autonomy, 260–265
Azrael (Jean-Paul Valley), 6, 52, 158
Azrael #2, 115

backward-looking moral reasons,
    91–92, 97
balance, 36–37, 267–270, 273, 275
Bane, 30, 115, 158
bat
    as Bruce Wayne's totem, 205–206
    subjective experience and, 171
    as symbol, 103, 132, 136, 138,
        139–140, 159, 201, 205–206,
        222, 223
Batcave, 42, 140, 184, 222, 228, 270
Bat Family, 240–241
Batgirl. *See* Cain, Cassandra; Gordon,
    Barbara
Bat-Knights, 97
Batman
    Alfred's care of, 183–197, 202

Batman (*continued*)
authenticity and, 201, 208–210, 221–232
balance and, 267–271, 273
basis of appeal of, 1–2
being vs. acting like, 167–178
canon of, 123
complexity of, 88–89
conscience of, 198–199, 200
as Dark Knight, 159–160, 208
determination of, 212–214, 221–222
dualities and, 64, 270
existentialism and, 188–189, 198
fear tactics of, 198–199
as fictional character, 117–125
fixed concept of, 162
Gordon's relationship with, 65–68
gothic and, 92
"grim and gritty" version of, 213
guilt of, 207–208
hatred of evildoers felt by, 28–37
as icon, 124–125
identity/persona of, 35, 129–141, 156–178, 201–205, 208, 210, 228, 240, 242, 245–246
inner circle of, 52, 159–160, 240–241, 246, 273
Joker as identical to, 142–155
Joker as nemesis of, 71, 80
justice's meaning to, 185–186
killing rejected by, 6, 7, 10–15, 52, 68, 92, 157, 158, 164, 176
"kinder, gentler" version of, 213
moral code of, 6, 91, 92, 199, 206
as moral exemplar, 114–125, 254–259, 260, 264
mortality and, 219, 221–223, 224
motivations of, 55, 89–90, 103, 168, 191, 213, 214–224
nonlegitimate actions of, 66–68
origin story of, 55, 59, 61, 85–99, 102–103, 108, 110–111, 157, 159, 163, 175, 219, 222, 230, 240
parents' murder and. *See* Wayne, Dr. Thomas and Martha
peak attributes of, 116–117, 119

personal isolation of, 29, 35–36, 37, 212–213, 240, 249, 271
personal traits of, 123–124
power source of, 170
promise made by, 86–99, 102–103
relationship with state of, 56–69
replacement of, 158–159
resolve of, 92, 246, 271
retirement and return of, 64, 98–99, 158, 207
sanity of, 135–136, 139
Superman compared with, 227, 229–238, 240, 248
Superman's friendship with, 239–252
as *Übermensch*, 248
unique calling of, 205
virtues of, 115–125
Wayne fortune and, 86, 101–113, 115, 131–132, 133, 202–203, 270
Wayne's billionaire-playboy disguise and, 90, 102, 213, 245
women in life of, 29, 35, 158, 160, 212, 213
Batman (film), 55, 88
Batman: Anarky, 63–64
Batman and Robin (film), 169
Batman Begins (film), 55, 89, 113n.2, 115, 122
Batman Returns (film), 87–88
Batman Superman Movie (film), 73
Batman: The Animated Series, 123
Batman: Two-Faces, 154
Batman: Year One, 32, 33, 59–62, 68, 102–103, 113n.2, 129, 132–133, 136, 157, 204, 222, 227
Batman: Year Two, 61–62, 65, 68
Batmobile, 19, 74, 228, 258
Bat-Tzu, 267–276
Batwoman (Kathy Kane), 160
Beauvoir, Simone de, 172, 173
"begging the question," 232–235, 238
Being and Time (Heidegger), 201–202, 215
"being-in-the-world," 187–188, 215–216
benefits-harms analysis, 107

Bentham, Jeremy, 15n.7, 20, 99n.3
Bertinelli, Helena. *See* Huntress
"better than" notion, 227, 228, 229
Black Mask, 44
Blind Justice, 29
Blüdhaven, 263
Booster Gold, 160
brain, 170, 171, 215
bravery. *See* courage
"Bread and Circuses," 47
Brother Eye, 246, 269
Brown, Stephanie (Spoiler), 272
"Bruce Wayne: Fugitive," 246
Buddha, 114, 119–120
Burton, Tim, 88
Butler, Judith, 141n.4

Cain, Cassandra (Batgirl), 52, 173
Camus, Albert, 200–201, 203
Captain America, 57
Carroll, Lewis, 135
Castle, Frank. *See* Punisher
"Castle of the Bat," 123
Cataclysm, 42, 277n.12
categorical imperative, 19
Catwoman, 29, 31, 96, 241, 269
causal responsibility, 73–74
Cavendish, Dr., 138–139
charity, 48–49, 89, 106–109, 111, 115, 202–203, 270
child rearing, 18, 23–24, 262
Chill, Joe, 67–68, 190, 230
Chilton, Mrs., 189
Chimp, Detective, 158
choice, 173–174, 217–219, 221, 223
Christian, Father, 48–50
Christian theology, 50, 133
Christmas Carol, A (Dickens), 100n.6
Chuang-Tzu, 268, 273, 275
Clayface, 94
Clown Prince. *See* Joker
Cold War, 57
Comic Code Authority, 160
comparisons, 229–238
concrete objects, 152, 153, 155
Confucius, 26n.8

Conrad, Joseph, 45
conscience, 198–210
consciousness, 93. *See also* subjective experiences
consequentialist ethics, 8, 20, 21, 25, 26, 29, 99n.3, 111
promises and, 90–92
Contagion, 42
courage, 23, 29, 115, 236–238
Crime Alley, 59
Crisis on Infinite Earths, 155n.1
Croc, Killer, 47, 49, 151, 215
Cruise, Tom, 14

Dalai Lama, 114, 119
Dark Knight, The (film), 73
"Dark Knight of the Round Table," 123
Dark Knight Returns, The, 28–29, 36, 56–58, 61, 64, 66–67, 68, 98, 123, 130, 135, 136, 139–140, 157, 165, 198, 207, 258–259
Dark Knight Strikes Again, The, 90, 166n.1
Dark Victory, 67, 68, 87
Dasein concept, 202, 205, 208, 215
Dawes, Rachel, 89, 90
death, 92–99, 219–223, 273
acceptance of, 208–209, 220–221, 224
authenticity and, 200, 203, 204, 219–221
postmortem harms and, 96–97
See also resurrection
Death in the Family, A, 98, 106, 112
deism, 50
Dent, Harvey. *See* Two-Face
deontology, 8, 9–10, 14–15, 16n.11, 19, 21, 25, 26, 99n.4
definition of, 9, 20, 29, 92
virtue ethics and, 22, 23, 24, 30
descriptions, 147, 150, 151, 152, 155, 162, 164–165
as comparisons, 229
desires, 77–78, 79
determinism, 75–76, 213, 214, 223–224

devotion, 185, 186, 187
Dick, Philip K., 14
Dickens, Charles, 100n.6
disillusionment, 176
Drake, Tim (Robin), 150, 174, 265n.4, 268–269, 271, 272–273
duty, 18–21, 186, 195, 200
situated freedom and, 173–174
supererogatory acts and, 108–109

earthquake, Gotham City, 42–43, 271
"Elseworlds" tales, 123, 154, 159, 160, 162, 218
Emile or On Education (Rousseau), 200
empirical science, 214
"End Game," 48
environmental influence, 130
Epicurus, 94–95, 96
epistemology, 14, 76, 166
equality
friendship and, 244–245, 246
moral, 103, 107
Essen, Sarah, 5, 60
essentialist conscience, 200
eternal recurrence, 137, 138
ethics, 6–25, 185
definitions of, 18–19, 20
See also deontology; utilitarianism; virtue ethics
evaluative comparison, 229–238
evil, 44, 95
Batman's hatred of, 28–37, 87, 89, 98
utilitarian approach to, 103, 111
existentialism, 187–189, 199–210

Fairchild, Vesper, 29
faith, 185, 187, 189–195, 196, 197
Falcone, Carmine ("The Roman"), 31
fallenness, 201–202, 204
family resemblance, 156–157, 161, 163–166
famine, 106, 108
"Famine, Affluence, and Morality" (Singer), 103
Fantastic Four, 212
Faulkner, William, 85

Fear and Trembling (Kierkegaard), 185
"Fear of Faith," 48
Feinberg, Joel, 5–6
fictional characters
as abstract, 152–154
as moral exemplars, 117–125, 165–166
Finger, Bill, 86
first-order desires, 77–78, 79
Flash, 244
Flash, The, 277n.14
Flass, Detective, 33, 34, 35, 60
Foot, Philippa, 8
forward-looking moral reasons, 90–99
Foucault, Michel, 72, 130, 131, 133–134, 135
Frankenstein story, 123, 159
Frankfurt, Harry, 75–76, 77
freedom, 172–175, 178, 201, 208–210
Angst and, 221, 222
as Kantian moral value, 260
free will, 72, 74–79
determinism vs., 213–214, 223–224
insanity as inhibition of, 80
Freeze, Mr., 52
friendship, 239, 240–252
"Fruit of the Earth," 47
future consequences, 111

games, 161–163
Gandhi, Mohandas, 114, 119, 120, 158
Ghul, Ra's al, 93
giving, 104–105, 106, 110–111
God, 129, 130, 133, 189–190
Golding, William, 45
Golonka, Big Willie, 62
Gordon, Barbara (Oracle), 52, 93, 159, 164, 171–172
as Batgirl, 5, 171, 173
Joker's paralysis of, 5, 71, 73
Gordon, James, 6, 29, 52, 65–68, 103, 116, 132, 147
affair of, 35, 60
character traits of, 33–34
Flass's brutality and, 33, 34, 35

Gotham City's anarchy and, 43, 46–50, 52
Joker and, 5, 48, 71
public safety and, 56, 59, 60
successor to, 58, 258–259
as virtuous, 31
Gotham City, 32, 87–90, 97, 101, 117, 135–136, 177, 198, 206
breakdown of social order in, 41–53, 271
governing chaos of, 55–69
hopelessness of, 103
pervasive fear in, 92
Superman as savior of, 56
violent crime rise in, 57–58
gothic, 92
Grayson, Dick (first Robin), 18, 52, 150, 158, 164, 166n.1, 240, 249, 254, 257, 258, 268–269
autonomy of, 262, 263–264, 265
as Nightwing, 263–264, 272
personality of, 271–272
Green Arrow, 93
Green Lantern, 116
Grounding for the Metaphysics of Morals (Kant), 16n.11, 259–260

harms
benefits vs., 107
not experienced, 96
hatred, 28, 29, 30–31, 33–37
Hauerwas, Stanley, 50
Haunted Knight, 87, 89
Heart of Darkness (Conrad), 45
hedonism, 94–95
Heidegger, Martin, 187–188, 201–210, 214–224
heteronomy, 260–261, 263, 265
Hinman, Lawrence, 109
History of Sexuality, The (Foucault), 131
Hobbes, Thomas, 42, 44–45, 46, 50, 59, 60, 61, 62, 63
Homer, 26n.8
human existence. *See* life
humanitarianism, 48–52, 103
Huntress, 47, 49, 52, 159, 240, 254

Hurricane Katrina, 41–45, 50–51, 53, 54
Hush, 6, 7–8, 10
Hush, 87, 89–90, 251

iconization, 124–125
identicals, 143–145, 146, 148, 149, 154
identity, 156–166, 188
construction of, 130, 131–140, 202, 204
essentiality of, 156
identical vs., 143
necessity of, 148–150
situated freedom and, 173–174
Identity Crisis, 277nn.7, 14
Indiscernibility of Identicals (IOI), 144–145, 146, 149
Infinite Crisis, 123, 246, 277n.14
inner/outer world problem, 215–217
insanity, 50, 70–73, 79, 80, 138–139, 174–175, 178
as construction, 72, 134–135
internalization, 23, 204
intrinsic values, 8, 20
irony, 189–190
Isaac (biblical), 189–190

Jackson, Frank, 179n.4
Jesus, 114, 117, 119, 120, 260
John, Gospel of, 188
Joker, 35, 44, 55, 69, 114, 131, 139, 140, 167, 170, 274
Batman as identical to, 142–155
as Batman's nemesis, 71, 80, 242
Batman's rationale for not killing, 6, 7, 10–15, 92, 112, 176–177
Batman's similarities with, 168, 172, 173, 175, 176, 177–178
film version of, 88
goals of, 64
Gordon's shooting of, 48
heinous acts of, 5–6, 8, 20, 25, 36, 48, 71–74, 98, 106
insanity of, 66, 70–71, 72, 73, 79, 80, 134–135, 175
moral responsibility of, 70–80

Joker (*continued*)
  "one bad day" of, 167, 174–176
  origin stories of, 79, 175–176
"Jurisprudence," 48
Justice, 87
justice, 69, 185–187, 190, 191
  social vs. personal, 186–187, 192,
    194–195, 196, 197
  as virtue, 29, 30, 115
Justice League of America, 245,
  246–247, 271
Justice Society of America, 57, 160

Kane, Bob, 86, 153
Kane, Kathy (Batwoman), 160
Kant, Immanuel, 16n.11, 19, 20, 26n.6,
  99n.4, 176, 259–265
Kent, Clark. *See* Superman
Kent, Conner, 272
Kierkegaard, Søren, 185, 187, 188,
  189–191, 193–196
Killing Joke, The, 70, 79, 167, 175, 178
King, Martin Luther, Jr., 200
Kingdom Come, 97–98
Knightfall, 6, 158
knights of faith, 192–195, 196
knights of infinite resignation, 191,
  193, 194–195
Kyle, Selina. *See* Catwoman

Laden, Osama bin, 200
Lane, Lois, 212, 240, 243
Lang, Lana, 67
language, 160–165
Lao-Tzu, 268–276
law, 131, 185–186
law and order, 56, 58, 66, 68
Lawless League, 160
Lazarus pits, 93
Lee, Jim, 153
Legends of the Dark Knight #1, 205,
  206, 207
Leviathan, 62
Leviathan (Hobbes), 44–45, 46, 50, 59
life, 215–219, 223–224
  authenticity of, 199, 203, 208–210
    balance in, 36–37, 267–270, 273, 275
    inner/outer world and, 215–217
    meaning of, 191–192, 196, 203, 222
    reinterpretations of, 201–202, 203
    as temporally ecstatic, 218, 219
    as "thrown-project," 217
    understanding of, 219
Loeb, Gilliam, 60, 61
Loeb, Jeph, 87, 88
Long Halloween, The, 31, 36, 87, 100n.6
Lord, Max, 15–16n.8
Lord of the Flies (Golding), 45
Lost (television series), 45
love, 185, 186, 187, 192, 196
  in balanced life, 36–37
  friendship and, 243
  selfless, 195, 197
loyalty, 185, 192, 195, 274
Luthor, Lex, 51, 53, 73, 117

Machiavellianism, 47
MacIntyre, Alasdair, 22, 23
Madison, Julie, 29, 158
"Man Who Falls, The," 206
marginalization, 72
May, Aunt, 212
meaning, 191–192, 196, 203, 216, 222
metaphysics, 130–141, 143–155,
    166, 177
Mill, John Stuart, 20, 99n.3
Miller, Frank, 56–58, 59, 97–98,
    113n.2, 123, 198, 222, 258–259
mind, 170, 214–215
"Minority Report, The" (Dick), 14
modal claims, 142–143, 145–149
modal properties, 153–154
Monk, 158
Montoya, Renee, 48
Moore, Alan, 70
moral actions, 8–10, 21, 23–25, 29–32,
    188, 199, 200, 251
  helping others as, 103–104
  intrinsic, 8, 14–15, 23
  promises and, 90–99
  supererogatory, 108–109
  use of wealth and, 101–113

moral code, 6, 91, 92, 129, 199, 206
moral education, 23–25, 255–264
moral exemplars, 114–125, 256–265
  fictional characters as, 117–125,
    165–166
  historical, 114, 117, 119–120, 122
  judging of, 259–262, 264
  learning from, 256–262, 265
moral "innocents," 11
moral judgment, 101–113, 199, 210
moral responsibility, 70–80, 103–111
  authenticity and, 200
  Batman's vs. Alfred's, 186–187
  causal responsibility vs., 73–74
  free will and, 74–78
  insanity and, 71–72
Morrison, Grant, 153
"Mr. Wayne Goes to Washington," 43

Nagel, Thomas, 96, 170–172
names, 147, 149, 150, 151, 152
Napier, Jack. See Joker
natural disasters, 41–42, 45–57
natural order. See state of nature
necessary condition, 157–159, 163, 164
necessity, 142, 145, 146, 150
Necessity of Identity (NI), 148–149,
    150, 151
New Earth, 146–148, 152, 154
New Orleans. See Hurricane Katrina
New York City, 57–58
Nicholson, Jack, 170
Nichomachean Ethics (Aristotle), 239,
    243, 255
Niebuhr, H. Richard, 50
Nietzsche, Friedrich, 63, 65, 130, 131,
    133, 135–141, 247–249
Nightwing. See Grayson, Dick
Nolan, Christopher, 87, 113n.2
"No Law and a New Order," 44, 47
No Man's Land, 42–57, 117
nominalism, 155
normal, 133–134
North American Kant Society, 15
noumenal world, 176
Nussbaum, Martha, 22

objective world, 214, 215–216
Olsen, Jimmy, 240, 243
Oracle, 52, 93, 159, 240, 249, 254, 257
"Our Vision and the Riddle"
    (Nietzsche), 137
Outsiders, 272

Parker, Ben, 86
Parker, Mary Jane. Ask Mephisto
Parker, Peter. See Spider-Man
Penguin, 44, 49, 50, 52, 66, 115,
    173–174
Pennyworth, Alfred, 29, 52, 63, 73,
    89–92, 147, 183–197, 240
  as knight of faith, 192–195
  Taoist principles and, 274–276
  way of being of, 215–219, 220, 221
personal justice, 186–187
Petit, William, 46–48, 49, 50, 52
phenomena, 168–171, 176–177, 178
Philosophical Investigations
    (Wittgenstein), 160–162
Philosophy and Truth (Nietzsche), 133
"picking out" objects, 147
Plastic Man, 247
Plato, 22, 23, 120
Poison Ivy, 52, 68, 76
Porter, Janice, 67
possibility, 142, 147, 218, 219
Potter, Harry, 94
power, 130, 131, 133, 137, 177
Principles of Morals and Legislation, The
    (Bentham), 15n.7
Prodigal, 158
promises, 85–99, 102–103, 240
Punisher, 86, 89

quantitative vs. qualitative evaluations,
    230–233, 238

reality, 176, 177, 214, 216
Reaper, 61–63, 189
relative ethical norms, 22–23
Requiem for a Dream (film), 79
resignation, 191, 193, 194–195
responsibility. See moral responsibility

resurrection, 25, 93, 159, 273, 274
retribution, 89, 91–92
  revenge vs., 88
  See also vengeance
Riddler, 30, 115
Road to No Man's Land, 42–43
Robin, 29, 52, 240, 249, 255, 268
  Batman as moral exemplar for,
    256–258
  Batman's spiritual quest with, 269
  ethics of creating, 17–26, 263
  first introduction of, 159
  identities of, 150, 163–165
  television portrayal of, 261–262,
    263
  See also Drake, Tim; Grayson, Dick;
    Todd, Jason
Rousseau, Jean-Jacques, 200

Sacrifice, 15–16n.8
Sale, Tim, 87
Sarah (biblical), 189
Sartre, Jean-Paul, 188, 200–201, 203
Scarecrow, 48–49, 215
Scarface, 44
Scratch, Nicholas, 43
second-order desires, 77–78, 79
self. *See* identity
Self (Heidegger concept), 202, 205
self-deception, 203–204
sense experience, 95, 96
"Shellgame," 51
Silver Age Batman stories, 160
Singer, Peter, 11, 103–113
situated freedom, 173–174, 178
Slote, Michael, 22
social justice, 186–187
social norms, 72, 131, 133–134
social order, 41–54, 60, 61
Socrates, 120, 199
soul, 129, 130
sovereign power, 45, 46–48, 50–52.
    See also state
Spider-Man, 34, 86, 212, 255
Spielberg, Steven, 14

"Spiritual Currency," 48
Spoiler, 272
state, 55–69, 199
state of nature, 42, 44–53, 60–62
subjective experiences, 168, 169, 170,
    171, 178, 214–215
subject-object dualism, 214–215,
    216, 223
suffering, 33, 37, 108, 191, 196
  Nietzsche on, 139
  utilitarian view of, 104, 105, 109
sufficient condition, 157–160, 163
Superdome (New Orleans), 43, 46
supererogatory acts, 108–109
superheroes
  Batman's singularity as, 34, 56–57,
    86, 99, 170, 212, 244, 246,
    254, 255
  Batman's moral authority as, 199
  changed conditions for, 165
  comparisons of, 227, 232–238
  duty of, 18–21
  murdered parent trope of, 159
  origin stories for, 85, 86
  realism of, 116
  refusing to kill by, 7–8
  Silver Age portrayals of, 160
  Superman's relationship with, 245
  training of, 24, 25
"Superhuman Registration Act,"
    69n.1
Superman, 34, 52, 61, 73, 88, 93, 116,
    165, 166n.2, 200
  Batman compared with, 212, 227,
    229–238, 240, 254, 255
  Batman's conflicts with, 249–251
  Batman's friendship with, 230–252
  as icon, 124
  legitimacy of, 56–57
  origin of, 56, 240
  personality traits of, 240, 241–242,
    248, 252
  weaknesses of, 251
Superman/Batman series, 87, 88, 89
superpowers, 240, 241, 245, 250

Batman's lack of, 227, 230, 233, 234, 237–238, 248, 254–255
bravery and, 237–238

Taoism, 267–276
Tao Te Ching, 277n.2
Teen Titans, 263
television Batman series, 261–262
Teresa, Mother, 114, 119, 120
terrorists, 41, 57
"they-self," 202, 203, 205
Thompkins, Dr. Leslie, 48, 49–50, 52
Thomson, Judith Jarvis, 8, 9, 10, 11
thought experiments, 15
Thus Spoke Zarathustra (Nietzsche), 63, 137, 239, 248
Titans, 272
Todd, Jason (second Robin), 6, 7, 18, 98, 150, 258
Batman's selection of, 19–20, 21
Joker's brutal murder of, 5, 20, 25, 71, 98, 106, 112, 273, 274
resurrection of, 25, 93, 273, 274
virtues and vices of, 24–25, 274
Tower of Babel, 246
Trainspotting (film), 79
transplant case, 10, 11, 12
trolley problem, 8–10, 11–13, 15
truth, 133–134, 136, 140
truthmaker, 117–118
Two-Face, 35, 44, 47–48, 52, 148
background of, 62, 63
bat symbol and, 140
insanity of, 70, 134–135
rules of, 131

Übermensch, 248
Under the Hood, 92, 93
unexperienced harms, 96
utilitarianism, 7–10, 12, 99n.3, 103–113, 222
definition of, 7, 20, 29, 103–105
judgment of acts and, 21, 25, 106
supererogatory acts and, 108–109
virtue ethics and, 22, 23, 24, 30

Vale, Vickie, 29
Valley, Jean-Paul. *See* Azrael
value theory, 227, 228–238
vengeance, 68–69, 87, 88, 114, 159, 198, 201, 207, 213, 219
wealth used for, 101, 102
vigilantism, 53–54, 58, 102, 136, 206, 213, 259
violence
freedom and, 174–176, 208
humanitarian nonviolence vs., 50–57
by nonstate actors, 57, 65–69
state agents' misuse of, 61
virtuous rationale for, 32, 33–37
virtue, 29–37, 192. *See also* moral *headings*
virtue ethics, 21, 22–26, 29–33, 255–256
Virtuous-Persons Theory, 30–31, 32
Virtuous-Thoughts-and Actions Theory, 31–33

Ward, Burt, 261
War Games Act Three, 277
Watchmen, 89
Wayne, Bruce. *See* Batman
Wayne, Dr. Thomas and Martha, 10
murderer of, 67–68, 190
murder, location of, 92
murder of, 28–29, 36, 55–56, 59, 85–99, 102–104, 111, 132, 133, 136, 157, 159, 175, 183, 189, 190, 201, 202, 203, 207, 208, 213, 214, 219, 221–222, 230, 240
philanthropy of, 89
resurrection of, 159
son's promise to avenge, 86–87, 93–94, 97, 98–99, 102–103, 240
wealth of, 101–113
Wayne Enterprises, 42, 106, 109, 175, 202–203, 212–213
Wayne Foundation, 110
Wayne Manor, 102, 140, 184, 205, 222, 270
earthquake destruction of, 42

wealth, 202, 270
  moral spending of, 101–113, 115
Weber, Max, 57, 63, 65
wei-wu-wei, 275
What Is Enlightenment? (Kant),
    260–261
"What Is It Like to Be a Bat?" (Nagel),
    170–172
White, Perry, 243
Wittgenstein, Ludwig, 160–165

Wonder Woman, 15–16n.8, 116, 246
World War II, 57

yin and yang, 268–269, 270, 272
Yindel, Ellen, 57, 58, 61, 66–67, 259
Yoder, John Howard, 50

Zatanna, 269
Zero Hour, 164
Zsasz, Mr., 49, 177